BACK FROM
DAMASCUS
LEAVING RELIGION BEHIND

Back from Damascus:
Leaving Religion Behind
Text © 2016 Cornel M. Hamm
Design © 2016 Inkflight

All rights reserved. No part of this book may be stored in a retrieval system, reproduced or transmitted in any form or by any other means without written permission from the publisher or a licence from the Canadian Copyright Licensing Agency. Critics and reviewers may quote brief passages in connection with a review or critical article in any media.

Every reasonable effort has been made to contact the copyright holders of all material reproduced in this book.

ink/light

Mailing address:
Cornel M. Hamm
2601 - 1438 Richards St
Vancouver, BC
Canada, V6Z 3B8

www.inkflight.com

Editor and Agent: Colin Hamm
talktocolin@yahoo.ca
Design by: A.R. Roumanis

Text set in Sabon.

FIRST EDITION / FIRST PRINTING

LIBRARY AND ARCHIVES CANADA CATALOGUING IN PUBLICATION

Hamm, Cornel M., author
    Back from Damascus : leaving religion behind / Cornel M. Hamm.

Includes bibliographical references and index.
ISBN 978-1-77226-259-9 (paperback)

1. Hamm, Cornel M.
2. Atheists – Canada – Biography.
3. Ex-church members – Canada – Biography.
4. College teachers – Canada – Biography.
I. Title.

BL2790.H34A3 2016   211'.8092   C2016-900895-9

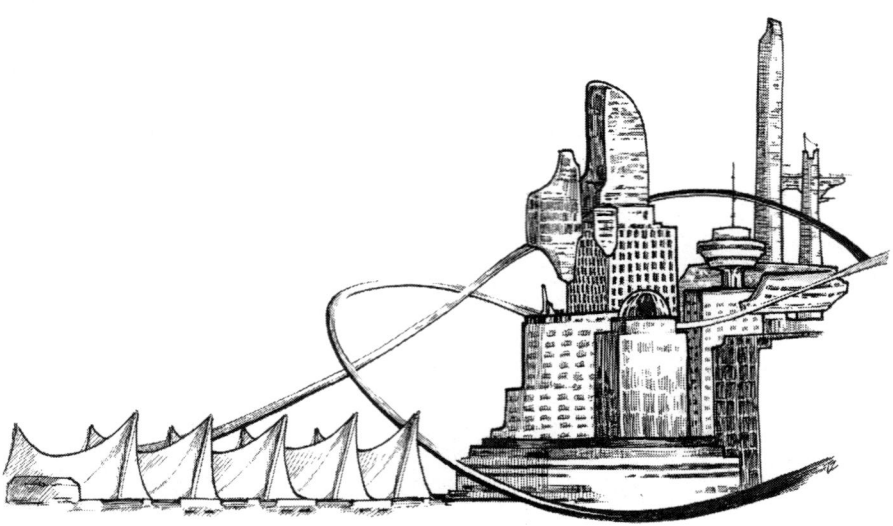

BACK FROM
DAMASCUS
LEAVING RELIGION BEHIND

An Autobiography by
CORNEL M. HAMM

VANCOUVER:
INKFLIGHT
2016

CONTENTS

   Preface 9

1 **Before La Glace**
    A Family Name 13
    The Mennonites 19
    My Parents Emigrate to Canada 24
    On To La Glace 28
    Pioneering in La Glace 31

2 **La Glace**
    My Birth 33
    Early Memories 38
    La Glace School 41
    Old Post School 45
    Church 50
    Getting Saved 57
    Our Family 66
    Farm Life in La Glace 80

3 **Chilliwack**
    First Impressions 92
    Sharon Mennonite Collegiate Institute 97
    My Five-Year Diary 104
    1948 – A Typical Year 105
    The Big Sin 115
    Grade 12 122
    The Fleece Test and the Religious Mind 130
    Leaving Chilliwack 142

4   **Three Hills (1950-1954)**
       Prairie Bible Institute   147
       First Year   151
       Witnessing with the Chilliwack Gospel Gang   154
       Year Two   160
       Year Three   173
       Senior Sermon and Higher Education   180
       On Tour   189

5   **Vancouver (1954-1963)**
       Normal School   205
       Elementary School Teaching   211
       UBC – Discovering Philosophy   218
       Secondary School Teaching in Vancouver   220
       Getting Married   227
       A Year at Columbia   233

6   **North Vancouver (1963 – 1984)**
    (Also London, Dawson Creek & Langley)
       A Year at Van Tech   237
       Two Years at Lord Byng Secondary   240
       My Best Ever Golf Game   244
       London   246
       Early Years at SFU   253
       Farming in Dawson Creek   260
       Langley and SFU Middle Years   270
       Melbourne   274
       An Inconvenient Love   278

7   **Burnaby and Yaletown (1989-2011)**
       Later Years at SFU   282
       Undergraduate Directorship   285
       Retirement   289
       Yaletown   300

8 **The Road Back**

    Losing the Faith and Growing Up 303

    Pockets of Disbelief 305

    The Embeddedness of Reason 307

    The Human Capacity for Delusion 311

    Need for Conceptual Clarity 315

    The Accretion of Disbeliefs 318

    Being a Non-Theist 326

    Myths About Non-Theists 328

    On Being Non-Religious 331

    Leaving Damascus 335

9 **The Road Ahead**

    Vision for the Future 341

    Public Education 343

    Health Care 348

    Democracy 349

    Environmental Sustainability 351

    Redistribution of Wealth 352

    Projects for the Planet 354

    The New Jerusalem 364

    Appendix 1 – Genealogical Chart 369

    Appendix 2 – Grandfather's Death 370

    Appendix 3 – Acknowledgements 378

    Index 380

PREFACE

MY MAIN PURPOSE in writing this memoir is to make available a record of my life for children, grandchildren, other relatives, and anyone else who is interested. I write also to undergo the exercise of self-discovery, self-enrichment, and self-development by reviewing, refining, and reifying my values, opinions, and ideals. In the writing of my life story, I also wish to leave some historical insights and information from my brief sojourn on the planet. Finally, I also hope to promulgate some ideas that arise from commenting on and reflecting upon some of the experiences I relate.

There is a sense in which the whole enterprise of writing one's story is a creative act and somewhat mythical. So I wish here to clarify how I conceive of and proceed with the writing of autobiography.[1] By no means is it possible or interesting to record all events in a lifetime. Not only would it take forever to do, but it would also be exceedingly tedious to read. Memoirists must perforce make a selection of what to record and relate. They will choose those events that to them seem important, relevant, and interesting according to some criteria which they also choose. Thus the writing of a memoir is necessarily a creative act, which gives the story a mythical ring, but is nevertheless not fiction.

---

1 I use 'autobiography', 'memoir', and 'life story' synonymously.

Memoirists have a number of options available to them in the writing of their stories. One such option is to write a somewhat fictionalized account of life, drawing largely on memory and documents, but nevertheless embellishing the account by imaginatively stretching the truth or omitting vital truths so that everything fits neatly into a compelling, dramatic story. We love to read stories because they have plots – beginnings, middles, and ends. All the characters and events feed into the plot, giving it movement and direction. In a good story there is nothing extraneous, nothing that doesn't help develop the plot. All the details – characters, geography, language and such – fit neatly together to form a unity around the author's central purpose. Autobiography written with this story-telling approach compromises the truth for the sake of the story line. It is autobiography written with a nod to art, to the publisher, to fame, and to royalty cheques.

Another approach to the writing of autobiography is to research thoroughly and record faithfully. To avoid error and to prevent embarrassment or affront, this kind of chronicler eschews personal opinions, emotions, feelings, reflections, and observations about the events recorded. The records have historical significance and may well satisfy family curiosity, but they often are dull reading and really don't convey to the reader who the writer actually was as a person. This is autobiography written with a nod to the historian.

A third approach is to write a story of one's life as truthfully as possible by choosing episodes deemed to be important by the author, including painful or even hurtful incidences in the interest of revealing the inner person, revealing, as they say in the business, 'warts and all'. Ray Mango, in his *Your Autobiography*, notes "truth is worth any risk of anguish."[2] Fictionalized content around some recognizable real life will not serve here. This is autobiography written with an eye to the truth in all its facets, including emotional truth about the inner person.

There are no doubt many other approaches to the writing of autobiography. Of the three approaches I have described, I attempt to use the third, which in a sense is a compromise between the first

---

2   Ray Mango, *Your Autobiography*, Collier Books, NY, 1993, p.16.

two. That allows me to comment on the episodes I choose to write about, including remarks amounting to observations, extrapolations, clarifications, interpretations, and even arguments. These musings at times give the work the flavour of what could be characterized as autobiographical essay.

Often memoirists use metaphors such as 'journey', 'road', 'unfolding', 'voyage', 'race' or 'calling' for their life's story. These notions connote forward movement according to a plan toward a predetermined destination as in a plot in a story. My brother, Peter, for example, in the forward to his memoir says, "By writing my story, the plot of life's incidences may become apparent".[3] It would seem he subscribed to the view that there is a pattern in life (the plot) which is given and directed from outside the self and that the "plot surfaces", is "discovered", "becomes apparent". I want here to resist the idea that a design in life becomes apparent, is revealed, is discovered by reviewing life's episodes and that memoir writing is the exercise of discovering the design, purpose, or plot. Our existential lot is to live and write our own story, if 'story' indeed it is. Life, in fact, is not at all like a story. At least mine wasn't/isn't. My life was full of many little stories often at cross purposes, full of contradictions and false starts with interludes of humdrum events not worth recording.

The story that emerges here is one I authored, not discovered. I authored it both in the sense that I chose in large measure to have the experiences I did in fact have and in the sense that what I am telling here is a selection of experiential material hammered into a hopefully coherent and readable account. Piecing together bits of my life into a tale with coherence and direction is an act of re-creating my life story, creating a new experience, a new reality. Writing my story has changed me and my perception of myself. Writing one's story is, like life itself, an exercise in self-enactment.

Before this turns into an essay on how to write autobiography, an exercise in "scratching where it doesn't itch"[4], I must conclude this preamble and get on with the real thing. "Time driveth

---

3   Peter M. Hamm, *Reflections on My Journey*, self-published, Abbotsford, 1993, p.vii.
4   The phrase is not mine. I came across it in my readings, but couldn't find it again.

onward fast, and in a little while our lips are dumb."[5] So before my lips are dumb and before my pen has ceased "to glean my teeming brain",[6] I must make it tell the story of my brief visit on this planet, tell it to anyone who cares to hear, anyone who cares to know about another human being's turmoil, struggles, and failures and, perhaps more rarely, also about life's successes, triumphs, and achievements.

Although my story is not one of extraordinary accomplishments nor of extreme hardship and debilitating failure, it is a unique story as all biographies are. Because I am most likely the only world expert and authority on my own life, certainly on my memory of it, I am the only one able to tell it. So that is what I write about to the best of my ability, straining my faltering memory for accuracy and researching documents carefully to ascertain the truth as far as possible. I hope that I will provide some inspiration, edification, and illumination; but if I fail at that, my wish is that it will at least be entertaining.

---

5 Tennyson, "The Lotus-Eaters".
6 John Keats, "When I have Fears that I may Cease to Be".

CHAPTER ONE

Before La Glace

A Family Name

CORNEY. Just plain Corney. That is what my many siblings called me at home, as did my classmates at school, and others who knew me. *Khornie* is how my parents addressed me, pronounced with a breathy "k", a rolling "r", with a touch of concern in their voice, and more than a hint of German, rising at the end as if to ask, "Are you in trouble again?" At Bear Lake Bible Camp they gave me the nickname "bacon", for bacon is better than "corny ham". Ha ha ha. So I quickly learned just to laugh with them. Cornelius is what it should have been, a name common among my forebears and no doubt originally after the first Roman convert to Christianity. But Mr. Larsen, local store owner and registrant, said that in this country the English version is Corney; and so that is how I was officially registered. Much later, I had my name legally changed to Cornel after a post-secondary institution responded to my request for an application form with "we don't accept nicknames on applications". Before I took up university studies, I completed a four year program of Bible studies to obtain the credentials (at least in some circles) for the designation of "Reverend", which I narrowly escaped becoming. Instead, after a year at Normal School qualifying to become a certified teacher, I became "Mister Hamm" in elementary schools and "Sir" in secondary schools, where some colleagues sometimes affectionately called me "Hammy". Then it was "Dad" or "Pa" and later "Grandpa" and even "Grumpy Grandpa". At university it was "Doctor" or "Professor". For a while on the farm, my doubting neighbours looked in on "the Prof" to see if he could make a go of it. He did. When they began to call me just "Cornel" I realized that I had earned their respect and had become an equal.

To this day some few of my friends and relatives still (or perhaps again) call me just plain "Corney". And I feel comfortable with all these monikers for they do after all represent who I am and sum up my life in a nutshell. There but for the details is my memoir. But before I provide those details I must step back in history and fill you in briefly on my heritage and the events that happened before I arrived on the scene in La Glace.

As noted, "Cornelius" (or Kornelius) should have been my name, since it appears so frequently in the families of my forefathers. My great-great-great-grandfather on my maternal grandfather's side was Cornelius Warkentin. Little is known about him except that he lived in the Danzig/Gdansk region of Poland and his sixth son, Dietrich, shows up in the lineage whence down the line appears my mother. I also had three great grandfathers named Cornelius. There was Cornelius Penner (1847-1935), on my paternal grandmother's side, who was born in the Borosenko colony in the Ukraine. He was a good farmer and preacher, like many in my family. There was great-great-grandfather, Cornelius Voth (1795-1859), on my maternal grandmother's side, who emigrated from Poland to the Molotschna colony in the nineteenth century. His son, by the same name (1832-1914) became my great-grandfather. He moved from the Molotschna to the Zagradovka colony, where his daughter, my grandmother, Katharina, met and married my grandfather Johann Warkentin. This Katharina deserves further mention, which I will get to in a moment. First let me add that many more Cornelius's show up in the lineage that represents my family tree. One such was my Uncle Kornelius (1909-1939?), my father's youngest brother, who on trumped up charges, was sent to Siberian work camps like so many others under Stalin's regime. In the last letter his wife received from him, written on June 9, 1939, he writes:

> *Lately I have been working with horses, hauling logs out of the forest to the shore of the 'Wishers' River, which empties into the 'Kama' River.*
>
> *I long to see you all. When I see children playing here (when walking or driving to work) my heart is almost torn out of my chest. But I believe I will see you again.*
>
> *Do not be overly concerned about me; and don't deprive yourself of your last possessions for me. I am not suffering. I have enough to eat.*[7]

They never did meet again. Sometime after that he perished, never to be heard from (or of) again. I find it hard to believe that he didn't suffer, for Siberian work camps were not generally fun places to be. More likely he was trying to prevent his family from further heartache.

Another would-be Cornelius Hamm is my double cousin (our fathers were brothers and our mothers were sisters), Neil Hamm, from San Jose California, where he prospered in machining and real estate. Neil emigrated to Canada just after World War 2 after harrowing experiences traipsing across Europe to the Western Zone of Germany. Neil and I have become close friends and golf partners.

Quite a lot is known and documented about my family tree or genealogical linkage.[8] Much less is known about the actual lives of my grandparents. I never met any of them. From the little that is

---

7 From the *Hamm Journals*, collected by my father Martin Hamm. These are on file in my study and available elsewhere.

8 Three major sources of information on my Mennonite heritage and family genealogy are: Martin Hamm's *Aus der Alten in die Neue Heimat*, Mennonite Press, Winnipeg 1971 (translated as *My Old Home and the New*, by Marianne Ewert Worcester, 1972); Peter Hamm's, *Reflections on My Journey*, self-published, 1993; and a short genealogical chart based on the California Mennonite Historical Society.

known I will remark briefly on two of them, my mother's mother and my father's father. Grandmother Katherina (Voth) Warkentin (1869-1915), born in Zagradovka, was an eighteen-year-old babysitter for the four children of a young preacher of a local church. The preacher, Johann Warkentin, a widower, went to his church elder, Voth, (Katharina's father) for counsel about what to do about his dilemma with motherless children. Voth advised him to marry. Warkentin replied, "Yes. If only I could find someone like your Katie!" Much to Warkentin's surprise, Voth then said, "Then you must ask her". He did ask and she accepted. My brother Peter, in his *Reflections...* writes:

> *Imagine an 18 year old woman assuming responsibility of instantly becoming the Mother of four children, along with marrying a man eleven years her senior! No doubt, being entrusted with the four children during the Sunday services demonstrated the trust placed on her capability of becoming their Mother and the Mother of yet another nine children of her own, not to mention the added four who died at childbirth or shortly thereafter. Those who personally remember Grandmother Warkentin speak of her with great affection... She was very seriously-minded (sic), religiously devout woman and had high expectations of her children. Sobriety was her watchword... Unfortunately she died probably due to inadequate medical attention... at the early age of forty-six after a prolonged illness resulting from an accident with a runaway carriage in which she broke several ribs and punctured her lung.*[9]

Grandfather Martin Hamm (1869-1919) was an evangelist by choice of career and a farmer out of necessity. Born at Cherson, he moved to Borosenko colony in 1877, married there and moved to

---

9   *Reflections...*, p.9.

Grandparents Martin & Helena Hamm   *Grandparents Johann & Katharina Warkentin*

Schoenau, Zagradovka in 1910. His oldest son, my father, Martin Hamm, writes of him, "In terms of personality, I would liken him to a small Luther or Menno. Before God, a worm; in his struggle with powers of darkness, a giant. He has been a blessing to many."[10] He was quite evidently a stalwart in the Mennonite community in the Ukraine, travelling widely to preach, baptize, counsel, evangelize, and attend Bible studies and conferences. Fearless in speaking his mind, he aroused the ire of his own church (Allianz) by insisting on baptism by immersion, the ire of the General Conference church for his denunciation of their formalism and apathy, and the ire of the Mennonite Brethren church for allowing all believers to participate in communion irrespective of denominational affiliation. Because grandfather was a significant figure and spiritual leader in his village, he was also a target for the roving Machno bandits who, following the Russian Revolution and civil war, criss-crossed at will the entire region of the Mennonite

---

10 *Reflections...*, p.6.

settlements, pilfering, raping, killing, and burning entire villages in search of plunder and revenge. On Dec 1, 1919 my grandfather was brutally murdered in his home village.[11] Both my father, and my brother Peter in their journals (and others too) have given detailed accounts of how it all happened.[12] It is not necessary here to retell that gruesome story. I will add only this notation from Peter's 'Reflections...'.

> *Apparently Grandfather was loved by everyone. One lady responded to the news of his death with the words 'Schoenau is just not worth as much to me if Mr. Hamm is not there'.*[13]

Among the occupations of my forefathers are the following: tailor, watchmaker, estate manager, preacher, oil miller, and (predominantly) farmer. A number of them also lived to a ripe old age, some well into their nineties.

Before I introduce you to my own parents, I need to say something more about my Mennonite heritage in general. Well might you ask, "What are all these people with German and Dutch sounding names doing in the steppes of Russia?" To answer that, I need to take another step back in history and tell very briefly the story of the Mennonites in general.[14]

---

11   An account of this, written by my father in 1927, is part of the *Hamm Journals* and is Appendix 2 in this work.
12   See Appendix 2.
13   *Reflections...*, p.12.
14   Very briefly because the story has been told over and over, not only by my own family, but by professional historians. Many good Mennonite histories are readily available to interested readers. See, for example, Frank H. Epp, *The Mennonites in Canada 1920-1940: A People's struggle for Survival*, MacMillan of Canada, 1982; or Andrea Schroeder, *The Mennonites: A Pictorial History of their Lives in Canada*, Douglas & McIntyre Vancouver/Toronto, 1990.

The Mennonites

MENNO SIMONS, from whom the name 'Mennonites' came, was a Roman Catholic priest in the Friesland area of the Netherlands, who broke away from Catholicism in 1536 over issues of mass and infant baptism. He and his followers believed in voluntary church membership upon confession of faith and in baptism by immersion. In this they were similar in outlook to other 'Anabaptists' in the Christian Protestant reform movement. But the Mennonites went a step or two further in their reform. In taking the Bible literally with respect to 'turning the other cheek' and 'ye are not of this world', they adopted a non-resistance (or conscientious objection) stance to war and lived a very simple rural lifestyle in colonies. Peter, in his *Reflections...* puts it this way: "discipleship [was] expressed in holy living with the ethics of love and non-resistance in all human relationships."[15]

For taking this stance, they were persecuted and branded unwelcome in Dutch Friesland. So they moved to East Friesland, Germany, and thence to more tolerant Poland around the area of Gdansk. (It was there that my great-great-great-grandfather, Martin Hamm, was born in 1742.) From the mid to late 1500's to about 1800, the Mennonites prospered in the Vistula Delta. Then, in 1772, the region came under the control of the militaristic Prussian, Frederick the Great. Immediately friction developed between the state and the non-militaristic Mennonites, who not only refused to serve in the military but also demurred from paying taxes to support the Lutheran state church.

By 1789 things came to a head when an edict was issued which forbade Mennonites to own land. Catherine the Great of Russia was aware of what was happening. Having long wanted to settle the steppes north of the Crimean Peninsula, she now lured the Mennonites into that area with promises of religious freedom and exemption from military service. It worked. The first of them began

---

15   *Reflections...*, p.2.

immigrating in 1778 to the Chortiza River, which empties into the Dnieper where Zaporozhye is today. By 1800 four hundred families had settled in the colony of Chortiza, farming over 89,000 acres in 15 different villages. They came in droves and soon daughter colonies were established in all directions. The biggest colony was Molotschna, where, by 1835, 1200 families in 58 villages farmed some 324,000 acres. My great-great-great-grandfather Martin Hamm settled in a village in Chortiza just after 1800. My great-great-great-grandfathers Cornelius Warkentin and Cornelius Voth (previously mentioned) settled in Molotschna. Molotschna's daughter colony, Zagradovka, was established in 1871 some 200 kilometers north west of the home colony. Here in the village of Schoenau my father and Mother grew up. Thus it was that my forebears came to Russia (now the Ukraine) together with many other Mennonites, who prospered there for 125 years or so.

Not all of them stayed however. After the Crimean War (1853-1856), Tsar Alexander II, reneging on the promises of Catherine the Great, introduced universal military service, and many Mennonites became agitated over the touchy issue. The reversal of the Russian stance on non-resistance triggered a response of packing up and moving on yet again, this time from Russia to North America. So between 1874 and 1880, 18,000 of them emigrated to the United States and Canada. Once again, at considerable cost, inconvenience, and emotional leave-taking, these Mennonites decided to uproot and move on for religious reasons as they had repeatedly done in their history. They were and are an extremely religious people, with their faith nearly always coming first. This strong faith they share in large part with other evangelical protestant Christian sects, but on the issue of non-resistance they stand apart from them.

The other issue that set the Mennonites apart was the more rarely discussed religious ideal of 'other worldliness'. By this I mean at least the following: (1) not caring overly much about possessions and riches (though not all Mennonites actually lived up to this ideal in their prosperous years); (2) living simple lives ('schlict' in German), not chasing after modernity and sophistication, be-

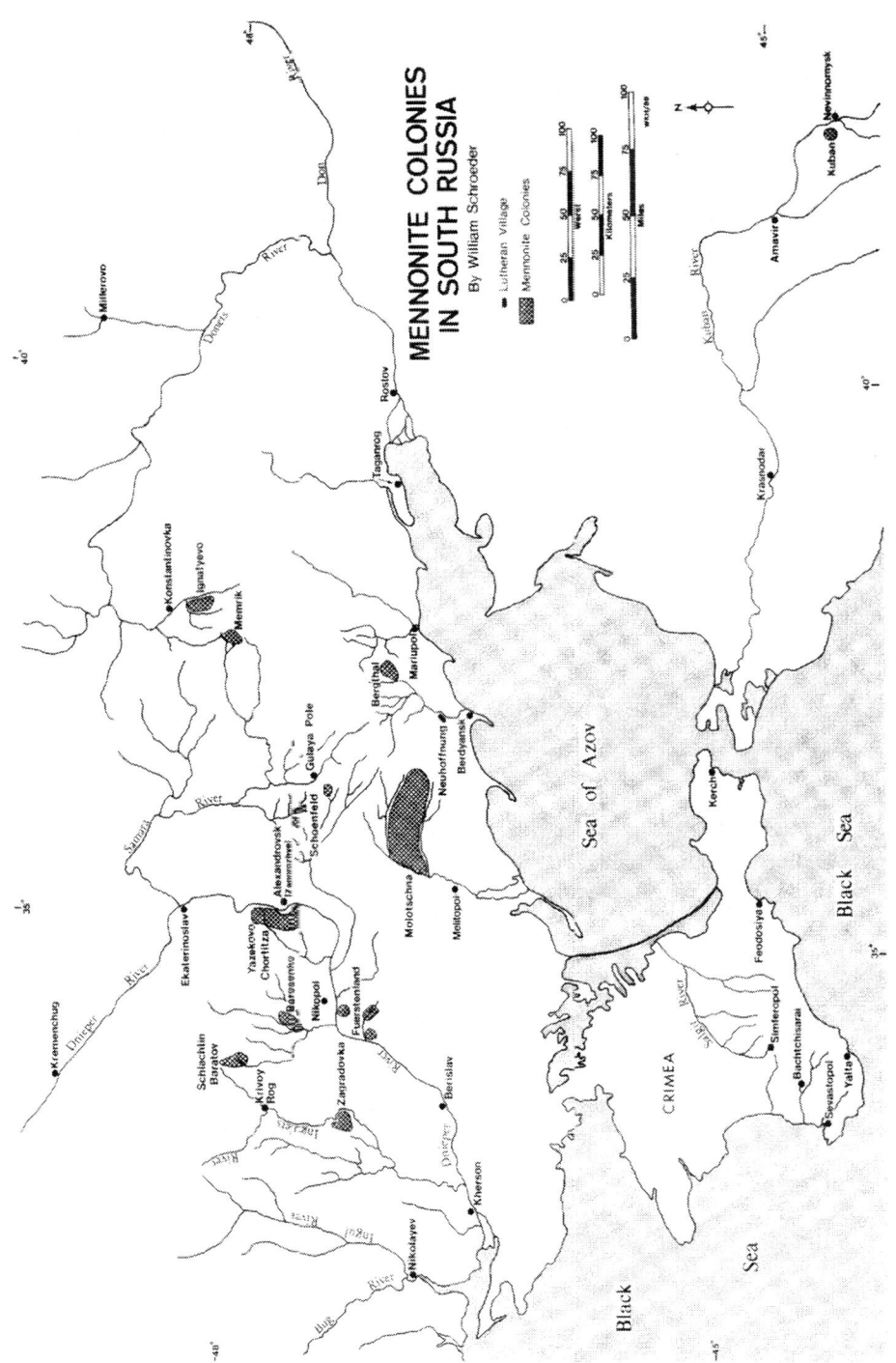

ing forthright, straightforward, honest, eschewing pretentiousness, guile, and dissimulation; (3) deliberately not following modern conventions and styles to advertise their otherness and their separateness from the rest of the world, letting the world know that in their view they have higher goals and intentions; (4) deep belief in and a longing for a much spoken of and sung about preoccupation with a better life after death, the real home awaiting those who keep the faith and survive in purity this veil of tears, this world where they have no fixed address. This 'other-worldliness' often took on different forms of expression from group to group and from time to time.

Often Mennonite churches split over the degree of worldliness permitted. In my own time I observed (in Pennsylvania, U.S.A.) churches breaking up over the colour of bumpers on cars, with white or chrome being the most worldly; red, a shade less worldly; and black, fully acceptable by even the most pious. Mennonites' separateness was also expressed in prohibitions against dancing, movies, TV (when it first appeared), gambling, card playing, drinking of liquor (not even a little wine is good for the Mennonite soul), sports on Sundays or joining any non-Mennonite team, swearing, dating for young people, and more. For women, immodest dress, perfume, showy jewelry, fancy hairstyles, and the wearing of trousers were all proscribed.

The point of it all was constantly to remind themselves that this life was but a short-term testing ground for the real world beyond. Theirs was an intense longing for a permanent, unspoiled (and unspoilable), peaceful, ideal, and eternal home; a home free of pain and sorrow, free of hate, war and suffering. This longing, born of wandering and persecution, is in the blood and marrow of Mennonites. This longing is expressed poignantly in the songs they sing or used to sing. It may be surprising to believers that non-believers still in nostalgic moments resonate with these sentiments even though they don't believe in any of it. One volume of the 'Dreiband' (a three volume hymn collection) is entitled 'Heimatklänge' (sounds or songs of home), though the theme rings true through the entire Dreiband:

Meine Ruhe ist dort im Heimatland
Wo Sorgen und Leid sind unbekannt

(My peace is over there in the homeland
Where worry and sorrow are unknown)

Later when the Mennonites joined forces with the American Evangelical movement, they seemed to resonate easily with similar ideas as expressed by the Charles E. Fuller Quartet in the song:

This world is not my home
I'm just a passing through
My treasures are laid up
Somewhere beyond the blue...
... I cannot feel at home in this world anymore

Similar idea, yes, but similar in overall outlook, I'm not so sure. I just can't imagine prosperous Californians chasing down the freeway on the way to the Rose Bowl in shiny new Cadillacs with the radio blasting, "This world is not my home, I'm just a passing through..." and actually *believing* it. Neither the melodies nor the language have the same poignancy of the Dreiband, expressing the historic longing of a people well acquainted with suffering.

Unless one understands this sentiment of 'other-worldliness', one cannot really understand the Mennonites at their core. If one does understand this central feature about them, then it enables one better to understand how easy and natural it is for children of the Mennonite community to believe and accept the whole doctrinal package in which this sentiment is embedded and expressed.

The ravages of civil war and revolution in the Ukraine following World War I and the Russian Revolution was devastating to the Mennonite colonies there, once again adding another note of sadness to their songs of home. Disease, famine, and violence claimed the lives of about 2200 of them during that time. The dread of Communism and the fear of losing the land and the livelihood that they had worked so hard to gain prompted many to seek escape from

Russia. It was high time to move on again. Between 1923 and 1927, 18,000 Mennonites, my parents among them, emigrated to Canada. That exodus was the beginning of the end of Mennonites in Russia.

My Parents Emigrate to Canada

AFTER THE BOLSHEVIK Revolution and the civil war ended in Russia and a New Economic Policy was introduced in 1921 by Lenin at the Tenth Party Congress, there began a time of relative calm in the country. Some private property was restored, restrictions on private trade ended, and forced grain requisitions ceased. The Ukraine Mennonites began to hope that their persecutions had ended as well, and that things would get better. Many who had been tempted to emigrate changed their minds. Others, like my father, kept emigration constantly in mind. But the new prosperity allowed him to get married, buy a farm, and start raising a family.

My father, Martin Hamm (1899-1982) was born on June 29, 1899 in Blumenhof, Borosenko, Ukraine near the city of Nikopol on the Dnieper River. In 1910, when Dad was 11 years old, his family moved to Schoenau, Zagradovka in search of better land and enhanced religious association. Dad did very well in school, his father instilling in him and his siblings a love of reading and learning and a yen for travel and adventure. At the same time, as Peter reports in *Reflections...*, "Grandmother catered individually to her children's whims and fancies. Dad admits they were thoroughly spoiled."[16]

Dad spent two years in Alexanderkrone, Molotschna, finishing high school and studying commerce. While there, he contracted typhus and nearly died. There too, he had a conversion experience that radically altered his ambitions in life. When he returned to Zagradovka, he began studying theology with H. Neufeld of Orloff. He had hoped eventually to study theology in Berlin and become a missionary, but that became impossible when the Russian Revolu-

---

16   *Reflections...*, p. 10.

tion and ensuing chaos intervened. With Grandfather's death at the hand of the Machnos in late 1919, Dad took over the family farming operations with his brother Frank. During this time he also became active in the local church as a leader of young people and the director of the choir. One of the choir members was Anna Warkentin, my mother, who was attracted to this devout young man. She didn't yet know it, but he was attracted to her too.

It was not customary for young Mennonite adults to date, but it was customary for a young woman to show affection by giving a gift to someone who was special. So for Christmas Mother knit and presented Dad with a coloured scarf. Thereupon, Lena, Dad's younger sister, became a go-between. By spring that year, they had arranged to meet in the garden, where Dad and Mother planned their future together. On August 28, 1921 they were married on Warkentin's farm in a cleaned and decked-out granary large enough to hold a huge gathering. Shortly thereafter Dad had to return to the draft board to complete his alternative military service. Dad writes in his journal *Aus Der Alten*:

> *We all carried as much food and provisions as possible. I also had 35 pounds of rye flour which was too heavy to carry. I went to market (in Nikolyev) to sell it. It was possible to trade it for almost anything. I saw two gold rings for sale, and when the proprietor saw the flour he was ready to part with them. I did not bother bargaining for them since he obviously needed the flour. What a coincidence to find that the smaller ring had 'Anna' engraved on the inside, my wife's name. She would be so pleased with the ring. When we had parted neither of us had any idea that it would be such a long time before we would be together again. I guarded the rings as though they were the crown jewels, until I placed one of them on her finger five months later. She wore it all of her life.*[17]

---

17   M.Hamm, *Aus Der Alten*, p.38.

Mother's father, Johann Warkentin, moved to Schoenau, Zagradovka from the Molotschna colony in 1879 and there settled on prime acreages and became a wealthy farmer. His farm was the largest in the village. In 1889, now a widower with four children he married Katharina Voth (as already related). They produced nine children, the fifth of which was my Mother. She was born in 1896.

Not a great deal of information on my mother's childhood and youth is available. A few things we do know. She was raised in a very pious and industrious family. There were many devotions, prayers, and Bible readings. Johann Warkentin himself was a preacher as well as a farmer. Mother attended village school to the sixth grade, after which she worked at home often helping with farm work, the large family being mainly girls. The girls also took sewing lessons. Mother, having a natural artistic flair and being extremely dexterous, throughout her life sewed beautiful clothing, which she designed herself. She also developed a special ability to care for the sick without formal nursing training. Mother was also very generous. Dad notes that on their first Christmas together after marriage, Mother had gone missing for a while. It later became apparent that she had skipped out to canvas villagers for donations so she could distribute hampers to the poor.

When Dad returned from his alternative service, he and Mother lived for a while in the family summer suite (*Sommerstube*) and had meals with the family, as was the practice. Then in 1922 Dad purchased his own farm on credit. They moved into their own home on September 15, 1922. Three of my siblings were born there, Lena, March 19, 1923, Mary, March 7, 1924 and John, June 12, 1925.

By 1923, Dad started making noises about emigration, despite apparent political order and stability. Mother objected strongly, "Had I known that you wished to emigrate, I would not have married you" she protested. But there was no holding Dad back. His suspicions that things would not return to normal, at least as the Mennonites knew it, were later borne out. Despite Mother's objections, Dad persisted in preparing to emigrate if he at all could. It took him nearly three years to put all the pieces together. Difficult times lay ahead for those who chose to stay put, which was the bulk of both the Hamm and Warkentin families. One exception was my mother's younger brother Peter Warkentin and family. They had already emigrated to Swalwell, Alberta in 1925. They would be there to greet my parents at Acme, the nearest railway stop, when my parents arrived in 1926.

Before emigrating, my parents had to get together the funds for travel. To do this and to be prepared to depart suddenly they sold their home and auctioned off most of their possessions. Then there were passports and travel permits to obtain both for leaving Russia and for entering Canada. The latter was the biggest worry. Dad, and Lena too, had eye disease (trachoma), which was extremely difficult to cure. Finally, with much relief and great jubilation, they were cleared for emigration.

After a tearful leave taking (for they believed they would never see each other again, which in most cases turned out to be true), they boarded the train on March 7, 1926 and left Zagradovka for good. They travelled via Moscow and Riga to Danzig. From

Martin Hamm family immigrating from Russia, 1926

there they took a ferry to London. They boarded their transatlantic ship, the 'Melita', at Southampton. It was a difficult crossing, with Dad and Mother both getting very seasick. It took 11 instead of the planned 9 days finally to get to Saint John, New Brunswick. After another examination of the eyes and another quickening of the heart, they were on their way by train to Acme, Alberta, where Peter Warkentin greeted them with open arms and introduced them to Canada.

On To La Glace

FOR THE BETTER part of a year upon arrival in Canada Dad and Mother and their children lived with the P. Warkentins on their farm near Sunnyslope, Alberta. As well as helping on the farm at Warkentins, Dad also hired himself out as a labourer, taking on such jobs as installing telephone lines, fencing, constructing, stooking, and threshing. He also rented a small acreage and put in a crop of his own. Dad notes in his journal:

> *The first while after our arrival I was not feeling very well, probably because of the change in climate. I was constantly tired, almost too tired to stand up. But we could not afford to be sick because workers were few and far between.*[18]

When his crop was ready for reaping, he bought a binder for $60.00 and cut and stooked the grain, getting it threshed for free in return for labour. Dad goes on to say, "When the summer and harvest were over I sat down to estimate what our possessions were worth. It added up to a grand total of $800.00. Surely that would be enough for a new start in Northern Alberta."[19]

---

18   *My Old Home and the New*, p. 49.
19   Ibid., P. 49.

During the summer and fall of 1926 Dad had searched for land in the Swalwell area near the Warkentins, but found it too costly. Also, he had been lured northward to the Peace River country by acquaintances from the old country. So after the birth of my brother Martin on Nov. 8 and getting more and more anxious to have a home of his own, Dad, in January 1927 took a train to Grande Prairie to investigate the possibility of moving north. First he had to find the Aaron Janzen family, who had bought a farm near La Glace, some thirty miles northwest of Grande Prairie. Dad tells the story of how he, plied with cards, maps, addresses, and/or descriptions of available land, walked nearly the entire 30 miles in the deepening snow, arriving finally after dark at the A. Janzens, where he was welcomed and where he overnighted. As fate would have it, that very night Janzen's sickly child died. It was a tragic way to get introduced to the community. In a day or two, there was a funeral at which Dad officiated and where he met other Mennonite folk. On his way back to Grande Prairie, he also met the gregarious Alexander Voth. Dad now knew that he could, here in La Glace, have great fellowship with like-minded people.

Now he needed to find a farm. He was shown a quarter section that appealed to him. It had 15 to 20 bald acres and most of the rest was heavily wooded with poplars, an indication of good soil. What to do? He decided that if he could purchase the land at $8.00 per acre ($1280.00 in all) then he would buy it, that being a sign that it was God's will.[20] The offer was accepted. Now he had to hurry back to Sunnyslope to fetch his family and possessions.

Back in Sunnyslope, the growing Hamm family made preparations for moving. Since the government offered the free use of a railway car for people settling in the north, Dad decided to buy some livestock and farm machinery (cheaper than in the north) to take with him. Here is how he described the contents of the railway car:

---

20 There is a fuller description of this later in the book in Chapter 3.

> *The horses were put on one end of the car with the hayrack as a protective wall. On the other end were the few pieces of furniture, implements, stove, and fodder. In the middle lay the cow, a container of water and other stuff (including potatoes). I rested comfortably on top of the fodder. The family would follow a week later and I wanted to settle the livestock and make the [place] liveable in the meantime.*[21]

At Sexsmith, the nearest railway station to La Glace, he loaded all the goods on a sleigh, four horses towing the heavy load, the cow tied on behind, and headed 'home' to La Glace, 18 miles away. With great difficulty, tipping the load several times and having to reload all by himself on the slippery melting snow, he finally reached his destination the following day.

Over the next few days he repaired and cleaned the one-room log cabin as best he could, settled in the livestock, chopped firewood, and bought more fodder. Dad says, "It felt so good to be living on my own farm at last. Now everything would be fine."[22]

Then the family arrived. For Mother it was quite a shock to move into such a modest dwelling. "The walls were dirty, newspapers were stuck into the seams of the log walls in good bachelor fashion, and there was no ceiling, only unfinished roofing covered with tarpaper. But it was warm inside because the beams had been well stuffed with moss."[23] That was how Dad described the cabin. He did not know it at the time, but that first night Mother cried herself to sleep in disappointment. Because she didn't want to discourage Dad, she never let on till much later. As Dad put it, "A noble woman".

---

21   *My Old Home and the New*, p. 55.
22   Ibid., p. 56.
23   Ibid., p. 56.

Pioneering in La Glace

THE NEXT FEW YEARS leading up to my birth in 1931 were years of grueling hard work, the severity of which only an experienced pioneering farmer can imagine. In that first year (1927) in addition to putting in and taking off a crop, Dad almost single-handedly cleared 40 acres of thick bush during the months of May and June and then in July and August did the breaking (with an inadequate breaking plow), including disking, root-picking, and burning. Then it was on to join a threshing crew to bring in some much needed cash.

In each of the years that followed, there was more land clearing and breaking to be done. Other work included: barn and house additions and renovations; fencing; sawmilling in winter for scarce lumber; church building; constructing of granaries and animal shelters; cutting, hauling, and splitting firewood; delivering grain to distant elevators, and much more. All of this was in addition to the not inconsiderable work of growing grain on increasing acreages as the land was cleared. The hard work paid off though, and our ever growing farm prospered, all the while our family growing along with it. Anna arrived on October 30, 1927; Frank on April 4, 1929; and Peter on August 26, 1930. Now there were seven children in the family and the house was extended again.

Everything seemed to be progressing nicely, when suddenly in the fall of 1929 the price of wheat began falling. At the beginning of the harvest season wheat sold for $1.00 per bushel. Later in the fall it dropped to $0.35. By 1932, wheat sold for $0.23 to $0.25 per bushel and oats for $0.08 to $0.10. During the year of my birth, Dad took four 250 pound hogs to market in Sexsmith. The usual hog purchaser was not buying; but feeling sorry for Dad, he advised Dad to try the butcher. The butcher gave him only $15.00 for all four! The Great Depression was in full swing.

Luckily for farmers, the lack of cash in the Depression era did not mean lack of food but it certainly meant financial difficulties including having an extremely hard time meeting credit and mortgage payments. Fortunately the government stepped in to prevent farm foreclosures if the farm was an otherwise healthy operation. So we managed to keep our farm and postpone and /or lower debt payments until better times arrived.

Meanwhile the stage was set for my appearing in the world.

CHAPTER TWO

La Glace (1931-1945)

My Birth

ON A COLD December night in the Peace River country just before Christmas in 1930, my father and mother, having already produced seven healthy children, engaged in a bit of frivolity (one would imagine, or at least hope) and got me going on a nine month trip towards my birthday. I showed up in the midst of threshing season on September 23, 1931.

The place of my birth was our farm house located two miles south and one mile west of the hamlet of La Glace, itself some thirty miles northwest of the regional centre of Grande Prairie, which is located about three hundred miles northwest of Edmonton, Alberta, Canada. I used to say flippantly, when asked where I came from, "hundreds of miles north of nowhere". And that's the way it seemed at times. Yet for me that modest farm home, that small hamlet and surrounds were very special, very dear. They still are. That was, after all, my only home for the first fourteen years of my life.

The fact that Euripides (480BC), Augustus Caesar (63BC), Kublai Khan (1205AD), Carl Munzinger (1842), Walter Lipman (1889), Mickey Rooney (1920) and Bruce Springsteen (1949) were all born on a September 23, the date of my birth, has no significance for me whatsoever. Of some significance, however, and worth mentioning, are some events that occurred the *year* of my birth. In the year 1931: Japan successfully invaded Manchuria, renaming it Manchukuo; Thomas Edison submitted his last patent application and later that year died; gangster Al Capone was indicted on 5000 counts of prohibition violations and perjury, and was sentenced to 11 years in prison; the Nazi Party continued its fateful rise to power in Germany; Lord Cecil of the British Government said "war is never so improbable" (eight years before the outbreak of WW2); the British Statute of Westminster gave complete legislative independence to Canada (and other commonwealth nations); Spain became a republic; New York's Metropolitan Opera broadcast an entire opera on radio for the first time; the USA began the construction of the Hoover Dam; and Mahatma Gandhi was released from jail and negotiated with Viceroy Lord Irwin the Gandhi-Irwin pact.

While these events did not and would not directly and immediately affect me, they nevertheless are the signposts of the historical time frame into which I was born, a backdrop for the stage on which I play my brief role. On that backdrop one sees the world in economic turmoil; world-wide shifting of political power; democracies like Canada, Australia, and New Zealand coming to full maturity; war and rumour of war not disappearing in the world; prohibition failing in the USA; and discoveries and inventions rising sharply.

The year 1931 also witnesses the following: Charlie Chaplin receives France's distinguished Legion of Honour; the Empire State Building opens; the cyclotron is invented by E. Lawrence in San Diego, USA; DuPont introduces synthetic rubber; the first infrared photograph is taken in Rochester, N.Y.; the first non-stop Trans-Pacific flight (Herndon and Panghorn) is made; Maple Leaf Gardens opens in Toronto; commercial teletype service begins (AT&T); the George Washington bridge opens connecting New York and New Jersey.

While the above events serve to present an historical perspective on the era of my generation, they, I believe, nevertheless do not represent the major determinants of my successes and failures in life. Yes, there probably are better and worse times in history to be born and to live. I think my time was relatively fortunate despite being born in the depths of the Great Depression in an unsophisticated rural community. I have always believed that the better and worse in life is in large part of our own making. No matter what the happenstance of birth, each new generation has to figure out how their world works, what social, political, educational, and industrial resources are available to them and bring to bear on the mix their own abilities, ambitions, and visions and hammer out a mode of life of their own. Nor do I believe in being born under a lucky (or unlucky) star or favourable (or unfavourable) configuration of planet and stars. Other elements than the time of one's birth come into play in the shaping of one's future. The environment, particularly the family environment into which one is born, has a profound effect.

So what were the circumstances of my birth? Since I was born in our farm house, everybody, including me, assumes that mine was an easy birth. More than likely that was true, but nobody knows for sure. Mrs. C. Friesen[24], Mother's best friend in La Glace, told me that Mother gave birth very quickly and easily. Who attended my birth? Nobody knows exactly. Very likely, Mrs. Gertrude Webber, a neighbor, was there acting as a mid-wife. In his autobiography my brother Peter writes:

> *It appears that by the time I was born there was a change in mid-wives and Mrs. Gertrude Webber... prominent member of the La Glace community was called to assist.*[25]

I do not see why there would be another change in mid-wives just over a year later so I am assuming that Mrs. Webber was midwife at my birth too, but nobody knows for sure. Was my father

---

24 I interviewed Mrs. C. Friesen in La Glace in 1992 and asked her specific questions about Mother. In other sections of this book I will have reason to refer to this interview again.

25 P. Hamm, *Reflections on My Journey*, p.24.

present at my birth? Nobody knows that for sure either. He was probably away threshing, for it was mid-week (Wednesday) and he would not yet have come home for the Sabbath. When Peter was born on August 26, 1930, Dad was at home bindering when signs of his arrival were evident. Dad then interrupted the harvesting and went to fetch Mrs. Webber and on the way also picked up Annie Janz, then a late teenager, who came to take care of the other children. Peter was the seventh child; I was the eighth; and two more were to follow. Peter writes:

> *Annie informs me that she rounded up the other children to take them for a walk, while Mrs. Webber attended to my birth. Although my own Mother attended to my daily care, Mrs. Webber returned for three successive days to assure Mother's satisfactory recovery. And Annie stayed for a full week to attend the other children.*[26]

Peter speculates that for three successive years such arrivals interrupted the all-important harvest, Peter's birth (Aug. 26, 1930), mine (Sept. 23, 1931) and Walter's (Sept. 11, 1932). However, there is no way he could have known this for sure. Even in his own case, he does not comment on what Dad did after fetching Mrs. Webber. Did Dad immediately go back to bindering? I would think so. Why wouldn't he? He would of course, stand by the ready in case Mrs. Webber were unable to cope or if an emergency arose, but as already noted, Mother gave birth easily. Dad would very likely *not* have interrupted harvesting in any serious way even during childbirth. A brief pause to get the personnel in place, yes, but not interrupt the momentum of the critical harvest work. It would seem to me uncharacteristic of him to take ceremonial or celebratory time off in the midst of the urgency to get the crop off the field in the brutally short growing season of the far north.

---

26   Ibid, p.24.

In his memoirs Dad simply says about my birth, "On September 23, 1931, Cornel was born."[27] He then goes on to discuss other Korenelius' in his and Mother's families leaving no hint of what were the conditions of my birth nor of his whereabouts at the time. If Peter is correct in assuming that Dad interrupted the harvesting to attend to our births, Dad himself just does not share that information. I simply do not know what role my father played at my birth. I also can't say how much I weighed at birth, what the weather was, what time of day (or night) it was, whether or not any layette items were prepared for me (probably not) or even if I was laid to bed in a crib or a box. I must say that I am curious about these things, including what my Dad was doing during the time of my birth, but I guess it doesn't matter much in the long run. I was probably an unremarkable healthy baby in a long series of such, inheriting diaper and crib, blanket and bib, from the previous baby and passing the same on to the next.

Though all of us siblings were patterned after the same genetic blueprint, we did definitely have distinguishing features right from the start. There is some evidence that I was a cranky and demanding baby. Peter observes, "my siblings remember me as being quiet, not such a 'cry baby' as one of my brothers..."[28] I once asked an older sister if I was that cry baby. She smiled without responding verbally but that was enough for me to assume that that was indeed me. Babies, of course, cry for a reason. Perhaps I felt discomfort more keenly and more frequently than my siblings. Perhaps I may have had allergies, unknown to us at the time. Some early photos of me remind me of some of the early photos of my son, Colin, who had various food sensitivities and lactose intolerance right from birth on.

Perhaps an incident will help explain my early crankiness. I have been told several versions of the story of how I, before I could walk, was sitting on Mother's knee while she was cutting bread for the family breakfast. I reached in and grabbed at the knife with the intention to take over the operation, resulting in a big mess. I still have a scar on the bridge of my nose to show for it. Perhaps even

---

27 M. Hamm, *Aus Der Alten* ... p. 76.
28 *Reflections...*, op. cit., p. 20.

then I just knew more precisely what I wanted and rebelled at the strictures preventing me from getting it. If I was an early cry baby, I have my reasons to believe that it didn't last long.

Early Memories

I THINK THE very earliest memory I have, at age three or so (who can say?), is my mother giving me a brief lecture. We are standing in our yard, where we usually parked the buggy. She is holding my hand when I ask her "What is behind the sun?" She says, "Heaven, a very nice place where God lives and where we will all go one day if we are good. If we are not good and don't obey God, we will go down to hell and suffer terribly. But if we are good we will be forever happy." How's that for a lesson in cosmology, theology, and ethics all simultaneously in less than a minute by an uneducated 'unsophisticated' woman! I believed every word. Mother and father were, of course, always right. When they told us not to touch the stove or we'd get burnt, they were right. So of course we also accepted the heaven and hell stories as well. It is very rational for children to believe their parents. Though it doesn't always happen, it is equally rational for people to discard their parents' beliefs when they grow up and find that there is no evidence for them. Anyway, I recall feeling a warm glow of cocooning comfort and security on that occasion. Not only would my parents protect me, but the whole universe was there to shield me against danger if only I was good. And I would be good. So I knew it must be true that: "God's in his heaven; all's well with the world." I walked away from that experience with an optimistic, almost Pollyannaish, outlook. Even when it rained we were cheerful, singing "*Es regnet; Gott segnet; Die Erde wirt nass*" (It's raining; God's blessing us; and the ground is getting wet). I think it is fair to say that, despite a melancholy blue streak running through the genes of our family, including me at times, I have had a relatively cheerful disposition most of my life. It may very well be that that attribute stems from those early years.

Peter and Cornel, 1932   Walter and Cornel, 1934

Peta Es Doot.[29] Another early memory concerns my brother Peter's 'death' and 'resurrection' when I was perhaps still only three years old. It was summer time. I remember playing with a toy horse on the south facing verandah when I heard the sound of tin screeching followed by a plop and a few seconds later Mother screaming for someone to fetch Dad, who was working at the church a mile away. Meanwhile Mother carried Peter out to the verandah, gently tossing him in the air again and again trying to revive him while she wailed, "*Peta Es Doot! Peta Es Doot!*" Was Peter really *doot* like the chicks and piglets we sometimes saw die in the spring? He didn't seem *doot* to me, only asleep. Then Mother, between wails, prayed something, and by the time Dad returned, Peter was no longer *doot*. He had fallen through the stove pipe opening in the 'middle room' upstairs, the protective tin having given way. It was customary for us to remove the stove pipes in summer for cleaning. So Peter was the attention getter for at least that day. Miraculously he seems to have had no short or long term ill effects from the fall. In the evening there was much talk about God answering prayer.

---

29 Low German (*Plautdietsch*) for 'Peter is dead', pronounced 'pight-ah ess doubt'.

It strikes me as interesting and significant that mother, in a time of crisis, switched to her 'mother' tongue, *Pläutdietsch,* a language related to German, halfway between the Anglo-Saxon dialect of German (which went on to become Old English and then evolved into the English language) and proper High German. Is it the case that our profoundest and deepest emotions are more precisely and poignantly expressed in our mother tongue? Do we all automatically revert to our original language in times of crisis? If so, what language would I revert to?

I was brought up almost completely bilingually, with both German and English being spoken in our household, though English eventually overtook the German. By the time I came along there was an established pattern of speaking English between siblings and German with the parents. It was decided by the La Glace Mennonite community before I was born that the *Pläutdietsch* would be dropped in favour of High German.

The language issue brings back another early memory. I am standing on a footstool at the kitchen table beside an older sister learning English names for the various kitchen items while drying the dishes with a tea towel. I then declare to my sister that I am ready to go to school, but she says, "not yet". Apparently all of us children helped with household and farm 'chores' from the earliest years, even before school began. Our chores in later years included carrying firewood, cutting kindling, carrying water, feeding animals, collecting eggs (one of my favourites), weeding the gardens, fixing fences, cleaning seed grain, and hauling fodder for livestock. Somehow our parents were able to instill in us a love of work and the completing of tasks. The worst shame we could experience was that of being thought lazy.

When I was about five, Mother took me on a tour of the farmyard to show me where hens were likely to lay eggs other than in the hen house, like at a straw pile or under the granaries. Soon collecting eggs became a hobby for me. One day, I saw a rooster pecking a hens head, jumping on top of her, and hitting her with his tail. I ran to Mother and told her the rooster was trying to kill the hen. When I described to her what had happened, she said, "Oh no, the rooster has to do that in order for eggs to hatch chicks." So I put two and two together and surmised that that was similar to the boar jumping the sow or the bull on the cow. "But don't look", Mother added. Just like Dad said, "Don't look!" when the boar did it to the sow. So, of course, that is exactly what we did. We learned (on a farm it is unavoidable to learn) about 'the birds and the bees' from an early age, not only the mechanism for sex, and the necessity of it for life to continue, but also that sex was necessarily bad and should not be enjoyed or observed. Early on the elements were put in place for the battle against eroticism even before the onset of puberty.

La Glace School

IN EARLY SEPTEMBER, 1938, in the same month I reached the age of seven, I entered grade one at La Glace School, situated on the northeast corner of Abe Janz's home quarter just over a mile away from home. During the first few months at school I remember that I felt very comfortable and that Miss Metcalfe, our teacher, was very nice. There were twelve of us in Grade One and we often crowded around the sand table for hands-on lessons. Other than that, I don't remember much.

It would be very likely that I, together with four or five siblings[30] walked to school, taking a short cut past the manure pile, past the nearest granary and diagonally northwest across the grain field in a perfectly straight line to link up with the dirt road that took us to the school.

The building itself was a typical one-room prairie schoolhouse with one wall of east facing windows and two walls of blackboard. It contained rows of desks on runners, a cloak room, a shielded space for the wood stove, an area for the teacher's desk, and some space for a sand table. At the back of the school yard

---

30 Perhaps one or two stayed home to help with the farming.

was a horse barn, very useful for feeding and sheltering the horses used for transporting us to school during extreme weather conditions. Halfway to the barn were the boys and girls 'comfort stations'. Just north of the school was our one piece of playground equipment with multiple grab-on handles attached to chains which hooked onto a rotating wheel at the top of a steel post. When not in motion the chains would hang straight down, but when children grabbed the handles and ran in a circle, the chains would flail out by centrifugal force. The faster we went the further out we spread until our feet actually left the ground and we were flying. Then we would let go to see how far we could jump away from the centre. Because the whole contraption was made of steel and chain, when we let go for our jump, the large steel handles and chain would crash into the steel pole and against each other with a terrific noise. Bang! Bang! How I remember that clang! How no one got seriously injured playing this dangerous game I don't know. Maybe they did.

In the winter we enjoyed another form of play, making and playing in igloos. The caragana hedge surrounding the school yard provided a perfect barrier for snow drifts to form and harden during blizzards. From these drifts we cut hay bale sized chunks of snow and formed them into igloos and connecting tunnels. The chunks were 'cemented' together with a bit of water which froze them together. With a hole in the top for air and a thick straw floor, these igloos became comfortable little play spaces. Often when it was not too cold we would grab our lunches and trade sandwiches (peanut butter for dairy butter, syrup for strawberry jam, bologna for zwieback) in our cozy little hideaway. Even in the harsh cold of winter, with many bodies huddled together, our igloos were warm and comfortable.

Apparently I didn't have much difficulty doing the school work, for on one occasion Miss Metcalfe asked me to show Abie, in Grade Two, how to do multiple column sums on the blackboard. So there I was in Grade One showing up a Grade Twoer. Or so I thought. Brother Martin later tactfully said that I got "all of them almost right".

One experience in Grade One that I remember very clearly is getting a strapping from the teacher that I liked so very much. It happened one morning before classes even began. Our family, doing the janitorial duties for the school, arrived quite early in the dark to start the fire in the heater to warm up the school before the others arrived. While waiting for the school house to warm, we entertained ourselves in various ways, doing math quizzes, reciting poetry, gazing at stars, or playing ink-bottle lid hockey with rulers between the desk rows. On this particular day, we were making farting sounds with our lips on our arms just to see who could draw the most laughs. Miss Metcalfe then arrived and quite sternly ordered us to quit. Just then my friend Henry came in from the porch and asked, "Why is Teacher so angry." I told him we were making noises like this, and then I demonstrated, not daring to use the word 'fart'. Miss Metcalfe heard me, and before I had time to explain she lashed me on the hands, blurting out, "This will teach you to be sassy!" Later when I explained all of this to Dad (and yes, he knew all about it, thanks to my ever vigilant siblings), he let me off without the customary reinforcement punishment and with only a mild reminder to be '*gehorsam*' (obedient). I interpreted that to mean that he agreed that the strapping had been unjust.

I got off lightly that time, but not the next time about a year later. This time the teacher more or less ignored the matter (if she knew about it at all) but my father was the one who administered the punishment – a good walloping. At school, on a mild spring day, my friends Abie and Ernie invited me during the noon hour to play 'doctor' in Ernie's caboose (a closed in box-like structure on two runners pulled by a single horse, which housed a comfortable seat and a functioning heater). This was the 'hospital' where doctors Abie and Ernie performed operations and set bones. I should have known better, for I was a 'good boy' because I was already 'saved'. They were 'bad boys', not having been 'saved', and probably up to some mischief again. While I was recuperating from an 'illness' in the 'hospital', it so happened that one of our female classmates showed up with a broken thigh bone. The break was high up near the pelvis, so quite a few pieces of clothing had to be removed. I watched with great interest as they got closer and closer to the mystery place, that tantalizing bit of female anatomy heretofore never observed. When I saw it, I was actually shocked because there was so little there. Sure, we already knew that boys peed through a 'pole' and girls through a 'hole', but was this all there was to the mystery? A little mound and a small slit and nothing else? How disappointing! It was not at all exciting or erotic.

It was all over in minutes. The bell rang for classes to begin anew. However, all afternoon I puzzled over what I had seen and couldn't concentrate on my school work. It all seemed so innocent, but apparently playing doctor had serious consequences. I knew that I had done something wrong, but what exactly was it that I had done to constitute the worst sin I had ever committed and would result in my getting the thrashing of my life? Just observing how half the human race is formed? In any case I somehow knew that I had brought great shame on the family simply from that innocent observation. To be sure Dad heard about this one. After school and during supper there was a big hush in our household. Everyone seemed to be pointing a silent finger at me. I knew that one of my older siblings had informed Dad and that Abie's father was coming over for a full discussion of the matter. A showdown was inexorably coming.

Sitting in the middle room, doing nothing but imagining the worst, I heard a cutter arriving in the yard. It was Abie's Dad. The discussion they had in the kitchen seemed to drag on and on, adding to my dread, though it was probably only a few minutes. When Abie's father left, I heard my name being called, "Khornie!" I answered and slowly approached as the dream-like sequence unfolded.

"Is it true that…?"

"Yes."

"Were you with Abie and Ernie…?"

"Yes."

"Don't you know that…?"

"Yes."

"Well then come with me."

Even though it was a mild spring evening, I was shivering as we walked silently past the garage to the patch of willows that grew alongside the slab fence marking out the garden behind. How I wished that it was summer and we were picking peas from the garden or even hoeing weeds in the potato patch. Dad asked me to pick a willow for the thrashing instrument, which he deftly cut with his pocket knife. The stick was about three-quarters of an inch in diameter and about eighteen inches long. Then my pants came down and I was whipped for the grievous sin I had committed. Streaks of fire burned into my buttocks. Of course I cried. Of course I was sorry. Of course I would never do it again. Of course God would forgive me if I truly repented. At long last it was over and I was sent to my tearful bed. I did repent and it did bring me some measure of peace again. That was seventy-seven years ago. It seems as though it happened yesterday.

By and large those first two years at La Glace community school were pleasant and I had made many friends. So it was quite disturbing when we heard rumours that the schoolhouse would be moved. A new school would be built on Lowe's bush quarter a mile south of us. That would mean that our big class would be split. It was thus with some sadness that we said our final goodbyes to friends at La Glace School at the end of June.

Old Post School

THE NEW SCHOOL on Lowe's quarter was called 'Old Post', a name not particularly flattering at first but a name we became very proud of later. It was so named because half a mile east of its location once stood a Hudson's Bay Company post where the Beaver Indians, inhabitants of the land before white settlers arrived, traded their pelts. These Indians were superior hunters, fierce warriors, peaceable, and honest. They surrendered their land by treaty in 1900 and no record of violence exists between them and the white settlers. George La Glace, their chief, restrained his tribe from using force against the settlers.

The old trading post was purchased in the late 1920's by our neighbor, Peter Wall, who dismantled it, moved it to his farmstead, and reconstructed it as the Wall's farm house. The Walls lived in that home until 1946. For years after that it stood on the old farm site as a rotting ruin. Then, beginning in 2001, an enterprising group of local citizens and the Grand Prairie Museum reconstructed the outpost to its original 1896 appearance and moved it to the Grande Prairie Museum's Heritage Village where it now stands.

Old Post School, 1949

Old Hudson's Bay Post reconstructed

My pride in the name 'Old Post' derives not from the bit of history just noted, interesting as that is, but from the actual educational achievements of the school during its existence. Old Post was very successful in doing what any free public educational institution in Canada (or anywhere for that matter) is designed to do – provide a modicum of general enlightenment in multiple disciplines, prepare children and young people with adequate skills to cope in society, implant moral and inter-personal attitudes that lead to a cohesive, harmonious society and at the same time give some of the children the background and opportunity for further study. This the teachers at Old Post achieved eminently. Of the children I knew during my five years there, most finished high school, a number of them (perhaps a disproportionally high number) completed a university degree, and at least four earned PhDs.

The number of children in the one-room school was upwards of thirty in all eight grades. Later when I became a school teacher I found it difficult enough to cope with 30 to 40 children in the same grade. How our teachers (Miss F. Smith for my Grade 3; Miss A. Kinderwater, Grades 4 and 5; and Mrs. L. Lowe, Grades 6,7 and part of 8) managed with eight grades is still a mystery to me. It took a great deal of skill and organization. It also required cooperation on the part of the children. I recall receiving help from an older student writing a report for a Social Studies project on Samuel Hearne's discovery of the Coppermine River in Northern Canada. Other times I might help grade mates (Elizabeth Friesen, Justine Wall, and George Konrad) with Arithmetic, which I found easy, sometimes finishing my Math for the full school year even before Christmas. This would allow time for free reading in the little closet-sized library. Among my favourite books at that time were: *Black Beauty, Anne of Green Gables, Call of the Wild, Wild Animals I Have Known, The Scarlet Pimpernel and Little David*. Some of these titles were given to us by Mrs. Lowe as prizes for such competitions as checkers, chess, ping-pong, or selling raffle tickets. Mrs. Lowe had a particular talent for instilling in us a love of reading books and reciting poetry. One way of achieving this was by reading to us orally every day just after 1:00 p.m. when afternoon classes began. Chapter by chapter she took us through *Anne of*

Green Gables and *Pinocchio* and other splendid stories. In that part of our English language studies called 'Oral Language', she had us make speeches and recite poetry from memory. She would also actually take us in her car after school to compete in elocution contests arranged by the wider community. I once won a prize for reciting poetry in a competition at Scenic Heights community centre.

We did not sufficiently appreciate Mrs. Lowe's qualities at that time but now I cannot praise enough this wise and talented person. She was the daughter of Walter McFarlane, who, with his crew, surveyed the Grande Prairie District in 1909 and 1910. She was married to Alex Lowe, a farmer who lived about a mile south of Old Post. Lillian Lowe obviously had a fine education and teacher training. She provided us not only with the basics (the three 'r's') but also with many extras, such as the competitions already mentioned. I recall enjoying immensely the all-day field trips onto the bush quarters adjacent to the school. On such trips we collected insects and leaves for scrap books and posters, and observed plants and animals, later to be described in our notebooks. In our spare time, and there seemed to be lots of it, we (including us boys) learned to knit and embroider. At Christmas we raffled off a patchwork quilt on which we had embroidered the family names of the entire school community. Another Christmas she had me sing a solo at the school Christmas concert. She was not so musically inclined, as I recall, but she did know how to get us to sing and act in plays. She selected the musical piece I was to sing and sent me home with it for my Dad (who was the church choir director) to teach me the song. So I entered the crude stage in the schoolhouse and fearlessly sang: "Watchman tell us of the night; with the star still burning bright…"

Mrs. Lowe carefully prepared us and coached us on many things, including competitions in the community sports day. She gave each of us nickels or dimes for spending on sweets. She was so kind and generous. Another feature of her total education program was what might loosely be called 'social education'. She taught a series of behaviours one could call 'virtues', such as honesty, thoughtfulness, kindness, politeness, perseverance, and industriousness. Unbeknownst to the students, she would select one such 'virtue' for emphasis for that particular day. At the end of the day, just before dismissal, she would name the virtue and name the winner, who received a star. I remember being the winner on a day when she had chosen 'politeness'. She said to me at that time, "One day you will be a gentleman."[31]

Despite her busy schedule teaching school and no doubt keeping farm, home, and garden in good repair, she nevertheless still had time for extras, including painting pictures and writing in our autograph books. Her entry in my autograph booklet on Feb. 4, 1944 speaks for itself.

Mrs. L. Lowe's autograph, 1944

In November 1945 we sold our farm in La Glace, Alberta and moved to BC. On my last day of school at Old Post, I stayed late after class dismissal to finish a project. Though I was free to go, I insisted on staying until the job was finished. Mrs. Lowe then said to me, "Your perseverance will stand you in good stead in the long run." Then she gave me my report card and we said goodbye.[32] Unfortunately, I never had the occasion to see her or speak to her again.

---

31 When I related this incident to a brother recently, he commented, "Perhaps it is not yet too late."

32 I have that report card to this day. It contains 45 entries of 'C' for commendable (the highest rating) in various categories. Armed with that I entered Chilliwack Jr/Sr High School later that month.

Church

IT IS ALMOST impossible to overstate the importance of the role of the church in my early life, in the life of the family, and in the life of the community. By 'church', I do not mean physical church attendance only, but all the many church related activities and observances. I think it is fair to say that I was thoroughly indoctrinated in those early years into one version of Protestant Christianity.

It is now fairly well understood what 'indoctrination' is, how it is conducted, and what the methods for this are. Not surprisingly, indoctrination is concerned with instilling doctrines, those defining and foundational *beliefs* (as opposed to responses and attitudes) of a creed, as in religion. These beliefs are essentially unverified and unverifiable and are introduced not by reason or evidence but by announcement by an authority who is not to be questioned. I have elsewhere commented on the methods indoctrinators use:

> "The methods indoctrinators use could be divided into three kinds: (1) those that are legitimate regular classroom teaching practices such as memorization, recitation, drill, telling, explaining, modelling, illustrating, instancing, repetition, monitoring, rote learning and so on; (2) those that are frowned upon as poor or unimaginative teaching but are also used by indoctrinators, such as no discussion, peer group appeal, failure to explain adequately, cynicism and brow beating, use of rhetoric, threatening, use of charisma and charm, use of coercion and punishment, use of social sanction and so on; (3) those of a more nefarious kind that are typically, but not exclusively, used by indoctrinators, such as selective use of evidence, over-generalization from insufficient instances, use of authority as 'stoppers' to discussion; toleration of inconsistency, contradiction and circularity of argument; suppression of counter-evidence; distortion of

evidence; use of programmatic definitions; failure to suggest available alternative points of view; lying; disregard for criticism; use of selected criticism; misrepresentation of the status of beliefs; isolation from contrary influence; use of 'loaded' questions, and so on. The reason that methods in this latter group are used is that the nature of the content of indoctrination demands it. The reason that inadequate explanation is used as a method, for example, is that the content is not adequately *explainable*. Such methods are regarded as indoctrination because of the nature of the content transmitted. Indoctrinatory methodology depends on indoctrinatory content."[33]

Most of these methods and others were used regularly in my early indoctrination.

It all started at home with family religious practices. We prayed (gave 'thanks') before every meal. In addition, every day before breakfast, there were longer morning devotions, including readings from the Bible and/or commentaries. Dad, or very rarely Mother in Dad's absence, would also question us on the previous day's readings, although assessing the merit of ideas or discussing the content freely was strictly not allowed. When we had special guests such as Aunts or Uncles or itinerant preachers, which was fairly often, we would have evening devotions as well. We would all gather in the living room where, after Bible reading and testimonies we would all kneel for prayer, with everyone expected to participate.

There was, of course, regular church attendance on Sundays too. The service proper began with '*Einleitung*', a member of the laity reading a few verses from the Bible and making a few comments on it as an introduction to the prayer meeting. Then there was an open prayer session during which any member of the congregation, man, woman or youth (not children), would take turns to speak an ad lib

---

[33] Cornel Hamm, *Philosophical Issues in Education: An Introduction*, Falmer Press, London, 1989, p. 101.

prayer as the spirit moved them (memorized prayers were frowned upon). This could last up to half an hour. Then followed hymn singing and performance by the church choir. The main feature of the service was the sermon, delivered by one of the lay preachers. La Glace Mennonite Brethren Church had three or four of these at different times and my father was one of them. Dad was also the choir director. The sermons could last up to an hour, but were usually shorter. As a child I found these quite tedious. We children, boys on one side of the centre aisle and girls on the other, usually sat in the front row or two. When our heads nodded with sleepiness, when we chatted or fidgeted, a hymn book or a Bible would smack us on the head from behind. A quick prayer and short song concluded the service.

Even before the service began, we all attended Sunday school. The older folk did Bible study in the main sanctuary, while the children, in age groups of two or three years, met in various rooms in the adjoining Bible School. Our teachers were carefully selected 'young people' of the church. Two of the teachers that I had were Elizabeth Konrad and Abe Siebert. We were taught Bible stories, Bible geography, and in later years catechism-like lessons. So we were expected to: (1) study the lesson as homework and be prepared to be questioned on it, (2) bring to class a Bible or New Testament, (3) memorize the prescribed verse and (4) bring an offering (usually a penny or two). My attendance record for the first quarter of 1945 shows that I fulfilled all of these requirements perfectly. I was, and I think we all were, quite highly motivated and enjoyed Sunday school. It helped that our teachers were also highly motivated and well prepared. I can still visualize the ingenious map Abe Siebert devised for studying Biblical geography. He drew a map of the Holy Lands on a large flat board of some kind. At the various places he wished us to identify (for example, Bethlehem, Jerusalem, or the Sea of Galilee), he placed a small light bulb but no actual place-name. If we could locate the name he called out, we could use his 'magic stick' to touch the spot and if we were right the light would come on. I remember Sunday school being fun.

Cornel's Sunday School attendance record

Cornel's Sunday School class (C. is second from r., back row), 1941

And there was yet more church. Naturally we observed and celebrated the main religious holidays: Christmas, Good Friday, Easter, Ascension, Thanksgiving, and others. Our leaders also selected certain Sundays as Children's Day, Mother's Day, Sängerfest (a singing festival), and so on, when services were held both in the forenoon and afternoon. Weddings, not surprisingly, were also heavily filled with preaching and other religious reminders. Added to all of that, there were periods of time, possibly three or four times a year, when the church conducted meetings each evening. Missionaries would arrive and report on their work and make their appeals. Evangelists would appear and hold their revival meetings. Itinerant preachers from the larger Mennonite communities such as Winnipeg and Coaldale would come to inspire and edify the faithful. Almost always we children attended those meetings too because usually there was something special for the children as well.

In summer even *more* time was spent on religious activities. We took turns attending the interdenominational Bear Lake Bible Camp, where, between periods of sports, swimming, and other outdoor activities, there were big tent revival meetings, Sunday

La Glace

La Glass Mennorite Church and A. Voth Silver Wedding Anniversary, 1941

school-like study sessions, prayer meetings, and competitive memorization and recitation of Bible verses. This was the season, too, when many of the English speaking Mennonite 'young people' (17 to 25 year olds) joined forces with the Peace River Bible Institute (PRBI) principal Walter McNaughton and cohorts to conduct Daily Vacation Bible School (DVBS) programs in various local public schools. Thus for several years there was a DVBS at Old Post, my home school. So a bunch of us from school attended, including the Janzen clan, our family friends. It was at one of these DVBS sessions that Jake Janzen, undaunted school prankster, brought in under cover a live rabbit which he released in the middle of the proceedings. The teacher, an Englishman who taught us to sing 'It is *summah* time in my *haaht*', became so furious that he closed up shop right then and there and sent us all home.

During one summer when I was about eight I took up the challenge of memorizing Bible passages for prizes. This was another PRBI scheme to shore up the continuous indoctrination. The idea was for children to recite from memory in front of a reliable adult selected passages from the Bible as advertised by them on radio CFGP, Grande Prairie and by other means. The adult would then vouch for us and send in a request for a prize. Usually the prize was some religious document, often paperback copies of individual gospels or even the whole New Testament, depending on the number of verses or chapters you could recite. I remember spending a good portion of that summer memorizing the third chapter of the Gospel of St. John and other scattered groups of verses like the beatitudes and the Sermon on the Mount. What strikes me now as worthy of comment is how little of the meaning of the content we understood or took in. Such is the nature of rote learning. Did I really know from memory the whole story of Nicodemus coming to Jesus by night for advice and yet not comprehend what radical ideas were being promulgated? Apparently so.

Only much later did I take note of the fact that Jesus is almost scolding Nicodemus for his obtuseness for taking Jesus literally. Jesus says, "Except a man is born again he cannot see the kingdom of God".[34] Nicodemus asks, "Can a man enter the second time into his mother's womb and be born?" Thereupon Jesus retorts, I imagine with raised voice, "That which is born of the flesh is flesh; and that which is born of the spirit is spirit. Marvel not that I said unto thee, ye must be born again." In other words, Jesus is telling us not to take him so literally. In spiritual matters the metaphor aptly serves. This insight was most helpful to me years later during Biblical studies when I grappled with the meaning of a text. I was reminded again and again not to take the passages so literally. Perhaps it was good fortune I had memorized that particular chapter.

More religious influence came from radio. CFGP broadcast quite a few religious programs, including McNaughtons PRBI hour and the Peace River Radio Sunday School, which had over 400 adherents throughout the area. We were allowed to tune in on some of these. The station also broadcast a Baptist program on Sundays and a short daily program by a couple, the Jewels, whose 6 year old daughter, Iona, singing solos was the feature attraction for us kids. I can still, in my mind, hear Iona Jewel sing "Jesus wants me for

---

34   *The Bible*, John 3:3.

a sunbeam; I'll be a sunbeam for him". From California, over the airwaves, came Charles E. Fuller and his famous quartet singing, "There's honey in Rock, my brother." We even tuned in to gospel programs from Texas and some mountain states.

In all these ways and more we were inundated with the Christian message. It must not be thought that I/we found this oppressive or excessive, at the time. On the contrary, we thought we were lucky to live in a country where freedom of religion was assured, where religion could be promulgated without interference. We, as Mennonites, thought too that we had the correct interpretation of the message while at the same time becoming more ecumenical in our stance and practice. It was the only world we knew. A non-Christian world outlook was not thinkable, not entertained as an option, and not discussed. The church and what it stood for was the all-pervading force, giving life itself meaning and purpose, including an explanation of the natural world, providing moral direction, consolation, and inspiration.

Getting Saved

EVEN AS AN eight-year-old in Grade 2, I knew that sooner or later I would have to do it. It was just a matter of when and where. I already knew what I had to do. Hadn't our parents, our Sunday School teachers, church ministers, itinerant preachers, and for sure Alexander Voth, self-appointed counsellor for the church's male youth, told us over and over again that unless we were 'saved', 'born again', 'converted', we would not enter heaven but go straight to hell and suffer eternal damnation after we die! And hadn't I already memorized in both German and English the appropriate Bible verses, "that whosoever believeth in Him should not perish..." (John 3:16) and "except a man be born again..." (John 3:3). Furthermore, hadn't every orator and preacher that we had ever heard reminded us again and again what we must do to be 'saved'? One such orator, B. Sawatzky from Coaldale, was a brilliant speaker and story-teller; words seeming to pour out of him even after he ran out of breath. It was fascinating to watch his lips and eyes moving even though we heard nothing anymore. Before he pitched into his main hell-fire sermon, he would do the 'children's hour' for us little kids, telling us simple stories of children being saved from damnation and looking forward to going to heaven. All we had to do, he told us, was (1) believe in Jesus, (2) confess our sins to God and ask forgiveness, (3) ask Jesus to come into our heart, and (4) announce publicly that we were saved.

One spring day at school shortly after the revival meetings for that year were finished, I asked to leave the room. We boys always used the horse barn, not the outhouse, where it was warmer, and we could keep an eye on the horses. As I made my way to the barn, casually noticing that a warm Chinook wind was melting the snow and causing our igloos to crumble, I recited in my mind John chapter three, which I had already memorized. Then I began to think about what Sawatzky had told us about getting saved. Suddenly it dawned on me that I could do this on my own without the help of an evangelist or preacher, without the church elders standing by.

The first thing I asked myself was, "Do I believe in Jesus?" The answer to that was "Yes, of course." Hadn't I always believed in Him ever since I could remember? The next thing I had to do was to ask God for forgiveness of my sins. I couldn't actually think of any sins I had recently committed, but I knew that we were all full of sin anyway because we inherited them from Adam and Eve, as the scriptures and elders had taught. This meant that I had to pray to Him. That would be no problem. I had done that before many times. "*Lieber Heiland mach mich fromm das ich in dem Himmel komm. Amen*" (Dear Saviour, make me pious so that I may enter heaven. Amen.) All I had to do was to find a place to kneel down, a tradition for serious prayer. So there amidst the complex odours of horse harness, horse sweat, and horse droppings, against the back wall of the barn, I knelt on some straw and asked God to forgive my sins and invited Jesus to come into my heart. The whole episode took only a few minutes. I remember feeling quite happy and proud as I marched back to the schoolhouse.

Now I had only one more step to take – make a public confession of my faith. I kept my little secret to myself until that evening just before supper when I ran into my older cousin, Margaret Goertzen, who was staying with us during the winter to attend the local Mennonite Bible School. When I met her at the head of the stairs I said, "Do you know what? I'm saved!"

"Really!" she exclaimed, "How wonderful! How did it happen?"

"I'll tell you at supper."

When we were well into the meal, Margaret announced, "I think Corney has something to say".

When all eyes turned to me, I simply said "I'm saved. Today at school in the barn I prayed to God to forgive my sins and asked Jesus to come into my heart."

Then there was much joy and chatter around the table because most of my siblings were already saved. They seemed to applaud me verbally; but also asked questions, particularly Dad. "Are you happy?" he inquired.

"Yes."

"Did you cry?"

"No."

"How do you know you're saved?"

"Because the Bible says that if you believe in Jesus, you're saved; and I believe."

And so on...

Word got out to the wider community very quickly. Very soon after the event, Alexander Voth took me aside after church and asked me, "Is it really true that you're saved?"

"Oh yes!" I replied, "It's really true."

A few weeks later he asked me again, "*Ist es noch immer so?*" (Is it still true?).

"*Jah! Jah!*", I replied eagerly.

And so it went over the next several weeks and months. Whenever Voth approached us newly saved, we knew he was going to ask "*Ist es noch immer so?*" This actually continued for many years to come.

So what is the 'getting saved' experience all about? (I speak here for myself but I also think that my observations are generalizable.) What I want to show is that it is *not* about radical (or even any) shift or alteration of belief, nor about radical change in behaviour, nor about profound emotional experience and outpouring. I further want to show that it *is* about: (1) making a personal commitment to live by the beliefs and values one already holds; (2) about making a public declaration of that commitment; and (3) about the accentuation of the Binker effect (to be explained below).

It should not be surprising that in being saved there was little or no change in my beliefs.[35] The basic tenets of Christianity were firmly in my mind before getting saved. I refer here to such tenets as: God exists with such attributes as all-good, all-wise, all-powerful, and all-knowing; the story of redemption through Christ's crucifixion is true; there is life after death; there is a heaven for the 'saved' and a hell for the 'unsaved' and a host of other minor doctrines representing evangelical Protestant Christianity. Rather than starting to believe these doctrines at the time of my getting saved, my 'conversion' experience was an acknowledgement of and re-commitment to the beliefs I already held. How did I acquire these beliefs? Through years and years of indoctrination by family, church, and community. When it comes to acquiring beliefs, we have little choice in the matter. Either we acquire them by rational demonstration, that is, by use of reason and/or empirical evidence in which case reason forces us to believe; or we acquire them, I am tempted to say, by force of social osmosis, and/or through the long processes of indoctrination by authorities. This is not the occasion for a full discussion of the role of will and choice in the formation of beliefs; I simply want to assert here that I do not remember ever not believing in those doctrines. My beliefs were not acquired sud-

---

35 I take the terms 'being saved' and 'born again' to be roughly synonymous. 'Becoming a believer' is something different, in that it is ambiguous, referring on the one hand to believing *in* something which is similar to making a commitment and on the other hand believing *that* something or other is the case. Believing *in* presupposes believing *that* in the 'being saved' experience. My contention that there is little or no change in *belief* refers to cases of believing "that"; doctrines, for example.

denly at the time of being saved, but slowly over a lengthy period of time and I surmise it to be so with most people who have been 'saved'. It seems to me entirely spurious to think (and sing) "How precious did that grace appear, the hour I first believed".[36] We do not come to believe in an hour, a day, a year those things that are foundational to our explanation of the universe and to the outlooks that shape our lives, our *Weltanschauung*. Beliefs, particularly religious beliefs, are not so transitory and capricious. I was metaphorically born in Damascus, alluding to the fact that I was raised believing all the things necessary to become saved. There simply was no need to change any of my beliefs.

Nor was there a radical change in behaviour. True, after my conversion I was labelled a 'good boy' while my unsaved friends were 'bad boys' and this may have had a small effect in reminding me to behave myself. But essentially even before I was saved, I didn't do what the 'bad' boys did (tell dirty jokes, cheat, swear, smoke, etc.) and did do what I continued to do afterwards (tell the truth, be kind, be fair, etc.). While I made the connection between being good and having faith, consistent with Pauline doctrine, I nevertheless also had a moral sense quite independent of religious faith.

My conversion experience was also not traumatic nor highly emotional. I do recall being quite happy and pleased with myself, mostly because I had achieved my conversion without the help of adults. Happy, yes, but nothing cataclysmic. Just a sense of accomplishment, knowing that I had done what I needed to do. What getting saved did mean was the making of a personal commitment to live by and acknowledge the beliefs I already held. It was an experience of coming to understand that I had all the ingredients of salvation at hand and all I needed to do was say "yes" and accept them. It was like coming to believe *in* what I already believed. It was like believing with my heart as well as my head. A commitment, to me at least, means to put ones heart into something.

---

36 From the popular hymn 'Amazing Grace'.

A crucial element of my understanding of conversion is to make a public declaration of the personal commitment. It is a sort of coming out of the closet, to join hands with fellow believers, to come on side. It was for me a bit like joining the church much later. The connection with other believers has a bolstering effect, strengthening the commitment and the beliefs themselves.

When, at the time of my being saved, I asked Jesus to come into my heart, it felt as though that was actually what happened. If not in my heart, at least my head. It seemed I could actually talk to Him and He heard me. This notion of having a homunculus inside you to communicate with in times of crisis or elation is a common human phenomenon. Richard Dawkins calls it the "Binker phenomenon",[37] so called after Binker, an imaginary friend in A.A. Milne's *Now We Are Six*. This phenomenon is the human being's capacity and propensity, particularly strong in children, to delude themselves into thinking that they have a ghostlike companion who communicates with them, befriends them, and watches over them. This Binker effect was not new to me at my conversion. I had often thought that Jesus was close to me and that I could call on Him for help in troubled times, as I did once when I had a bad nightmare. That was before I got saved. But after being saved, the capacity to call on Jesus was heightened, sharpened, and accentuated.

To a small extent my getting saved experience was similar to Saint Paul's on the road to Damascus; but in other respects it was very different. To clarify and elaborate on this, I may need to remind some readers what the "road to Damascus" experience is all about. Not even all Christians read the Bible these days, or read it only selectively; so I will briefly retell the story of Saul of Tarsus as recorded in Acts 9 and 22.[38] Saul, a Jew from the town of Tarsus (in present day Turkey), was on his way with his accomplices to Damascus in Syria to take on and try to eradicate a new cult of Jesus

---

37 For a full discussion of this phenomenon see Richard Dawkins, *The God Delusion*, Mariner Books, 2008.
38 In this memoir all allusions and quotations from the Bible refer to the King James Version (KJV).

followers centred there. As they approached Damascus, swords at the ready, Saul was suddenly struck by a blinding light and thrown to the ground. A voice spoke to him and said "Saul, Saul, why persecutest thou me?" In Saul's mind the voice was that of 'the Lord', namely Jesus of Nazareth, who ordered Saul to proceed to Damascus, seek contact with the disciples of Jesus, and await further instructions. Blinded by the light, Saul was led into the city of Damascus by his accomplices. There Saul's contact, Ananias, restored Saul's vision and baptized him as a believer. Saul now became one of the faithful, changed his name to Paul,[39] and much to the amazement of everyone, started proselytizing on behalf of Jesus. He was, of course, to become the famous Saint Paul of the New Testament, spending the rest of his years spreading his version of Christianity throughout the Near East, Greece, and Rome.

Paul's life-changing conversion happened suddenly on the road to Damascus. My getting saved experience in childhood was unlike Paul's radical conversion. Getting saved for me merely solidified and confirmed the beliefs I already had. *My* radical conversion came later in adulthood as I slowly examined and changed my beliefs, gradually leaving religion behind.

Over the years the 'road *to* Damascus', story has come to acquire, not only for religionists but generally, three central characteristics or definitional attributes. First, the phrase refers to a radical reversal of belief or point of view, a conversion (from the root word 'converse', meaning 'opposite'), a complete about face, a gaining of a new perspective. Second, the about face concerns a significant aspect of one's life, a change in life's orientation and direction on important issues such as politics, religion, education, or ethics. Changing allegiance to a sports team is not a 'road to Damascus' experience. Third, the turnabout comes suddenly, swiftly, through some kind of dramatic, non-rational, epiphanic, even mystical, experience, as opposed to a thought out, prolonged reflection on the issues.

---

39 It's an interesting coincidence that both Saul and I changed our name by one letter, Saul on his way to Damascus and I on my way back. That, however, is more coincidental than symbolically significant.

In my story, *Back From Damascus*, I want to retain the first two elements of the symbolism (the radical about face on a serious issue) but not the third, the suddenness and capriciousness of the change. My conversion was *not* a non-deliberate, non-rational, non-reasoned instant reorientation as connoted by the blinding light and the mysterious voice. Figuratively speaking, I was born in Damascus; born to Christian parents, raised to believe the Christian story. If the road *to* Damascus experience represents a sudden, dramatic, convulsive change of *heart*, the road back from Damascus, at least for me, represented a slow, methodical, deliberate, reasoned examination of beliefs; a change of *mind*.

When St. Paul was converted on the road to Damascus he had a radical about face experience. I did not. I evolved into my faith. In that sense I had been in Damascus for some time. Does that mean that my experience of being 'saved' or 'born again' was not genuine? Not at all. I didn't need an about face. I believed in the Lord Jesus Christ just as genuinely as did St. Paul, only he needed to be transformed to get there. I was born there, lived there, brought up there. What I am arguing here is that the vast majority of religious followers (of any religion) don't have or need to have a Pauline conversion to be true believers. The road to Damascus experience is very rare and mostly unnecessary. People generally come to their religious beliefs through a slow process of indoctrination and have little choice in the matter. If you take the Bible literally, "Believe in the Lord Jesus Christ and thou shalt be saved" (Acts 16:31), then I was saved. I had always believed and I was saved by virtue of my upbringing about which I had little or no choice. If that is so, then one of the major doctrines of the Mennonites is seriously compromised, namely the idea of baptism by dunking only upon adult confession and examination of faith. If we, as I claim, come to our faith through a process of indoctrination, and not by choice, not by force of compelling evidence, then one might as well be baptised into the faith at birth or shortly thereafter, as the Anglicans, for example, do. If there are no grounds for religious belief other than those based on the Bible and on authority, then waiting for baptism until your late teens makes little sense. If faith is not based on evidence, then evidence will not accumulate to make faith stronger. Waiting an extra decade or two is just a decade or two more of indoctrination and reinforcement of the faith. Lloyd Ratslaff makes the point nicely:

> *Who knew what they were doing when it was being done to them... I had no idea what I was doing down at the river any more than a blanketed boy at an ornate font.*[40]

Our upbringing was a matter of acquiescence to parental and social pressures. There was only a very small element of choice involved with that. The way into religion is easy. All you need to do is accept your parents' and your church's teachings. That is not a big choice to make, if it is a choice at all. It is even quite rational to do so. Believing what your parents say and obeying their instructions is a sure and natural way of survival. And if along with religious instruction there is also repetitive religious observances, social pressures, and coercion, one can almost guarantee faithful followers. Many are those who keep the faith of their parents.

The way out of religion is far more difficult to achieve. For that one needs to reject parental teaching. That is a difficult choice to make. It requires lengthy examination of inherited doctrines. It comes as a result of much hard independent thinking, reading, and studying. It means trusting your own judgement and having courage to go against the grain, against the family, against huge social pressures. It means being willing to embrace radical changes in life.

Alluding to Saint Matthew's description of the straight and wide gates and ways, it makes one wonder who are the few that struggle against the flow of the masses and find the narrow gate leading to life and who are the many that march in unison along the broad way leading to destruction. I would put it this way:

---

40 Lloyd Ratzlaff, *The Crow Who Tampered with Time*, Thistledown Press, Saskatoon, p. 66.

> *For wide is the gate and broad is the way of popular inherited religion leading to destruction and many there be which go in thereat; because strait is the gate and narrow is the way leading to liberation from religion and a better life on Earth, and few there be that find it.*[41]

Our Family

I FEEL FORTUNATE that I was part of a large close-knit family. Family affection, between parents and children, and between siblings, was not something we talked about or overtly demonstrated with physical or verbal expressions of any kind; we just understood without words or actions that this affection existed and that the family unit as a whole functioned as a wall of protection against a sometimes hostile world. We just *knew* that when anyone of the family was away, such as when Mother was in the Grande Prairie hospital, or when Walter was away with his severe injury, or Martin away to Gretna, Manitoba for school, that there was a serious chink in that wall. Even though we siblings were supposedly arch enemies in our day to day disputes, rife with verbal and sometimes even physical sparring, the moment anyone was gone, we couldn't easily bear their absence and wished them back. Sure, we siblings had our fights, but in the end they were always smoothed over and we came to some kind of resolution, often with parental help. I just couldn't imagine any one of my family members not being there. Not one of us ten children were doted upon or favoured in any way. Our parents treated us with respect and absolute fairness. None of us had privileges or penalties not warranted. It is possible that I had more physical punishments (thrashings) than any of my siblings (my brother John might dispute that), but that doesn't mean that they were not deserved or unfair.

---

41 Paraphrasing Matthew 7:13,14.

La Glace

M. Hamm Family, 1942

Father and six brothers, 1942, La Glace

Back from Damascus: Leaving Religion Behind

Father and six brothers, 1952, Chilliwack

Mother and four sisters, 1942, La Glace

A characteristic of the family was a high level of organization. *'Ordnung'* (order) was an often heard word from Dad. We each had our place at the table, Dad at the head, boys (oldest to youngest) at the south wall and lower end, Mother and the girls (oldest to youngest) on the kitchen side and little Margaret between Dad and Mother. We each had our little shelf to hold our few possessions, always neatly arranged. We each, as soon as were were old enough, had our chores to do, helping with household work (including but not limited to cleaning, doing dishes, and hauling wood and water) and with farm-related work (including feeding animals, harnessing horses, and milking cows). We each had turns going along on family outings such as our yearly summer pilgrimage (in later years) to Tofield to visit our relatives; also on shorter trips to Sexsmith, Grande Prairie, or Saskatoon Island to pick berries and swim.

If *'ordnung'* was our watchword, then smooth efficient operation of farm and family was the result. Work, order, obedience,[42] and frugality paid off; and we prospered as a result. We even became proud of our appearance (we boys in our suits and ties) on Sunday at church; proud of our comparatively meagre possessions (eventually a car *and* a threshing machine); proud of our performance at school, always trying to be first in our grade (and often achieving it); proud of our reciting, singing, and other Sunday School achievements. I learned early on that one of the worst offences we could commit was to bring shame on the family and somehow damage our reputation.

Dad was without question the head of the household, consistent with Christian doctrine and the Mennonite interpretation of such. He was dominant and demanding, Mother was submissive, and we children obedient. It was difficult to oppose Dad, particularly early on, although we kept trying, particularly in our teen years. Dad took the view that it was better to be too strict than too lenient. I think he took this view also because he was busy trying to

---

42 Dad boasts that all his ten children learned obedience by the time they were two years old.

raise his big family *and* play his important role in the church. Just before leaving Russia, he had qualified as a teacher and had tried his hand at it. He would have loved to be a teacher in Canada too, but the language barrier and the pressure to immediately provide for the family forced him into farming. He became good at farming largely because he was ambitious and worked very hard at it. In his scholarly ways, he kept careful notes on farm operations – dates of seeding and harvesting, growing days required for various grains, yields of various acreages, prices, weather, and so on. That served him well. When my oldest brother John was able to take over most of the already successful grain farming operation, Dad ventured into beekeeping too. He was daring and willing to take risks, but not in a foolhardy manner. He had painstakingly studied beekeeping in the long winter months when we were more or less forced indoors.

Despite Dad's tendency to domineer at home, he also had the ability to be charming and affable. Easily excitable and sensitive he made friends easily, and generally people liked him. His accomplishments were many: successful farmer, beekeeper, father and grandfather, preacher, choir director, Saturday German school teacher, and writer. Here is how my brother Peter describes him:

> *In temperament, he was sanguine and choleric; he was intelligent and creative, especially in writing and composing doggerel, and innovative on musical instruments. He was well-read with a broad range of interests (in travel, politics, explorations, beekeeping, archeology and theology); and he had a broad worldview with liberal leanings. He assumed leadership among his peers and encouraged youth in their exploits. He had many friends and was widely known among Mennonites through his writings.* [43]

---

43   *Reflections...*, p. 19.

Dad was a complex person. Though he was stern and tough at times, he was also genteel and kind. Perhaps because I had already experienced the worst in punishment Dad had to offer quite early on, I no longer feared him later. After one of the thrashings I got, I asked him if he, like God, would forgive and forget. With tears in his eyes, he said "Yes, of course". Then I knew that he had a soft spot, which I then learned to exploit. Often in winter evenings Dad and I would play chess or checkers, after which, particularly if I won, he would share some nuts or candy or halvah from his seemingly never empty secret stores that he kept hidden somewhere in his desk, which we were told never to explore.

Later, in my teen years I was able freely to discuss with him subjects such as evolution, witnessing, ecumenicalism, and even dating. On almost all of these topics I came to agree with him more or less. In recent years my younger brother Walter told me that often I stood up to Dad to present the case for us younger sons; and Dad listened and compromised. That surprised me. Maybe Walter was right and I had forgotten. In any case my relationship with Dad was usually quite smooth and genial.

My relationship with Mother was quite different – more reserved, more formal, more distant. Perhaps that was because she often seemed tired, sad, or even depressed. In this, my brother Peter and I agree. Here is how Peter describes her:

> *Mother was disciplined and industrious, efficient and thorough, perfectionistic with high expectations. She was serious, truly pious, and humble; and she was generous, caring and self-giving. Melancholic in disposition, she was reserved and submissive. She was meticulous in detail and artistic, especially in her handwork. Her worldview was narrow, her opinions largely inflexible, and her leanings conservative. She truly complimented Dad in many ways.* [44]

---

44 Ibid.

Perhaps Peter is right in saying that Mother was melancholic in disposition, but there is some evidence that she was not always so, or perhaps so only in the later years of her life. In my interview with Mrs. C. Friesen in 1992, alluded to earlier, I got a very different conception of who Mother was before Peter and I arrived on the scene and formed our impressions. I asked Mrs. Friesen my questions in English and she replied in German:

"Was Mother perennially sad and unhappy?"

"*Nein. Immer fröhlich!*" ("No, always happy!")

"What kind of relationship did my Dad and Mother have?"

"*Gut. Aber sie sachte mir, 'Er hilft nicht mit die Kinder. Er sitzt nur und liest immer'.*" ("Good." But she also told me, "He doesn't help with children. He just always sits and reads.")

As the interview continued, I learned the following about Mother from Mrs. Friesen. She was very busy, but still always willing to help. She was kind-hearted too. She gave birth very easily without being sick or headachy. She had fingers like a machine and could knit faster than anyone in the neighbourhood. She even told Dad to speak up in his sermons. She could do most everything well – cook, clean, sew, look after kids, all of that; always had visitors on Sundays and gave good lunches. Mother, not the siblings (until much later), looked after the children; and the Friesens and Hamms did almost everything together. This seems like a pretty feisty woman to me, not at all sad and depressed.

Yet, I recall with clarity an incident that disturbingly points to the assessment Peter and I, and indeed all the later children, had of her. The scene is in the living room at LaGlace where Mother is sitting on a rocking chair on the far side of the pot-bellied heater, slowly, almost imperceptibly, rocking back and forth, her hands nimbly knitting something or other (Stockings for the soldiers? Scarves for the mission sale? Anklet socks for some family member?). Her quick fingers fly automatically. Her eyes and her mind are on something other than her knitting, for her knitting needed no eyes. With a concentrated look on her face, she seems deep in thought about something profound long ago and far away. After tossing a handful of sunflower seeds into her mouth, she expels the shells with extreme skill. Like a lace on a shawl stretching from her shoulder to her knee, a long concatination of sunflower shells, hung together by her spittle, embroider her ghost-like form. Her dark eyes are distant but not vacant. Is she thinking of the days in the old country where, with her many sisters, she is dressed in splendid finery, hair coiffed in the current style? Is she dreaming of better times to come, an end to this endless cycle of poverty and children? Sitting on the cold floor some distance from her, I stare at her face, at her black hair combed straight back and tied neatly in a bun, at her perfect white teeth, at the corners of her mouth slightly drooping. I want to go over and ask her, "What are you thinking about? What are your wishes for the future? How can I be a better son? What would make you so happy that you couldn't keep from laughing?" But I didn't dare. I didn't dare to pierce her introspection, her splendid isolation, her reverie. It was in any case none of my business. Perhaps she would be cross and send me to bed. So I didn't find out what she really thought and dreamt of. I didn't then, and I never did. From that day until the day she died she remained somewhat of an enigma.

Years later, when I sought help for some mid-life crises, the counsellor offered the view that I had been an abandoned child, coming as I did, the eighth out of ten children. Of course I vehemently denied this. Mother was ever so caring, giving all she had for her family. We were well fed, well clothed, well looked after in every way possible. The dialogue between the counsellor and me then went something like this:

"That doesn't mean you weren't emotionally abandoned."

"I wasn't."

"Tell me about your mother."

"She was diminutive, dark-haired, a little bit plump; she had..."

"I don't want a description of her; I want to know what she was really like. Tell me about her dreams, visions, tastes, ideals, preferences. What was your Mother's favourite colour?"

"I don't know."[45]
"What was her favourite food?"
"I don't know."
"What colour were her eyes?"
"I don't know."
"What would she have liked to do more than anything else if she weren't saddled down with caring for her huge family?"
"I don't know."
"What were her ambitions for you specifically?"
"I don't know."
"What made her happy more than anything else?"
"I don't know."
"What do you think she might have been had she had the opportunity for education and personal fulfillment?"
"I don't know."
"Do you think you knew your mother and were intimate with her?"
"I don't know."
"Do you still think you were not an abandoned child?"
"No, I don't think so."
"Did you know that sons who are abandoned by their mothers often have difficulty with forming intimate relationships with women?"
"I've read that."

The point the counsellor was trying to make with me was that my difficulties in achieving an intimate relationship with women was traceable to a lack of bonding between me and my mother. I suppose that that is a possibility, but to explore that would take another whole book and another lifetime of psychoanalysis.

It is interesting and worthy of note that both my brother Peter and I without thinking twice refer to our parents as 'Dad and Mother', not 'Dad and Mom' or 'Mom and Dad', or 'Mom and Father'. Why the more friendly, less formal term 'Dad' for my father and the more formal term 'Mother' for my mother? Does this

---

45 I knew that my Dad's was green.

suggest that my relationship with Dad was more friendly than with Mother and that I was more aloof with Mother? Perhaps. And yet, as I alluded to earlier, my earliest memories are exchanges with my mother. There is much left to explore here even at my advanced age.

I want now to introduce to you my siblings. Before I say my little piece about each of them, I will give you the result of a little thought experiment I tried out. I forced myself to give each of my nine siblings a one-word description. No-one of course can be fully or accurately described by one word. In fact the four adjectives I attached to my four sisters could easily be used interchangeably to describe any of them. The one word I do use just slightly outweighed the others. Here goes: Lena, kind; Mary, friendly; John, protective; Martin, stimulating; Anna, industrious; Frank, generous; Peter, disciplined; Walter, smart; and Margaret, nice.

It is widely known that Lena (born March 19, 1923, Ukraine) is a perfectionist in cooking, sewing, and housekeeping, and judging by her accomplished and successful children, she also had to be a wonderful mother. All that notwithstanding, I think her predominant quality of character is kindness. For example, more than once, she was the only one of my siblings who sent me a birthday card.

I recall one incident from my childhood, probably at age seven or eight when she took me for a bicycle ride one evening just for pleasure. About half a mile from home, I carelessly stuck my bare foot into the spokes of the front wheel of the bicycle. My left big toe was cut, with blood spurting amok. I was injured and it was my fault, but it was Lena who was crying because she was sorry for the happening. That about says it all.

Mary, (born March 7, 1924, Ukraine) is said to have been in charge of me at times in my early years, getting me dressed and cleaned for church, as Lena was for Peter. Perhaps that is why I have a special affection for my second eldest sister. Or is it just because she is so affable and friendly to everyone? Having brought up a beautiful family of her own, she is manifestly competent, organized, accomplished and confident; and to this day a delightful hostess.

Until I read George Orwell's '1984', I always thought that 'big brother' had a positive meaning. For a while, I couldn't even understand the novel, while reading the book during lulls in Vancouver's PNE parking attendancy, because I always thought that a big brother was a valuable asset rather than a liability. Then I realized that John, my real big brother (born June 12, 1925, Ukraine) was *not* Orwell's 'big brother'. Mine was kind, thoughtful, protective, and overall a good role model for us younger ones.

Martin (born November 8, 1926, Sunnyslope, Alberta) was always, in the best sense, stimulating. He, having travelled and attended high school in Gretna, Manitoba, when nobody else had, brought in a bit more of the outside world. He shared with us his love of classical music and poetry (both in German and English). I remember to this day lying in the sun on the grassy slope leading to our favourite swimming hole in Bartsch's creek with Martin reciting the lines:

> There lies a vale in Ida, lovelier
> Than all the valleys of Ionian hills
>
> Oh Mother Ida, many-fountained Ida,
> Dear Mother Ida, harken ere I die.[46]

For years and years the lines kept ringing in my ears, even with no clue as to what they meant until much later in adulthood. With Martin, I probably had the best discussions and arguments on the topics that mattered a lot to both of us, namely education, politics, and philosophy. I hope he takes it as a compliment that I could argue with him as I could with few other siblings. He is also always a fun and challenging travelling and gaming companion.

Anna (born October 30, 1927, La Glace, Alberta), rather than Annie, as she now prefers to be called, was and is an unrivaled model of work and dedication. She sacrificed so much of herself,

---

46 Tennyson, 'Oenone'.

first for the good of our family (making lunches, picking berries, tending gardens) and then for her own. Even early on she was preoccupied with thoroughness and the completion of tasks. In March of 1944 she wrote in my autograph booklet:

> *It's not the number of times you have failed in your task,*
> *It's the number of times you have tried that will tell.*
> *It's not the amount of hard work you have done,*
> *It's if it's done truly and well.*

On the rare occasion that I actually did so, I considered it a great achievement to have picked more pounds of berries than Anna did in one day, even though I started much earlier and continued much later. She was the personification of efficiency and industry, and she did it all with a caring and giving attitude.

Frank (April 30, 1929 – October 6, 2009, La Glace, Alberta), prankster and joker of the family, I would characterize as the most generous of all my many kind and generous siblings. He was, from the earliest days, always willing to go the extra mile, do the extra chores; and he continued that throughout his life. He loved to play jokes and rarely could we younger ones put one over on him; but one time we did. It was a matter of honour among us siblings attending Old Post School, not to tattle on each other if we got into trouble at school, unlike in the La Glace School days. One day Frank did have to stay for a short while for some misdemeanor. We knew Frank, speedy as he was, would run as hard as he could to catch up with us on our walk home from school so that he wouldn't be noticed as missing and have to 'fess up. So all us siblings hid behind some willows in Bartsch's Creek and held our hands over our mouths to keep from giggling as Frank raced by. As we intended, he arrived home well ahead of the rest of us and was forced to tattle on himself. When we arrived howling with laughter, rather than being upset he joined in the laughter, thinking it was a great prank. Even Mother joined in.

Peter (August 26, 1930 – August 16, 1993, La Glace, Alberta), seemed to take life more seriously than the rest of us. From the earliest times, I recall his taking on difficult tasks and sticking with them to completion. I must have been eight or nine years old when I observed him struggling through a thick volume the reading level of which was much ahead of his years (was it George Elliot's *The Mill on the Floss* or Dickens's, *David Copperfield*?). He stuck with it to the very end, looking up difficult words in the dictionary throughout. He was tenacious alright. Once in a friendly wrestling match, I had him around his neck to the point where he was losing colour. I asked him if he would give up, to which he replied, "Even if you kill me, I'll never give up." So I had to let him go; what else could I do? He was clever rather than brilliant (none of us were), a good student, dedicated and meticulous. He had a lot of what the Germans call '*sitzfleisch*' and it saw him through to his PhD and beyond. He was a highly disciplined person to the very end, completing his memoirs shortly before he died of renal cancer.

Upon rereading Peter's *Reflections...* recently, I got the impression that he was restless, constantly on the move. He seemed never completely content or at ease, always struggling in matters of faith as well as vocational direction, not really enjoying the potential satisfaction of his successes as a missionary. I was particularly surprised (not having noticed in prior readings) at his use of Tillichian language [47] in describing an aspect of his faith. At times, he talks about an anthropomorphic God,[48] yet at other times he talks about a non-anthropomorphic deity. Was he struggling with post-war continental liberation theology, which is essentially camouflaged agnosticism? Was he trying to balance that against the more rigid Mennonite evangelical theology? Was this the essence of his ambivalence, the source of his restlessness? And was the decision to stick with the latter despite some possibility of doubt his ultimate act of discipline? These are speculations of course, but possibly not wide of the mark.

---

47   Paul Tillich, theologian, does not think of God as a person but as the "ground of being", which Peter quotes and seems to agree with.
48   My term, not his.

Walter (born September 11, 1932, La Glace, Alberta), my only younger brother and closest to me in age, came along with plenty of grey matter, which he used to great effect in our inevitable verbal sparring matches early on. I call him 'smart' not only because he is quick and precise in thought (suitable for his career in teaching Mathematics) but also because he has good judgement and makes wise choices. Despite a physical disability (he lost his right hand in a terrible accident when he was eight), he was and is as capable as any of us were in jobs requiring flexibility, dexterity, and speed. One of his hobbies is building things which he does better than most of his capable brothers and almost as well as Frank, who was a professional and master craftsman. Walter also has a myriad of desirable qualities of character. He is unselfish and giving of his time to help others in many ways, from hosting and chauffeuring to bookkeeping for the church and singing for many years with the Vancouver Bach choir. Not only smart, but generous too.

The baby of the family is my youngest sister Margaret (born November 17, 1933, La Glace, Alberta). She tagged along immediately after four males in a row. She was 'nice' right from the start. I can say, with great satisfaction, that I can't remember quarreling with her, not even once. I recall playing hopscotch in the spring mud with her once, not because she particularly wanted to, but simply because I asked her. I had wanted to try out some new rules that I had learned at school from a book. Sometimes 'nice' has a slight pejorative sense but that is not at all my intent. I mean to say that she has many attractive qualities and characteristics. She has an exceptionally pleasant smile, a friendly personality, and an outgoing manner to go along with her thoughtfulness, generosity, and sensitivity. Clever too. She can put together a neat little sermonette or prayer in an instant. Had she wanted to and had she had the opportunity to, she could have become an excellent nurse or teacher, or anything for that matter. As it was, she chose to become and indeed became the perfect minister's wife and accomplice.

Farm Life in La Glace

CAN YOU IMAGINE living in a house that has no electricity, no running water, and no indoor plumbing? Now can you imagine what that really means considering that this house is situated in the frigid climate of northern Canada? Can you imagine not having any of the electrical devices that we now take so utterly for granted? Imagine also a Canada before family allowance (cash from the government simply for being born), before credit cards, employment insurance, social welfare, government health care, old age security, and easy access to secondary schools and higher learning. If you can imagine all of the above then you will begin to understand what life was like for me in La Glace for the first fourteen years of my life.

What did we do for water? We carried it by pail from the pump house a few hundred yards away. What did we do to keep warm when it was 40-50 degrees below zero?[49] We stoked up the McCleary oven in the kitchen and the pot-bellied heater in the living room and didn't stray too far.

La Glace farmyard, circa 1936

---

49 At around 40 degrees below zero, Fahrenheit and Celsius are roughly the same.

More La Glace farmyard, circa 1938

The provision of wood for the stoves was a huge undertaking. It started with the felling of trees in late winter or early spring. Usually we used poplar but sometimes spruce or larch. We then had to haul loads and loads of logs to our yard and begin the massive job of sawing them with a crew of half a dozen or so neighbors into 16" lengths. Later, when they were half dry, we would split them, resulting in a huge mound of green firewood to be dried in the hot summer sun. We then stacked and stored the dried wood on the verandah for the next winter always just around the corner.

In the bitter cold of winter when we got up in the mornings, with pee pots frozen and a ½ inch of hoar frost on the inside of the bedroom windows, we would shout down to Dad from upstairs, "*Ist der Heitza warum?*" (Is the heater warm?) If the answer was "yes", we would rush down in our Admiral Bird long-johns and huddle around the fire while we clothed ourselves for the outside world.

What did we do to keep our clothes clean and our shirts ironed for Sundays? At first, all the washing was done on a rubbing bar but later in the mid to late thirties, much to the relief of those who had to do the scrubbing, we acquired a gas-powered washing machine. As I recall, its arrival was a day of celebration. For ironing, we would heat up several big iron blocks on the kitchen stove, having to exchange them every few minutes to maintain adequate heat.

What did we do for bathing? In the winter, once a week, we would place a portable tin bath-tub beside the heater in the living room and heat water on the stove for the big event. In later years when we had a radio, a special treat was to sneak in a listen to a Leafs hockey game while we were bathing. We had plenty of hot water; one tub-full for the six boys and one for the four girls.

The nearest hamlet had no street lights; in fact, there weren't even streets. The dirt roads were considered very good if they had some semblance of a ditch, let alone being gravelled or paved. Even in later years when we actually owned a car, we could use it only when the roads were dry in summer and not at all in the winter.

It was not the best of times, but it was certainly not the worst of times either. Our deprivations, if that is what they were, definitely did not detract from our happiness. Did we think of ourselves as poor? Not at all. In fact, we were better off than many families around us and considered ourselves fortunate.

A large part of family life played out around the dinner table. Mother and the sisters worked hard to get the food on the table and the rest of us hoped to deserve to be there to enjoy the spoils. Some of the meals were fantastic, like roast goose with *bubat* (fruit stuffing), or one of my favourites, *kleeta mousse*, a milk broth with pellets of dough. Apparently, on at least one occasion, I fell asleep at the table during one of these fine meals and dunked my chin into the hot soup, and cried while everyone else laughed. G*lums verenke* (perogies), *wurst bubat* (stuffing), *nudeln* (homemade noodles), smoked sausage, and roasted '*zwieback*' (two layered buns) dipped into *prips* (homemade postum) were some of my favourite foods from that time.

We weren't rich by any stretch but we ate well, as do most farmers, especially at Christmas and on holidays. New Year's Day we typically had deep fried, raisin-filled, doughnut like blobs, that we simply called New Year's cookies. They were delicious. At Easter we were treated to *paska*, an egg-rich, icing-laden, white cake, which was also very tasty. But in the main we ate noodles, root vegetables, a tiny amount of ham or sausage and little or nothing by way of dessert.

Dad was not inclined to have our cows bred to produce milk all year, so we had an overabundance of milk, cream, and butter in the spring and summer, which we would sell, but none in the winter.

In winter we often had only *schliesa malch* (skim milk), which we got from our neighbors, the Bartschs and Voths. With lots of vegetables, little meat, and lots of skim milk, we probably had quite a healthy diet by default, though unbeknownst to us at the time.

I could not give even a nearly accurate account of my childhood years in La Glace without emphasising the importance of Christmas celebrations. We always welcomed holidays and special events such as Good Friday, Easter, *Kinderfest* (a church related children's day), Thanksgiving, and Halloween. At these events there were always fun and games, and more and better food, such as ice-cream at kinderfest, and apples at Halloween; but nothing came close to rivalling Christmas. The celebration unfolded in three phases. First was the school Christmas Concert, which was not merely a concert, but included singing and acting out plays, not even necessarily related to Christmas. The exciting part for us was the arrival of Santa Claus with his proper red and white gear and his "Ho Ho Ho!" Did we recognize the voice? You bet we did, Arnold Christianson again. He would then pick up the presents from under the tree and call out our names at random to come forward and pick up our mystery gift exchange package. Only then did we discover the secret of who had picked our name. This was followed by Santa giving each of us a small brown paper bag filled with goodies – mostly peanuts and candies.

That all took place days before Christmas Eve, so we had plenty of time to scour the local landscape for a suitable Christmas tree for our home. On the day of the 24th our many hands helped decorate the tree, mostly with last year's decorations and a few new ones, mostly homemade. In the early evening and in the dark we headed off for church, the horses decked out with bells. After arrival we heard, but couldn't see, other sleighs approaching as we tried to guess whose team it was. Sieberts? Friesens? Konrads?

When the service began we children sang the songs we had practiced and memorized so faithfully several Saturdays before under the skilled direction of Mr. C. Friesen. These songs, among which were *Oh Tannenbaum, Oh Tannenbaum; O du froeliche, O du selige; Ihr Kindelein Kommet; Stille Nacht, Heilige Nacht* , still ring in my ears at Christmas to this day and I still know most of them from memory. Almost all of us children recited a verse or two as well. When it was all done, someone (I remember Mr. P. Konrad being one) would light real candles with real fire on the real wonderful smelling Christmas tree. (I don't think the Fire Marshall would allow that these days) It was now time to receive another bag of goodies, usually handed out by Mr. C. Friesen.

Better still than at school or church was the spread of treats – oranges, apples, candy, nuts and even halvah – we got the next morning at home together with our much anticipated major gift from Dad and Mother. After doing the chores and just before our breakfast of roasted *zweiback* we would line up in front of the living room curtain, ready to be shown to our plateful of goodies and the unwrapped gift alongside. We were always overwhelmed at how Dad and Mother could manage to be so generous in so difficult a time. We were very seldom even slightly disappointed with our gifts. After yet another service at church on Christmas day we hurried home, often with visitors, to play with our new toys and eat and eat away at our new and treasured collection of sweet stuff. Christmas day and the days following through to New Year (when we had yet more church and even more goodies) were ever so joyous and memorable. Christmas truly was the most wonderful time of the year.

Christmas was not the only time and opportunity for merriment. Unless there was an afternoon service on special occasions or the once a month communion, Sunday afternoons seemed to be reserved for visiting time. Either we went visiting to another family from church or they visited us. How our parents arranged who visited with whom without telephone or mail, I'm not sure. At least some arrangements were made on the spur of the moment. Usually guests came for lunch, after which the parents chatted in the living room and the children played. Indoors, we often played Monopoly, crokinole, dominoes, checkers, other board games of various kinds, or with our new Christmas toys. Outdoors, we skied, skated, sledded, or played hockey (on the packed snow, with no skates, using curved willows for sticks and frozen horse turds for pucks).

On one occasion in mid-winter when the Konrads and Friesens were over, we boys decided to go tobogganing. We headed to a new steep hill at Bartsch's creek, tied together several pairs of home-made skis (for we could not afford to buy skis or even a toboggan), and piled on for the descent. The first run in the powdery three-foot deep snow was slow, as we made trail. By the third of fourth run we had carved out a trench about two feet deep, and the run was packed and slippery. All of us joined in, whether actually on the toboggan or not, with the speed of descent approaching lightning-quick. What fun that was! We called it the 'Jericho Road' for some reason or other. When darkness set in, we wearily trudged home, our soaked outer clothes squeaking as Jack Frost did his work. By the time we got home the arms and legs of our clothing became mini stovepipes, forcing us to walk like the tin man from 'The Wizard of Oz'.

In summer, but not only then, other outdoor fun included games such as hide-and-seek, anti-I-over, scrub (the softball kind), tag, croquet, prisoner's base, and the inevitable hop-scotch. Even though it was more of a girl's game, we all played. And of course, with Bear Creek (Bartsch's Creek to us) so nearby, we had an ample supply of swimming holes, which we used not only for fun but also to cool off and clean up. There were also many outings (i.e. going more than two or three miles from home) by buggy, or later by car, to the towns of Sexsmith, Beaverlodge, or Grande Prairie, or to go wild blueberry, raspberry, or strawberry picking (these trips were not only for fun). A memorable yearly outing was riding in the box of the Sieberts' truck to Saskatoon Island, where by noon we would fill all the available containers with berries and could then spend the rest of the day picnicking and swimming. We were amazed how well Dad could swim way out in the deep through the crashing waves.

After we bought our 1928 Hudson car in 1936, Dad and Mother with several children (we took turns) made their yearly pilgrimage to Tofield, just south and east of Edmonton, where Mother's brother and two of her sisters and their families lived. These trips, as each of us siblings recall with relish, were memorable, eye-opening, and hugely enjoyable.

Our life on the farm did provide some opportunities for fun but it wasn't all leisure, travel, and recreation. Far from it. These fun activities were only made possible because Dad, with the help of my older brothers and sisters, particularly John, ran a very well organized and efficient farming operation. We had a mixed farm, with emphasis on grain production. Grain farming has a rhythm of its own, with sequences of jobs dictated by season and weather. In the Peace country, latitude 55 degrees north, one of the most northerly grain growing areas on Earth, the growing season is short with frequent early frosts in fall. That means that it is essential for farmers in this area to hit the fields in spring as soon as the weather allows.

For us it meant that we had to round up and feed the horses and get them ready to plow and harrow as soon as possible. Two teams of horses (Dan and Baldy, our trotters, and King and Charlie, the favoured work team) were kept in the barn all winter for work and transportation. The rest of the horses ran wild, eating snow and devouring straw stacks one after another throughout the neighborhood. Someone always knew where the herd of horses was and reported on them. Then, in early spring, they would be rounded up, sorted out and taken home for grain feeding. On one such wintering, our mare, June, met up with a stallion (unknown to us, but probably an Arab) and produced 'my' horse Birdie.

After the field was prepared and the seeding done, another harrowing followed. That done, hopefully by early to mid-May, one breathed easier and the hectic pace slowed down a bit. Then followed the cultivation of summer fallow, which for us amounted to about one-third of our cleared acreage. Midsummer was really quite a relaxing time, relatively speaking, when Dad and Mother went on their Tofield trips and most of us, at least for a few weeks, basked in the sun between swims. When Dad returned from travelling he turned his full attention to the binder and threshing machine. He spent days, together with Mr. Siebert (with whom we jointly owned the threshing machine) going over every inch of the machine looking for parts needing to be adjusted, replaced, or re-machined.

I recall on one occasion Dad hurriedly walking to the house, announcing that he'd have to go to Sexsmith or Grande Prairie for parts. After begging and obtaining permission to go along, I had to wait patiently and watch as he deftly shaved himself with a straight edge, hoping he wouldn't cut himself. He didn't. I asked him why he had to shave. He just said, "You never show up in a public place without looking your best." The reason I so desperately wanted to go along was to get Dad to stop at the Buffalo Lake general store to buy a nickel's worth of maple buds (chocolate). It was rumoured that the storekeeper there gave even bigger bags full than did Mrs. Larsen at La Glace.

The moment that the grain was ripe enough to cut, the pace of activity picked up again, even more hectic now than in spring seeding time. As soon as we were able, we were required to help with the farm work. We younger boys now began to experience the real work of farming on top of the regular chores we did (all without pay of course). At first, maybe at about age nine or ten, Peter and I, after school, followed Lena and Mary around the fields placing a single bundle on each side of the stook.[50] Later I would prepare and take to the field an exchange team of four horses, a job I hated because I was scared to harness the big work horses.

The 'mixed' part of our mixed farm was the raising and fattening of hogs and steers in numbers allowed by our facilities and pastures. Somehow we always managed to have enough feed for the pigs over the summer before the new crop came in, but just barely. It may have been mysterious to me at the time but it was almost certainly a result of careful planning. One summer, however, we did run out of grain. Fortunately we still had a good supply of potatoes, so we cooked them, cooled them, and fed them to the pigs. We also raised chickens, ducks, and geese, mostly for our own consumption.

With the older boys taking over more and more of the farm duties, Dad now was freed up to pursue his love of beekeeping, a hobby at first and then a prosperous side-business to farming. After

---

50   A 'stook' is a pile of little bundles of straw with the grain still attached, arranged in such a way so that it dries before threshing.

a slow build-up, Dad eventually owned some 150 hives, which he serviced with the help of Anna and Martin and eventually Peter too. John and Frank more or less ran the farm. Beekeeping during the war years, a time of sugar rationing, turned out to be quite lucrative. We were now definitely heading out of poverty. Both our fortunes and our work patterns were changing. We were all growing up and beginning to seek our own opportunities for vocations and our own directions in life.

Dad was well aware of this and began looking elsewhere for openings for his huge family. Martin had already gone off to Manitoba to complete the last two years of high school at Gretna, a prestigious Mennonite private school. Dad and Mother were very much hoping that we children would all become good Mennonites, or at the very least good evangelical Christians. In the summer of 1945 Dad and Mother took the opportunity to attend a Mennonite conference in Yarrow, B.C. (in the Fraser Valley near Chilliwack). There, they found what they were looking for: a community of compatible Mennonites, a more benign climate, good farming potential, and opportunities for high school and Bible school. There was even a distinct possibility of a new private Mennonite high school being built. When our parents returned to 'the Peace', they were full of enthusiasm for this new 'land of milk and honey' and started exploring the prospects and possibilities of moving there.

Dad's enthusiasm can be measured by his own depiction of the new found land.

> *Everything was in full bloom; the raspberries were flourishing. The weather was lovely; the trees were laden with fruit. It felt like paradise. [Southern] B.C. came close to what we remembered of our home in Russia. Our hearts warmed with the idea that perhaps we could include it in a chapter of our lives...*
>
> *All our friends who had moved here seemed to be very happy. They had running water in the house, electric lights, bathrooms, etc. Everything was idyllic. The*

> winters were short, there was a big Mennonite church, a Bible School, a high school and so on. Our life in the north was so much more rustic...
>
> We went back and told everyone how wonderful it was in B.C. We were at it again at the dinner table...[51]

It appeared as if our parents were ready to make the big move, and they probably were; but they also wanted the opinions of the children. So it was decided that as soon as the harvesting was complete and the beekeeping done, Dad, and as many of the older siblings as could fit into the car, would take a trip to the Fraser Valley to see for themselves what a wonderful place it was. Before that trip all of us children were very reluctant to leave our home in La Glace, and were suspicious of the motives of some of the families with 'B.C. fever' that had already moved. All that changed, however, after that fateful exploratory trip. Everyone became convinced of the merits of moving, everyone except for me. Dad and my five older siblings (not counting Lena and Mary who had already married by this time) took up all the space in the car, so I could not join them.

The three week absence of Dad and all the older siblings provided me with valuable experiences and insights that I could not have gained had I been able to go along. I was now the oldest sibling at home and took charge of doing the chores and seeing to other farm work. This was quite thrilling. Finally I counted for something, no longer just a number in a series. I also got a chance to go threshing for the first time. For a long time I had wanted to stay home from school and be part of a threshing crew. The B.C. trip was premised on the completion of the harvest; but just before the last field was cleared of bundles, the rains came and halted the threshing. Dad even wanted to cancel the trip because of this, but Nick Siebert, our brother-in-law (Mary's husband) promised that when the weather broke, he would take care of the last bit. And that's how it turned out. Just after the BCers departed, the weather cleared and in a few

---

51 *Aus Der Alten*, p. 89.

days Nick came by to ask me to take a team out west to help him complete the threshing. I couldn't have been more delighted. Jake Janzen, Nick, and I finished the harvesting in a couple of days. After cleaning up, Nick asked me to drive the tractor (towing the threshing machine, 'Old Bess', to which were tied King and Charlie towing the hayrack) back to Nick's homestead. Proudly I did so, feeling quite the man. But I nearly had a disaster. Not having discussed with Nick the route I should take, I decided to take the short cut through the soft-bedded waterless creek. Half-way through I knew this was a bad mistake, but there was no turning back. I nearly tipped over the whole outfit, which would have been ruinous to my reputation, not to mention the family fortunes. It was a hair-raising experience, but I lucked out and made it through.

The gang came back from BC early and with great excitement. Along the way, it had been decided that we would move. Rather quickly we sold our land and prepared to auction off all of our possessions other than a few personal effects. Dad had to sell his precious beehives. Rover, our dog, had to be put down. Birdie, 'my' horse was going to be auctioned off. Even my mandolin was put on the block. All our livestock would be sold and many of the animals were dear to us. We had lived with them and communicated with them over the years and it was sad to say goodbye to all of them. We would miss more than just the animals though, for there were many familiar things and places that were precious:

> *To house and garden, field and lawn*
> *The meadow-gates we swung upon*
> *To pump and stable, tree and swing*
> *Good-bye, good-bye to everything*
>
> *And fare you well for evermore,*
> *O ladder at the hayloft door*
> *O hayloft where the cobwebs cling,*
> *Good-bye, good-bye to everything.*
>
> *– R.L. Stevenson, from 'Farewell to the Farm'*

On a cold and snowy November day we had our farm sale. I was not happy as I watched beast by beast, item by item, disappear never to be seen again. I was not happy about leaving La Glace, despite the enthusiasm of my parents and siblings, despite assurances that all would be well once we got to BC. All did turn out well and I did eventually like BC but that was still to come. We spent our last night in La Glace at the Siebert's old place.

Early the next day, with our 1937 Chevrolet packed to the gills, Dad, John, Frank, Peter, Walter and I, said good-bye to Nick and Mary, and Martin (who stayed behind to attend Bible School) and headed north on a detour. We had to travel north to Watino to wait for a train with a flat deck to take us across the Smokey River, the ice not yet solid enough for an ice bridge at Bezanson, the regular crossing. By the time we got across, it was late afternoon. Our plan was to drive all night and reach Tofield the next morning to visit our relatives there before continuing our journey through the Crowsnest Pass (high in the Rocky Mountains on the BC/Alberta border) and via the USA to Chilliwack, BC. Having just eaten something, we packed ourselves into the car and headed out with John at the wheel. Even with the Chevy's heater going full blast, we plied ourselves with blankets against the cold, and with the snow pelting down behind us we headed out into the darkness away from our old farm never, except for brief visits, to return to La Glace.

CHAPTER THREE

Chilliwack (1945-1950)

First Impressions

CHILLIWACK, a relatively small city approximately 100 kilometers east of Vancouver, is situated in the heart of the beautiful Fraser Valley of British Columbia. It has a mild climate and very fertile soil. Thus it is most suitable for all kinds of farming and other industries. This, and the fact that many Mennonites were moving there in the late 40's, attracted my parents; and so we too moved there in 1946. It was in Chilliwack that I spent my tumultuous teenage years between 1945 and 1950. Though these five or so years represent only one sixteenth of my life span (so far) they are proportionally of far greater significance, being crucial formative years. For better or worse, and in large part, my Chilliwack experience made me what I became.

Upon leaving La Glace en route to Chilliwack, we slept fitfully in the cold car on our way to the Warkentin's in Tofield, Alberta. There we rested and visited for a day or two before continuing on through Calgary to the Crowsnest Pass, the safest route through the Rockies in the southeast corner of BC. From there we connected, as quickly as possible, with the US Hwy 2 in Idaho and on through the St. Steven's pass in Washington state. I was tremendously impressed by the beauty and majesty of the mountains which I had never seen before. Once through the towering mountains to the western side of Washington state, we began to witness first-hand what we would find in the Fraser Valley for years to come – relatively warm weather, rain, more rain, and even more rain, green fields late into the fall and even winter, and the ever present smell of 'Fraser Valley gold'. For a week or two before taking possession of the farm Dad had purchased a few miles away from Chilliwack city, we stayed in a house near the rise of the dramatic mountains east of Vancouver. There I got the first whiff of the distinctive smell of western red cedar. It seemed too that I could even smell the rain. Ubiquitous rain, cedar, and the ever-present aroma of cow dung were my first memories of B.C. I was also very impressed with the amenities we enjoyed: running water in the house, including hot water; indoor plumbing, including a real bathtub; electricity, including lots of real electric lights; a warm house and even a milking machine. Could it get any better than this?

Within a few days of our arrival, we were on a crowded yellow school bus, taking us to Chilliwack High School (CHS) over gravel roads. I was amazed that even though it was winter, there was no snow. Armed with an exemplary report card from my old school, I approached principal Graham with trepidation, wondering where he would place me. He asked me where I was from.

"La Glace", I said.

"And where is that?"

"Peace River, Alberta."

"Come with me."

We said no more as we marched down the seemingly never ending corridor to the last classroom at the corner of the school. After he knocked on the door, a very pretty young female teacher appeared. He introduced me to Miss Snow and quickly disappeared. Miss Snow then explained that the class was just beginning a spelling test and suggested that I try some of the words even if I hadn't been prepared. I tried. As it turned out, I was the only person who spelled them all correctly. Apparently this was some type of 'opportunity class' for slower learners. Had Mr. Graham mistakenly put me in the wrong class? Had he misread my report card, perhaps taking the C's as mediocre grades rather than as 'Commendable'? Miss Snow later explained that I didn't really belong in that class but it was the only Grade 8 class that had any space left.

In a few days, another Albertan, this time from Lethbridge, came to join the class in similar circumstances. Jake Geddert came to be my friend and long term acquaintance, with whom I spent years competing for top spot in the high school, Sunday School, and later in Bible School. We worked, played, sang, and studied together for many years. Jake's strength as a student was his fantastic memory. Later in life he became a librarian at Prairie Bible Institute. I am grateful to Jake for his friendship and for his prodding me on in my studies even though our adult lives took off in different directions.

CHS, despite Jake's friendship, was a bit of a cultural shock. Among many new things, we quickly learned: to say 'Hi' instead of 'Hello', to save up a nickel to join the others for a 'revel' before we boarded the bus, to fight our way through crowded hallways to get to the next class when the buzzer sounded, and to shun wearing a cap outside even when it rained. Everything seemed so strange and confusing compared to the cosy one-room school in La Glace. It also seemed odd that we should have to acquire gym clothing and do exercise indoors. And what about that strange game called 'basketball'? I had never seen or even heard of such a thing. Why did we have to bounce the ball when running with it? That seemed so unnecessary. Eventually I learned to really like it. Although some of the elements of school were the same as before, we Hamms were advancing by leaps and bounds in this new culture.

Sure enough, CHS, just like other schools, had its bullies. The one in my class quickly realized that these Mennonite kids coming in from the Prairies were pacifists and didn't fight back as readily. So once again we were fair game for the usual punching and pestering. As once before at Old Post School, I chose to deal with the problem instead of just enduring it. This time I used different tactics. Rather than ask a friend to help me beat up the bully, as I had done before, this time I decided to give him a treat. I invited him to join me at noon hour to go to the favourite local candy store. After buying each of us a revel we sat down and discussed the whole bullying problem. I simply told him I didn't like it and would much sooner be his friend rather than enemy. It worked. Not that we became close friends, but at least the bullying ceased.

Church life early on in Chilliwack was also a bit of a shock. Suddenly we were in big churches, packed with parishioners and balconies bursting with a huge number of young people. Large choirs sang beautifully, accompanied by piano, unheard of back in La Glace. Here too were more interesting and gifted preachers and Sunday School teachers. These churches also attracted many itinerant evangelists and singing groups, like L.E. Maxwell and the Janz Quartet from Prairie Bible Institute. We had experienced some church services in English before, but here they were more frequent. Home services with local lay preachers were still always conducted in German. Lest we assimilate completely with 'the English', we were actually sent to Saturday School (held in the local church) for the purpose of improving our written and spoken German. My father and Mr. G Penner were our teachers. It was decided that learning German was more important than planting strawberries or spreading manure, important though that was. I am grateful that my father made that decision.

That first Christmas in Chilliwack also seemed very strange. There was no snow, and it didn't even rain. Riding a bike on a warm sunny day to visit a friend on Christmas day seemed totally surreal. Never again would I experience those snowy and wonderful Christmas celebrations we had had in La Glace.

It took a while to become comfortable with all the newness and the unfamiliar but eventually we settled into a not too different routine of school, chores, homework, church, farm work (after school and on Saturdays and holidays), more church (in the evenings), choir practices and endless visiting. Once the routine was established, the five months I spent at CHS completing my Grade 8 vanished quickly. I remember very little of the actual school work other than memorizing long sections of Sir Walter Scott's *Lady of the Lake* and struggling through the novel *Ivanhoe*. Even before completing my Grade 8 at CHS, we were given to understand that next year we would be attending a new private Mennonite school in Yarrow. So when we said goodbye to CHS at the end of that year, it was supposed to be for good. However it didn't exactly turn out that way.

Before we would discover what the new school would be like, there was a summer's worth of work to attend to. We were now introduced to some new kinds of farming: strawberry and raspberry picking, planting corn and hoeing weeds, haying with fork in hand (rather than by machine), picking hops and beans, stomping corn silage, and even picking wild blackberries on occasion. The latter we did on our few days off. We sold the berries in Chilliwack city for pocket money.

Our days were not all drudgery. Except for the rigidly daily milking and regular chores, we never worked on Sundays. So Sunday afternoons were visiting times. Only seldom did we not have visitors or go visiting with other church members. We young teenagers played games (softball, for example), biked to Ryder Lake or Little Mountain, tagged along with older siblings to local swimming holes (but not to the popular Cultus Lake or other public swimming places where girls and women also swam in far too revealing bathing suits), played board games indoors on rainy days, climbed the nearby mountains, or just sat around telling stories.

Sunday visiting, Chilliwack, 1949

It wasn't only on Sundays that we enjoyed some recreation. Every once in a while Dad would declare a day or two as days off. He himself had the 'wanderlust' and a yen for travel and adventure. So on one Saturday it was arranged that we, with the Hiebert family (males only), would hike up Mount Cheam, the 6000 foot snow-capped beauty starting a range of jagged peaks between Chilliwack and the USA. On another occasion we drove up as high as possible on Mount Baker in Washington state. Another time Dad and five of us siblings took the ferry to Vancouver Island where we toured Victoria, visited Butchart's Garden, and gazed at the stars through the lens of the local observatory. These were memorable and exciting experiences for us, particularly because they were so rare. They were rare because the farm work needed to be done and extra money was needed to be earned so we could pay our debts and pay for tuition at private school. In contrast to our older siblings, all four of us younger children (Peter, Walter, Margaret and I) insisted on continuing our schooling until high school graduation and beyond. With Anna and Frank staying at home to help on the farm (in actuality running the farm), and with the rest of us pitching in when we could, we all somehow managed to satisfy Dad's requirements for us and each of our own wishes too. Anna and Frank, in fall and winter, attended Bible School and the four youngest of us attended Sharon Mennonite Collegiate Institute in Yarrow.

Sharon Mennonite Collegiate Institute

THE MENNONITE churches of Yarrow, Sardis (now Greendale) and Chilliwack joined forces in 1945 to create their own private school, called Sharon Mennonite Collegiate Institute (SMCI, or just 'Sharon' for short). It was modelled after the Mennonite Educational Institute (MEI) in Abbotsford. SMCI was located in Yarrow, a small town, then almost exclusively populated by Mennonites, huddled at the base of Vedder Mountain, approximately a dozen miles southwest from where we lived in Chilliwack. For the first

Sharon Mennonite Collegiate Institute (SMCI), 1948

year of its operation, and part of the second, the school consisted of a group of buildings on the site of Yarrow Mennonite Church. During my first school term there at SMCI (Grade 9), we as a class were in a separate building (converted from a farm building) just east of the main building (a former Bible School), where the rest of the school classes were housed.

While this was going on, a brand new school was being built about a mile east and somewhat north of the Yarrow church. This new school opened on October 10, 1948 during my Grade 10 year. I recall sitting in a classroom examining the wall I had helped paint the summer before. Much of the materials and the labour that went into the building were from voluntary contributions from the community. Dad even called a halt to farm work for a few days so that he and a few of us brothers could volunteer our labour for the cause. I was placed under the supervision of Mr. Boldt, a professional painter from our church. He taught me how to apply the paint smoothly, avoiding streaks. The school's construction was in many respects a labour of love. That fact was just another reason I was so disappointed when the school was sold just a few years later.

The purpose of the private school was primarily to continue with our indoctrination into the fundamental tenets of evangelical Christianity in a setting that protected us against ideas that might challenge our faith. Thus, included in our schooling were courses in *Glaubenslehre* (religious studies), Bible, and catechism, memorizing a great deal of the material without scrutiny or discussion. However, this school wasn't just a run-of-the-mill Christian school. It was a *Mennonite* school, so another purpose was to broaden our understanding of Mennonite culture and traditions, including the German language, the mother tongue. The required provincial curriculum was also included, almost as an afterthought.

If the indoctrination and enculturation in the end partially failed, it was not for lack of trying on the part of our dedicated and well-intentioned teachers. Preoccupation with religion and religiousness was intense. Every day began with morning devotions, usually conducted by one of the school staff members. Tuesday noon's were reserved for 'voluntary' prayer meetings, led by one of the senior students. Fellowship meetings, also 'voluntary', were on Friday at noon at which students prayed, sang, spoke, and gave testimonies. The latter was a source of tension for me. How often I thought I felt the Spirit moving me to speak up, but I was too nervous and shy, going home for the weekend with a bad conscience.

SMCI Friday Fellowship Meeting, circa 1948

In addition to these regular services and religion classes, visitors from other Christian schools (a number of them from just across the border in the USA) would come by and deliver a religious program. When missionaries and itinerant preachers showed up, which was often, regular classes would be cancelled at the drop of a hat to give them the opportunity to spread their religious messages. School plays, dramas, and speaking competitions all provided even more opportunities to get in a religious plug. For example, when I was in Grade Eleven we, together with the Grade Twelves, organized a noon hour 'speaker's corner' to practice speech making and presentation. I volunteered to give a speech (actually a small sermon) on the topic of 'Remembering and Forgetting', basing it on a Biblical verse, "The wicked shall be turned into hell and all the nations that forget God."[52] Another biblical notion that I included was the idea that when God forgives, He forgets. The speech was essentially a study in the pros and cons of both remembering and forgetting. Students and teachers alike took every likely opportunity to cultivate religious fervor and Christian faith. Despite the relentless reminders to get saved, stay saved, and rededicate our lives to Christ, we by and large did not feel spiritually bullied or oppressed. We were fully convinced that we were on the right track to becoming good Christian Mennonites.

I agree with my brother Peter:

> *Thus, while on the surface nothing dramatic appeared to occur, almost imperceptibly our parents' desire was being fulfilled. Through the exposure to Christian principles in the private school and the faithful participation in the weekly church services, we were being socialized to their value system and a Christian orientation for life. And little by little growth in our Christian experience was being realized.*[53]

If the emphasis on religion at SMCI was intense, hardly less so was the emphasis on secular academic studies and sports. If I recall correctly, my strongest academic subjects (probably because of good teaching) were mathematics and geography. English and history were moderately well taught. The weakest part of the curriculum were the sciences. Despite the fact that inspector Turnbull examined and approved our lab books (so that we could move on to the next grade without taking provincial exams), we nevertheless had a pau-

---

52   Psalm 9:17.
53   *Reflections...*, p. 60.

city of science equipment. A general lack of interest in the sciences was pervasive. We took science courses because they were required not because they inspired us. I wish that we had been provided with a better science education such that I could read physics and quantum mechanics now with better understanding.

On one occasion in Grade 10 when I wrote an exam in General Science and received a perfect grade, Mr. Dyck, our science teacher and later principal of the school, complimented me on the result and asked me if I was going to become a doctor. "Oh, no!" I said "I'm going to become a minister." I had already made up my mind. The professions which held the most prestige at SMCI, the ones that were the most suitable for Christians, were some form of ministry, teaching, or medicine (for men) and teaching and nursing (for women). In light of that, it is surprising that we did not receive more thorough instruction in science and English. I do not recall that evolutionary theory was an issue. I think that most of us believed that evolution and creation were compatible.

In the belief that a strong body and a strong mind work together and that the body is the temple of the Holy Ghost, SMCI placed a lot of emphasis on sports. The entire school was divided into four 'houses', each including members from all the grades (grade 7 to 13)

SMCI Athens House Basketball Team (C. is far r.), 1948

and each having Greek state names: Athens, Corinth, Macedonia and Sparta. Each house was further divided by age groups: bantam, junior, intermediate, and senior. The houses competed with each other in various sports, such as softball, soccer, tennis, field events, and especially basketball. In this way almost everyone was on some team or another. Almost every noon hour (when there weren't prayer or fellowship meetings) some team would be competing against another, sometimes even two or three teams both indoors and outdoors.

In addition to the house teams, SMCI also had school teams in a few sports. These teams competed with other high schools such as MEI and CHS. Thus I noted in my diary on October 28, 1948 and February 2, 1949 respectively:

> *Abbotsford (MEI) soccer team played Yarrow (SMCI) this afternoon. Walter and I reffed the game. Everybody said we did a good job of it. Felt proud and popular.*
>
> *In the evening we sneaked[54] out and in again from home to see SMCI beat CHS in a basketball game. We won 32-30. Very exciting.*

CHS, the public high school, was several times the size of our little private school so that made it all the more exciting if and when we won.

Toward the end of my Grade 11 year at SMCI we got word that the school would likely not operate the following year and would be sold. That came as quite a shock. Just when I had nicely settled in, and had become comfortable with my position in the school both academically and socially, I would be uprooted yet again and have to start my final year of high school in a strange setting. I had really grown to like SMCI. What bothered me more than anything else was the fact that the school was closing for financial reasons. If our Christian education was so important, couldn't our parents (and we too) put out a little more and sacrifice for the sake of our

---

54 'Sneaked' because Dad would not have given us permission to attend such a 'worldly' event.

spiritual well-being? I suppose at least some of the school officials, including my father, thought just that.

The main problem was that the market had dropped out in the raspberry industry. Some of us, who in addition to the berry crops, had dairies to back us up, could have managed. However in Yarrow (particularly) and Sardis, farming, the favourite occupation for Mennonites, was mostly done on small acreages devoted entirely to berries. When the berry market crashed, there really was no way forward for the parents of the majority of the students. There was just no money for tuition. I did not understand that at the time and so I bade farewell to SMCI with a heavy heart.

What are my overall impressions of my three foundational years at SMCI? Despite some reservations as to the overall academic effectiveness of the school, I do look back on those years with pride and fondness. We had developed a certain 'esprit de corps' and we honed excellent work habits that served us well into the future. The study habits that I developed there – concentrating on the task at hand, persevering through thick and thin, completing tasks, going for help when needed, and self-discipline – helped me cope with academic studies throughout my life. I do wish we had received better instruction in English[55] and the sciences but what we lacked there we would partially make up later with hard work. The strength of the school lay in its ability to foster personal and character development. Above all, I learned to be self-confident, courageous, and self-assured. I felt that I could do anything whatsoever I put my mind to.

Our 1948-49 annual, *The Laurel*, had this to say about me beside my photograph:

> A youth with a purpose high and strong. A youth with a will to conquer wrong. A spirit of self-reliance and independence.

Someone, I think, got it mainly right.

---

55   I don't even remember who my English teachers were at SMCI as distinct from the vivid memories I have of the excellent instruction we received from Mr. P. Penner the next year in Grade 12 at CHS, the public school.

My Five-Year Diary

WHATEVER POSSESSED me at age fifteen to keep a diary I cannot possibly imagine. If I had any delusions of grandeur such that somebody someday might want to look into my development, I certainly don't remember. Perhaps I just wanted to chronicle my feelings, thoughts, and actions to see if I had kept my resolutions; perhaps I just wanted to keep a record of dates and details of work and play; perhaps I wrote to challenge myself to take life more seriously by becoming more aware of what I was doing and how I was using my time. Maybe I was just following a fashion of the time. My brother Walter, for example, also kept a diary at that time. I can only guess at what my reasons might have been. In any case, I had until early this year (2010) a tattered brown leatherette-covered lockable diary with entry spaces for five years. Of the 1826 available spaces, one for each day covering the period from Jan. 1, 1947 to Dec. 31, 1951, I made entries for 1581 of them. To pack in as much information as possible into the available four lines (4" x 7/8") I used codes and abbreviations, even inventing some of my own. 'Thought' became 'thot', 'DM' meant 'Dad and Mother', 'Y' indicated a girl I liked, and so on. Most of the spaces left blank were in the last two years, probably because I was just too tired at the end of the day or I was losing interest. That still left the diary 87% complete.

Upon recent review, I found the diary to be exceedingly boring, embarrassingly badly written, and blushingly self-revealing. There were in it passages that I didn't want anybody to read. I cringed at some of the things I said about myself those many years ago. Most of the diary is now destroyed.

1948 – A Typical Year

IN THE YEAR 1948, there was an entry for every single day, the only such year; so I am concentrating my sharing of the diary with you on this year. I noted things such as when I went to school and when I didn't for reasons of illness, farm work, other work, or non-statutory holidays (i.e. Church functions). Surprisingly, I discovered that I had attended school (SMCI), only 145 days in 1948. Why did I miss so much? I stayed home for twelve days to work on the farm. I also missed school for several weeks because of severe flooding in parts of the Fraser Valley. We worked on the dykes for a good part of that time. That year I also spent a few days in the hospital and a few more weeks at home to recuperate from an operation to remove a nasal obstruction. Missing that much school was potentially a serious limitation to my education, though most likely I made up for at least some of it.

So what did occupy the heart and mind of a normal, healthy, sixteen year-old Mennonite farm boy in the Fraser Valley in 1948? Not surprisingly, school, religion, farm work, weather, sports, and, of course, girls and sex.

Here are some selected, perhaps typical entries:

> *Mar. 15, 1948, Sun. Very nice day. Had bad boil on my chin. Did no chores. Peter and I stayed home from church. Jack Braun came over for a little while. Listened to radio and got a real blessing. Did Home Work – lots of it.*

> *Mar. 25, 1948, Thurs. Last day of school before Easter. Peter stayed home to go to Vancouver. Got report cards. Had 2 B's; and the rest A's. Was satisfied. Had blessing in Fellowship meeting.*

> *Apr. 14, 1948, Wed. A nice day. Had a bad cold. Practiced quartet in the auditorium. Liked XY more. Listened to last hockey game of the season. Leafs got the Stanley Cup.*
>
> *Oct. 14, 1948, Thurs. Piled high with work to do. Not satisfied with my behaviour in school. I'll make a new start. After school cut some clover till the mower broke. Dad again opened my letter. Very angry with him and the Mennonites.*
>
> *Oct. 30, 1948, Sat. Filled silo at Dykes in the rain. Got soaked. Did a lot of homework in the evening. Thanked God for my endurance and will power.*

It is understandable that farmers are concerned with weather, as frequently it was the weather that determined what kind of work or play we undertook. That said, the fact that I made 156 entries about the weather in the diary in the space of one year is to me now astonishing. Weather not only influenced farm-related work but also my moods, as is still the case today.

It has already been mentioned that I stayed away from school for twelve days to work on the farm which included cutting corn, hoeing weeds in the berry patches and spreading manure. In addition to the work on our farm, I missed most of September to work in the hop yards[56], both picking hops and working long shifts at the kilns. I didn't start my Grade 11 year until September 28th.

Of course we almost always put in full days of work on our own farm on statutory holidays and in summer. For the year 1948, I made 103 entries of doing farm work, most days from 8 a.m. to 5 p.m., and often in the evening as well. Some days were cut short

---

56 About 90% of the hops grown in the Fraser Valley go to beer production but since we were good Mennonites and frowned upon the consumption of alcohol, we always imagined that we were working on the other 10%.

because of inclement weather. When work on our farm was not urgent, we would often help others, usually without pay, and they in turn would help us.

Our dairy operation, of course, required relentless attention to 'doing the chores'. Twice a day, seven days a week, 365 days a year, thirty or so cows had to be milked and fed and the sanitary conditions in the barn maintained. Two or three of us boys could get these chores done in about 1 1/2 hours. Most of the time, thank goodness, several of us were involved, but as noted 23 times that year I did these 'chores' all by myself.

Fortunately, I liked hard work, as I have for most of my life. Doing strenuous physical work is exhilarating and just as rewarding as committing a poem to memory or solving a math equation. And we indeed often did memorizing and milking at the same time. A job of any kind well done is its own reward.

I recall trying to become the local raspberry picking champion that year. Usually my sister Anna (now Annie) was the top picker out of the twenty or more pickers at our place. And local rumour had it that no one in the neighborhood could pick berries by hand as fast as she could. She could pick 250 or more pounds of raspberries in a single eight hour work period. I had often tried to beat Anna but had never done so. The best I could ever manage, even with supreme effort, was a tie. I decided one day, when the berries were bearing at their best, to challenge her record and try for 300 pounds. With my cousin Neil's help, I picked from early morning until late, from dark to dark. Here is the diary entry for Wed., July 14, 1948:

> *Was up at 5:00 a.m. to pick raspberries with Neil. My aim was to pick 300 pounds, but I got only 271 lbs. even though I worked hard.*

Neil brought me my meals, brought me empty flats, and stacked up the full flats (22 in all) at the weigh station. I had hoped that at 14 pounds or so per flat, I would have enough to reach my goal. Upon weighing, I was disappointed to find that I had only picked 271 lbs., not the 300 lbs. that I had hoped for but it was still enough to beat Anna's record. Why did I work so hard at it? Just for fun. Just to be the best.

I also tried to be the best at school. At SMCI there were four of us, all boys as I recall, that vied for top marks in various subjects. At times I reached the top, mostly because I was diligent in doing homework. In my diary entries for 1948 I made eighty references to doing homework, sometimes long into the night. Often, too, I did homework at recess and noon hour at school so that I could attend special evening church services and choir practices and *still* have all my homework done.

To say that we boys at home were very conscientious about doing our homework is seriously to understate the case. After Frank left home to work for himself, Dad suggested that we younger three boys (Peter, Walter, and I) each by turn drop out of school for a year to help on the farm. We vehemently objected. We assured Dad that we would get all the farm work done if only we were allowed to stay in school. So Dad took more than a casual look at our report cards to count up the A grades. It was understood that if we were not serious about our studies, then we would be pulled off the school bus.

Here are some of my diary entries relating to homework:

> *Jan. 20, Tues. – Decided to work very hard at my studies so one day I can do a D.D. (Doctor of Divinity) degree.*
>
> *Mar. 2, Tues. – Memorized poetry while doing chores. In the evening wrote a short poem about work.*
>
> *Mar. 24, Wed. – Did homework till late, 10:30. Then read* Clearing in the West.
>
> *May 10, Mon. – Played 'Rook' in the evening. Felt sorry because of the waste of time.*

May 13, Thurs. – Did Math homework till 11:00 p.m. just for fun. God helped me find the answers.

Oct. 13, Wed. – Lots of homework. Did all the chores alone.

Oct. 14, Thurs. – Piled high with work to do.

Nov. 7, Sun. – In Sunday School I was very sleepy.

Dec. 10, Fri. – Got up at 3:30 a.m. to study and memorize in German 'Lied von der Glocke'. Stayed home from choir practice to study.

Dec. 16, Thurs. – Today we wrote Math and 'Kirchengeschichte' (Church History) exams. Got 100% in 'Kircheng...' Studied hard again in the evening. I'm nearly going crazy from studying so much.

A typical day of work in the year 1948, say in winter, would be as follows: rise at 5:30 a.m.; do chores till 7:00 a.m.; 7:00-7:15 change clothes, shave, clean up; 7:15-7:45 morning devotions and breakfast; 7:45-8:10 prepare for school, take milk cans to the road; 8:10-8:45 take school bus to Yarrow; 9:00-3:30 school; 3:30-4:00 after school activities; 4:00-4:35 bus ride home; 4:40-6:00 work in barn and/or farm depending on the weather; 6:00-6:30 dinner; 6:30-7:30 more chores; 7:30-10:30 homework and/or reading time and sometimes game time. On evenings when there were church services, prayer meetings, choir practices, or other special services of one kind or another (missionaries in town, revival meetings, visiting preachers, or singing groups), then our homework would be delayed until after the service. Only seldom did we wish or get permission to skip these services. On such days, and one could count on at least one or two per week, bedtime came late, often midnight or later. Yet we had to be up again at 5:30 a.m. to start all over again. No wonder I frequently felt tired.

I noted in my diary on no less than 29 occasions that I felt tired or lazy. It might have been that I was then, as I still am now, struggling with a condition of hypothyroidism, discovered decades later when I began routine medical check-ups. However it was more likely that my condition of weariness and lethargy were caused simply by too much work and not enough sleep. My diary provides some evidence.

Gleaned from the diary entries for the year, I chronicle my moods and attitudes as follows: tired and lazy (29 times); determined to work harder, to live better or to prepare for the ministry (53 times); spiritual blessing or felt being 'called' (19); humbled, stupid, or unpopular (21); proud (22); lonesome (1); doubting God, Bible, or church doctrine (7); excited (4); unhappy (12); verging on depressed (4); happy (63). Today I am quite surprised by these tallies. When I think back now, I remember more the turmoil and stress of youth and the unending chores rather than happiness, the prevailing mood, it would seem. The evidence suggests that I must have been a happy-go-lucky guy despite the pressures of too much work and too much church.

We seldom missed church on Sundays or any of the other many types of services. We would have to mount a serious case to Dad for us to be given permission to stay away, though we were usually allowed to skip church if we were sick. I note that I skipped Sunday morning services only four times that year and only seven times on Sunday evening. Other mentionings of church related activities in my diary are as follows: Young People's Meetings (27); prayer meetings (7); SMCI Fellowship meetings on Friday noons (17); special church services (44); choir practices (19); quartet singing (9); listening to religious radio broadcasts (17); '*Hausbesuch*', pastoral visits at home (2). These entries, it must be noted, almost certainly, do not represent the totality of church-related activities but only the ones that I was impressed with at the time and felt the need to record.

Church was not the only thing on my mind. As would be expected, I was also constantly interested in girls. Although sex was certainly mixed up in it, my interest was not primarily of a sexual nature. My interest was mostly one of assessing young women's qualities as potential marriage partners down the road. I remember thinking many times that I would eventually have a more loving and happy home than the one I was brought up in. And so from the point of view of a future partner I would grade and record my female interests with words like 'liking', 'really liking', 'loving', 'really loving' and 'very attracted to'. Not that the 'spicy' ones didn't turn my head too. They did. But sex was something secondary and mysterious. I still hadn't learned, and wouldn't for a long time, to link 'dirty' sex and 'clean' marital love. The idea of expressing love through sex was a difficult concept for me given the way we were taught to view sex as 'dirty' and marriage as almost 'holy'.

The girls, young women really, that I fancied were all Mennonites of course and all the same age or a year or two older or younger than I was. There are six entries in my diary referring to looking forward to a happy marriage someday. Another five times I refer to my keen interest in girls in general, no names mentioned. However, I mention girls, rate them and add some other small comment such as 'they smiled at me', 'talked to me' or 'didn't look at me', 103 times. At other times, I went on to note that I had changed my mind and 'didn't like her' after all. And so it went for an entire year, up again, down again, on again, off again, in leaping vicissitudes, just like the swing in my moods.

It would not be fair to mention names but at least six girls were on my radar that year as documented in my diary. Some girls get mentioned many times, others but once or twice. A few years later, one of them would become a serious interest to me but also a painful disappointment. This interest in girls would only increase over the next few years, shifting only slightly when I entered public high school (CHS) in Grade 12, to include 'English' (non-Mennonite) girls.

Some typical entries about girls I liked include the following:

> Jan. 22, Thurs. – *Liked Y quite a lot*
> Jan. 23, Fri. – *Loved X very much again.*
> Jan. 26, Mon. – *Thought X didn't like me anymore.*
> Feb. 20, Fri. – *I gave X a Valentine. Hid it in her book.*
> Mar. 3, Wed. – *Fancied both Y and Z a little more.*

> *Apr. 12, Mon. – X smiled at me in school. She seems to like me, as does Mr.. Toews.*
> *May. 11, Tues. – I think I'm in love with Z.*
> *May. 21, Fri. – Didn't know whom I liked better, X, Y, Z, or A.*
> *July 19, Mon. – I think I love A.*
> *Sept. 1, Wed. – I really think I don't love any girl.*
> *Oct. 19, Tues. – Still liked both Y and A but also X a little.*

My interest in girls and my interest in sex seemed to be two distinct categories of interest, which it would take me a long time to integrate. That sex was wicked had been ingrained in us since childhood. Hadn't we been told again and again not to watch animals mating? And when we discovered that human beings did 'it' too, and when puberty arrived and we ourselves were able to and desired to do 'it', we were told that 'that' was a big sin. That the 'big sin' was an overarching theme in the diary significantly understates the case. The issue was immensely important and also troublesome. I discuss it below in a separate section.

I often mentioned sports activities in my diary in the year 1948. That I was interested in sports is undeniable. Sixty-one times I note that I participated in some sport or another. In my limited spare time at home, I often played softball, soccer, basketball (in the hayloft), and badminton. These we also played at school. When not actively involved in sports, I would listen to sports radio broadcasts (hockey, boxing, and baseball), watch school and interschool team games, and referee games. I probably had a reputation for fair refereeing, for numerous times I would be asked to referee.

I also participated in track and field events. One sports day I came home with five ribbons, three first's and two second's. A lengthier entry reads:

> *May 24, Mon. – Big day for me. Sports day. Excellent cloudless weather. I won three first prize ribbons – broad jump, relay race, mile race – and two seconds.*

While running felt God's presence. Our house won the softball cup. I played 2nd base, hit well, and scored three runs. A family dispute started between Dad and Mother and the rest of us. Did chores (alone) after coming home at 7:30 p.m. because Frank was away. Henry G (cousin) was over in the evening to take Martin back to Osoyoos. Tired and sleepy.

It was some sort of fluke that I was entered in the mile race, the last event in the morning before the softball tournament in the afternoon. I had not trained for nor planned to run in that race. It just so happened that I was standing beside the senior leader of our house (the Athenians), when he called for the mile race participant from our house, who could not be found. We needed to have somebody in the race because points were awarded just for participating. John Ratzlaff then turned to me and said, "You're going to run this race. It doesn't matter if you don't finish; we need the points." Reluctantly I decided to do so to please him even though I hadn't trained, had on the wrong shoes for the track, and was wearing wrong clothes. I had already changed to long trousers after the earlier events and there was no time to change back.

Before I even had time to think how I should approach the race, I heard the starting whistle blow, and we were off. I was not an experienced distance runner but I was eager and so I sprinted out of the gate. I immediately decided that I would run as fast as I could for one lap of the ¼ mile circuit around the playground and then call it quits, pull off to the side and then wave the other runners on. Might as well have a little fun with this odd spectacle. I was probably two hundred yards ahead of the pack when I felt my breath waning and my energy fading. But just as I was completing that first lap, I caught my 'second wind' and my energy returned.

I had often felt this phenomenon when working hard on the farm, pitching hay, or chasing cattle. Suddenly it felt as if I had switched to automatic, as if no further effort was required for my legs to keep churning out the yards. So I didn't stop. In fact, I surged ahead, forging an even bigger gap between me and the now spreading pack. I wasn't even thinking about the race any more. My mind was back in La Glace with my horse Birdie, my feet unconsciously flying under me. Soon I had completed another lap. And then another. I looked back as I turned a corner and saw the other runners gaining some ground on me. Right then and there, I decided that not only could I finish the race, but I could *win*. Quickly, I asked God to help me. I did not look back again. As I turned the final corner, hearing other boots pounding the ground behind me, I heard a familiar voice somewhere from the sidelines "Rrrrun Khorrrnie rrrun!" The rolling r's were unmistakably from the tongue of Mr. Alex Voth, our old spiritual advisor from La Glace. I just had to win this one for Mr. Voth and put out my best effort. I did. I won, and quite handily at that, to win my third first prize ribbon of the day.

Interestingly, the following year, having trained this time, I entered the mile race again, this time on purpose. I only came in second, my aching thighs barely carrying me to the finish line. I had most likely overtrained.

Another theme in the diary of 1948 is one of preoccupation with illness. Despite access to wholesome food and lots of exercise on the farm and at school, I nevertheless was quite frequently ill, much more so than as an adult in middle age or even old age. Twenty-five times I note that I was ill enough to curtail some planned activity or church service. Frequently I mentioned who, whether family or friends, was in hospital and for how long. Illness of other family members I mention eleven times.

Not only family illness was recorded but also family quarrels and disputes. Disputes with Dad were frequent. When listening to non-religious radio broadcasts, for example, Dad would criticize them as being too 'worldly' for us Christians. I would protest. I mention quarrels with Dad nine times, with siblings six times and quarrels with Mother, none.

Reading was another activity that seemed to have been significant to me. Eleven times I mention reading the Bible and eighteen entries allude to my reading other books of religious character, such as Charles E Fuller's literature or L.E. Maxwell's *Born Crucified* and

In His Steps. There are seven entries of my reading non-religious fiction such as Orczy's *The Scarlet Pimpernel*, P.C. Wren's *Beau Geste* or John Bucan's *Greenmantle*. Thirteen entries mention reading in general without mentioning book titles. All of these were in addition to required reading for school or Sunday School.

My preoccupations and interests for the year 1948 persisted (and possibly even intensified) throughout the entire 5 year period of keeping the diary. I was obviously extremely concerned with sin and piety. The main issues during that period of my life are summed up in three questions: what will I become? whom shall I marry? and how can I achieve salvation? Hence the concerns for things like getting good grades in school, scouting for and choosing a good post-secondary school, acquiring and maintaining good social graces in order to win a marriage partner, engaging in physical fitness and clean living, keeping the faith and eliminating doubt and sin. As I reread my diary now, I observe that the earlier years had a general lightness and sense of fun compared to the later years, when I became even more earnest, worked even harder, was even more duty-bound, and even more committed to religion.

The Big Sin

ONE MIGHT WELL imagine that the 'big sin' of my youth would be an extreme human evil, something like murder, rape, or grand theft or in a religious context perhaps declaring atheism among the faithful or cursing the Holy Ghost. Surely 'big sin' ought to be something juicy like treason, conspiring against the crown, or cheating on one's income tax. But no, the 'big sin' in our community was something extraordinarily common, utterly mundane, innocent, and even banal. The sin was so ghastly that it couldn't even be mentioned, only referred to as 'it'.

If only the clergy, church elders, and parents had concerned themselves with the real evils of the world such as poverty, unfair distribution of wealth, crime, disease, war, racism, or feminine inequality; if only they had spent all that twisted energy, interest, fervour, and commitment to solving real human problems, they might well have made a real difference in ameliorating the human condition and help build a bit of heaven here on Earth. But no, their business was that of trying, and largely succeeding, for a while at least, to control minds and bodies by laying on painful and damaging guilt trips over one of the most innocuous of human peccadilloes.

Long before moving to Chilliwack we knew all about the birds and the bees. What farm boy didn't? It was almost impossible not to get introduced to sex education early, living as we did on a mixed farm with many kinds of animal life around us. When the big rooster 'jumped' the hen and flattened her to the ground, we knew that such 'attacks' were necessary for the eggs to produce those cute little chicks. We soon learned too that if we were going to have pink piglets with curly tails and darling big-eyed calves, that the boar would have to mount the sow and put that pink curved thing into her and the bull would need to make a mad leap on the cow with a hefty push. We were told not to watch the matings. We began to understand that sex, even among farm animals was something 'nasty', something we shouldn't talk about, describe, or observe. When we discovered that human beings did 'it' too, we were told that sex (and nudity) was definitely sinful except in marriage, where God tolerated sex because that was the only way to perpetuate the species.

One of the very earliest memories I have about nudity takes me back to age three or four. I was sent upstairs away from the others because I guess I was too intent on watching Mrs. Friesen, Mother's best friend, breast feeding her baby. You may also recall that I was strapped in Grade Two for 'playing doctor' and seeing too much of the female anatomy. We knew anyway from Sunday School pictures of Adam and Eve that all the interesting parts were covered with leaves. We also knew that Adam and Eve did something to produce children, something connected with original sin, something wicked.

We actually learned more from watching the animals. We even copied them. Out behind the barn at school, somewhat innocently, we 'played horse' with some pretending to be mares and others pretending to be stallions. Only much later did I really know what all of that was about.

One day when I was about eleven or twelve another lad a few years older than me, taught me in the hayloft how to do the "sweetest thing of all". It was indeed pleasurable but we never talked about it again. Nobody talked about 'it' except in hushed tones and indirect allusions. I don't think that our parents were ever aware that we knew how to do 'it' all by ourselves.

As youths we didn't even think about, let alone dare to try to have sex with a real partner. We didn't, or at least I didn't, even dream of such a thing. At that time the 'big sin' was strictly self-gratification. Such activity gave us new found and profound pleasure. However, abstention from that was supposed to be virtuous, helping us to achieve heaven.

It was in Chilliwack that the heavy guilt trips were laid on the thickest by church and parents. We were now deemed to be old enough (I was fifteen) to become acquainted with the 'young man's problem'[57], with the awful evil charged in our loins. Church elders would pull us aside to warn us of the danger of 'yielding to temptation' or doing 'it'. They plied us with literature such as *What a Young Man Ought to Know* or *The Way of Man with a Maid* to underscore the warnings (much too late might I add). What the books did provide was a vocabulary for what we had already known and experienced. Now we knew that 'pleasuring the self', 'self abuse', 'autoeroticism', 'masturbation' and 'onanism' were all names for doing 'it'. Our elders themselves could never bring themselves to use such language so in our circles the concept of masturbation was confined to 'it' or 'that'. We heard over and over, "You shouldn't do it!", "Christians don't do 'that'!", "You must not yield to temptation." It was generally understood that terms like "getting the victory", "getting control", "living a clean life" and "having a pure

---

57 I don't recall it ever being referred to as a 'young women's problem'.

heart" all referred primarily to abstaining from doing 'it'. If doubting the truth of the Bible, and the very existence of God were the gravest sins that the Devil could tempt one with, then the temptation to do 'it' certainly seemed to come a close second.

If you did 'that' without confession and forgiveness from God, you would certainly go to hell. Our salvation depended on 'getting the victory' over temptation. Even here on Earth we could suffer serious consequences for doing 'it'. We were taught (it is now hard to believe) that failure to 'get the victory' could lead to catching venereal disease, becoming blind, or even going insane. The books that were given to us to read all confirmed that. And I believed that right up until I was nearly twenty years old.

Clerics, church elders, parents, self-appointed youth counsellors and Sunday School teachers all joined forces to warn us against the perils of this terrible evil. The resulting guilt and fear of perilous consequences cancelled out the pleasure of doing it. Or nearly did – we kept doing it anyway – which of course only brought on more guilt. How we could have been so guilt-ridden over such a petty matter, I now just can't imagine. Had we been thieves, liars, cheaters, hoodlums, vandals, or gangsters, there might have been cause for guilt and merit in seeking forgiveness. But no, we weren't tempted by any of that. Overcoming 'temptation' was virtually synonymous with overcoming temptation to do 'it'. Apart from doing 'it', we were little angels.

The guilt thing ruled our inner lives. As young men, we did not discuss 'it', we just assumed that we were all struggling with the same dilemma. Many decades later I learned that one of our acquaintances at the time seriously considered *chopping off his member* to avoid any further sin and guilt, in order to assure his salvation. Such grip and control did the church have over us. It was even fair game for church elders to ask in open meetings on examination for baptism if you had achieved complete victory.

For some, including my father, the 'big sin' was viewed as a private matter between you and God. I do not recall his ever asking me if I had done 'it'. He probably would not have punished me either. I coped by confessing and asking for forgiveness time and again in private before God. How many times did I swear to God that I would never ever do it again if only He would forgive me one more time? I was morbidly obsessed with ridding myself of this overwhelming and depressing guilt.

Because the business of overcoming sin was the most important part of my inner life, I faithfully recorded my victories (few) and defeats (many) in my diary:

> *Feb. 12, Thurs. – Mr. Peters spoke to us about the 'young man's problem'*
> *Feb. 13, Fri. – Decided to live cleaner and better.*
> *Feb. 14, Sat. – Had great temptation to sin, but did not. Thank God.*
> *Mar. 11, Wed. – Read 'What a Young Man Ought to Know'. Asked God to forgive my sins and to prevent me from getting disease.*
> *May 14, Fri. – Was afraid of venereal disease because of the pimples on my back and stomach.*
> *May 23, Sun – Yielded to temptation. Didn't know if I sinned or not. I think I did. Repented and God forgave.*
> *July 4, Sun. – Read 'Sex and Love Life'. This book told me many things about females. I also read that masturbation did me no actual physical harm.*
> *July 20, Thurs. – Read 'The Path to Noble Manhood'.*

Having yielded to temptation on average more than once per week, it was becoming obvious, in 1948 at least, that in my war between hormones and holiness, hormones won hands down. Hormones just plainly invaded and conquered one's will power. Our testosterone-laden young bodies demanded a legitimate sexual expression. But none was to be found. Our natural desires were turned into guilt by the teachings and attitudes of the religious zealots who surrounded us. Even our involuntary wet dreams were turned into self-loathing. Even what couldn't be helped was wrong.

It would only get worse over the next few years. Through my Grade eleven and twelve years it became increasingly clear to me that I was being 'called' to some sort of Christian ministry. If that was to be the case, then the efforts to stop this evil 'self-abuse' would have to be doubled and re-doubled so I would be a pure and worthy servant of the Lord. I began to wonder why we were given all this magnificent equipment and the strong urge to use it when, if we did, it was such a big sin requiring humiliating expiation. I took the view, so typical of the religious mind, that this conundrum was God testing us. It was all about testing our love for Him, our obedience and submission to Him, fulfilling thereby the requisites for eternal salvation and exemption from everlasting damnation.

When in Grade 12, in addition to completing the regular University Entrance program, I chose to write four Senior Matriculation exams, achieving a first class standing with an average of 'only' 80.5%. I actually believed that I had gone partially insane (as evidenced by my marks being so low) as a punishment from God for having yielded to the 'big sin' so often. Here is the telling entry from my diary:

> *July 25, 1950, Tues. – Got my Senior Matric exam results. Was very disappointed. It was my fault though and I couldn't blame God for not helping me. I sinned too much.*

It is difficult now for me to imagine I believed all of that after not only more than successfully graduating from a better than average secular public high school but also fulfilling all the requirements to go on to higher learning.

When, after leaving high school, I spent the next four years attending Prairie Bible Institute (PBI), as the first sequence of training for the Christian ministry, here too, the issue of 'the young man's problem' came up again and again. I recall the principal of PBI, Mr. Maxwell, calling men's meetings in the men's gym some Saturday nights to discuss the problem of 'temptation'. Again, no technical or clinical language was used, only vague allusions, yet everyone knew precisely what was meant. Perhaps that suggested widespread practice indeed. "How did the clerics know?", I wondered. We were encouraged to exercise frequently, take cold showers, pray and eschew 'dirty thoughts', as if that would make any difference. Why imagining being with someone you might fancy was a 'dirty thought' I didn't understand then and I still don't. The clerics knew best.

I recall asking about 'wet dreams'. (What sneaky things hormones are! When, through prayer and extreme force of will, you overcome temptation, then the hormones do 'it' for you.) I simply asked, "Are wet dreams sinful?" I never could get a clear answer but it was generally assumed that they were.

When in my senior year, as an assistant to the Dean of Men, I asked the Dean if I might circulate a questionnaire amongst the male student body to inquire into the frequency of masturbation and wet dreams. My purpose was to discover if wet dreams actually resulted from dirty thoughts and what was the nature of those dirty thoughts. Without hesitation, the Dean refused. It was not right to question the nature of those dirty thoughts; it was already 'known' that they cause wet dreams (which was not my experience) and that a questionnaire of that sort would simply exacerbate the problem. He encouraged me instead to pray for victory over the temptation for myself and my fellow students. What an interesting, disinterest in facts! How common it is of the religious mindset to think of 'facts' as being only revealed by the mysterious mind of God rather than ascertained by evidence and research.

The 'big sin' was a huge guilt trip laid on us by clerical control freaks, who took prurient interest in our lives and used threats, guilt, and coercion to make us conform to their narrow mindset. We were really supposed to believe that the normal practice of masturbation and the involuntary phenomenon of wet dreams would endanger one's achievement of salvation and eternal life, that if one 'did it', one directly sinned against God and would need to seek forgiveness; that failure to get forgiveness would lead to eternal damnation; that God would punish us with venereal disease, blindness, and/or insanity for simple bodily functions. On the one hand, these beliefs are laughable lies to be dismissed with contempt. On the other, they are spiritually, and psychologically damaging and amount to cruel invasion of privacy and a serious encroachment on personal freedom. When packaged together with religious doctrines of salvation and hell-fire, this whole issue results in tortuous guilt and permanent psychological damage, the amount and extent of which is incalculable.

I myself feel robbed of years of potentially guilt-free happiness in my youth. The references in my diary to failure to overcome sin, to my inability to truly find God, to deep doubts about my mental capacity, to depressive states of mind, to great anxiety about the welfare of my soul and more, all stemmed from my inability to control this manufactured 'evil'. What I know now to be simply hormones and biology, I truly believed then was the inability to control sin and that masturbation was a significant barrier to my finding salvation, that I so desperately wanted and otherwise was well on the path to.

In the final analysis, however, I did get the victory; not over temptation, but over the notion of 'it' being a sin.

Grade Twelve

OUR YEARS of youth are turbulent and stressful almost by definition, for these are the days of choosing a career, seeking a mate, and finding our general direction in life. However, I have reason to think that mine were more than usually stressful and tumultuous, particularly my Grade Twelve year.

On September 6, 1949 I re-entered Chilliwack High School (CHS) after having spent the previous three years, Grades 9 through 11, at the private Mennonite school (SMCI) in nearby Yarrow. What should have been one of the best years in my life because of the prospect of graduating from high school, turned out to be one of the worst, at least in terms of stress, anxiety, and general bodily weariness. Academically the year went reasonably well, but I could have, perhaps should have, done much better had I not had what seemed to be several strikes against me.

In the first place, there were problems of adjusting to a new school and new classmates. It wasn't just a different school but a whole different culture. At SMCI our class was a family of thirty or so students well known to each other, each of the same faith, knowing also where we stood in academic competition and social position. Suddenly we were all thrown into a graduating class of upwards of 120 strangers, all coming from diverse backgrounds. If the Grade 12 class resented the sudden influx of thirty additional students, they certainly didn't show it. It was all a big melting pot. As it turned out we integrated fairly well and I learned a lot from my new fellow students and the very fine new teachers. Though ultimately I benefited from the move to CHS, it was nevertheless stressful at a time when I already had plenty of stress. Not only did we join a new student body at CHS but in mid-year we also entered a brand new school building as well, just a few blocks away from the old, over-crowded building where I had attended in Grade 8.

Another strike against my succeeding as well as I did was my unwise choice of not taking a study period[58], instead deciding to take the heaviest academic load possible. In fact I decided to write four Senior Matriculation government exams at the end of the school year: Math, Biology, History, and German.[59] Even with such a heavy school work load, I might have succeeded much better, had I not also had a very heavy work load on the farm.

At that time, my older brothers Frank and Peter were pursuing their own ambitions and not available to help on the farm. Peter was away at Normal School, learning to be a teacher, and Frank was off running his trucking business. Thus I became the chief milker on the dairy farm. That was no small job, for it required between three and four hours of hard labour per day, every day. No exceptions. In addition I also missed a number of school days to do other work on the farm. Weather permitting, we would always work full days on Saturdays and holidays too.

---

58 At SMCI I never took any study periods, always opting for extra credits.
59 I studied German on my own, often drilling myself and doing memorization work while I was milking cows.

Did that take away from time for church activities? Not at all. Church related activities were always at the top of the priority list. I still regularly attended Sunday services, morning and evening, as well as Sunday school. I also sang in two church choirs, which of course required rehearsal time. I also attended the many evening services during the week when visiting preachers spoke and singing groups performed. On such occasions I would do my homework after the service, sometimes long after midnight. On top of all of that, I also discovered at this time the 'Inter School Christian Fellowship' (ISCF) and became heavily involved, eventually becoming the singing leader. But that was not enough, I also joined both the CHS Glee Club and the male choir as extracurricular activities.

Other issues that worked against me at the time were girlfriend problems, problems of low self-esteem and guilt, friction with my father (who, despite my devotion to the church, thought that I was straying too far from my Mennonite upbringing), and religious doubts, even doubting that I had indeed been 'called'. It was true that I was moving away from the narrow confines of the Mennonite religious outlook, taking a more ecumenical stance.[60] I wasn't rejecting Mennonitism, I was just embracing a larger and different view of Christianity. However the ground beneath me, the bedrock of my faith, was shifting, adding to my stress and inner turmoil.

In addition to all of that, CHS was closed the entire month of January 1950 because of an horrific blizzard. When it opened again in February, we had to attend extra classes after school to make up for the lost instructional time. I don't believe that we actually did make up for that loss of instruction but we sure tried.

My Grade 12 year was one of the years during which I was still keeping my diary. While I didn't have an entry for every day like I did in 1948, there were still entries enough to paint a picture of that school year:

---

60 I took easily to an ecumenical position and I later learned that both my Father and Grandfather were of similar bent in their early years.

Chilliwack blizzard, January, 1950

Oct. 14, Fri. – All this time (Sept 25 – Oct. 14), I did not write in my diary. I was very busy doing chores, working in the fields, filling silos, going to school and doing homework

Oct. 19, Wed. – Hurried after school to lay concrete foundation for the chicken house. Very tired. Did the chores. Then went to church for a revival meeting. Mr. Hooge spoke on repentance. After church did homework till 2:00 a.m.

Dec. 12, Mon. – Got to know and like a number of English girls.[61]

Dec. 19, Mon. – These days had to stay late at school for Glee Club practices. On one of these days I met and talked with a bunch of Yarrow girls. I told them I disliked Mennonite traditions and reform was needed. Perhaps I said too much, for word got back to Peter in Vancouver that I had gone to the dogs.

Mar. 3, Fri. – A bad day today. I felt as bad as I had ever felt. Did poorly in Math test and got only a C+ in my essay in English. I think maybe I am mentally ill.

Mar. 8, Wed. – School was good today. At noon played chess with Jake Hildebrandt. We didn't finish. I had a chance anyway. In the evening gave up studying and went to church.

Mar. 19, Sun. – These days I am being tempted terribly to give up my faith.

---

61 Meaning non-Mennonite.

Mar. 23, Thurs. – Felt confident and intelligent. Maybe one day I will be a great political leader, solving questions of war, etc.

Mar. 25. Sat. – Frank and I hauled manure and spread it. Between loads I studied.

Apr. 4, Tues. – Liked school a lot. Got a good mark in a Math test. Beat J.H. and most of the others. English class is especially good. "Man must either be a God or a beast to live alone; but he is neither..." He (Mr. Penner) always makes us think.

Apr. 24, Mon. – At school I realized how ignorant I am. I really must study harder. After school hoed strawberries. In the evening did my homework well. Stayed up till 11:30 pm I'm happy. A successful day.

Apr. 25, Tues. – Liked school even though I was drowsy.

Apr. 26, Wed. – I'm always tired these days. So much work to do.

May 2, Tues. – Am worried about all the work I have to do. I'm afraid that I'll forget all the memorization I do in the barn. Don't know why I feel so terrible.

June 13, Tues – Not happy. Can't see my way through all this work.

June 15, Thurs. – did not do much on this our last day of school. Got my poor report card.[62] So I reaped as I sowed. I hope I will sow better in the future.

---

62   It was actually not that bad, three A's and two C–'s, all in academic subjects.

I know now and perhaps I should have known then why I felt 'terrible'. It was simply a matter of being overworked and underrested, but that was hard to see then in that time of stress. Often I functioned with only four or five hours of sleep. I estimate that my farm work alone added up to a 35-hour work week. When you consider that I was also completing my Grade Twelve year, including four fifths of a First Year University program at the same time, it was as though I was doing *two* full time jobs. And that doesn't even count the many religious activities that I was also involved in at the same time.

I should explain why I participated so much in church-related activities. For some time I had believed that I was being 'called' to take up Christian ministry of some sort. However I also knew that I could not follow on strictly within the narrow confines of the Mennonite Church. For example, I could never understand why dancing or having some wine was *'verboten'* (strictly forbidden). So I readily and eagerly took on any opportunities to broaden my horizons within Christianity with organizations such as the ISCF and Youth For Christ with their more ecumenical stances and more liberal practices. At the same time I wanted to convince my home church that I was not leaving the faith but wanting to bring in new ideas. Thus I took every opportunity both to show my loyalty to Mennonitism and at the same time to spread my wings just a little. This all made for a very time consuming assortment of church related activities in addition to everything else. It is no wonder therefore that I only got a C+ on my English essay, my favourite subject at the time. I had insufficient time to ponder and prepare, to revise and rewrite. First draft hand-ins were often the order of the day.

Even with all the stress, weariness, and anxiety, I very much enjoyed all my courses and my teachers, and gained many insights that I wouldn't have gotten at SMCI. Miss Keith, the librarian, challenged me on my views on conscientious objection (no Mennonite teacher would have) when I argued that a book I reported on, *Fighting for Peace*, was a contradiction in terms. Mr. Penner, as already noted, got us thinking critically in English class. Always too, there was the redoubtable Mr. Doell who shook up our orthodoxy and made history come alive in Social Studies. How well I remember the plight of workers during the Industrial Revolution and how unionism eventually helped form the middle class first in England and then too in the USA, Canada, and elsewhere. I was very moved, and still am, by Oliver Goldsmith's lines:

> *Ill fares the land, to hastening ills a prey,*
> *Where wealth accumulates, and men decay.* [63]

It was there and then that I began to form political ideals of social justice and equality of opportunity. I was then and still am ambivalent about the constant fight between the left and right in politics. On the one hand, I detest sloth, dependency on others, inefficiency or carelessness with the spending of public funds. As well I admire the success of the hard working and ambitious. On the other hand, I naturally side with the underdog, those who don't have a fair chance at success. I consider the wide discrepancy between the rich and powerful on the one hand and the poor and powerless on the other as an abomination and a great injustice. I think it is fair to say that philosophically I am a left leaning and temperamentally right leaning.

Fellow students also taught me much. Often we informally debated ideas arising from classroom instruction and reading. I recall looking forward to long noon-hour walks, deep in discussion, to downtown Chilliwack with our class genius, Jacob Hildebrandt. We discussed such (for me) esoteric matters as: Is religion the opiate of the masses? Are Freud's id and superego equivalent to the voices of Satan and God? Is the notion of God nothing more than an anthropomorphic projection? These were for me very heady and daring questions to ask – and I liked it! None of these would have been discussed or even entertained at SMCI.

Grade Twelve had its highs as well as its lows, its happy times as well as unhappy, its achievements as well as disappointments. Despite what I am calling "unusually stressful and tumultuous" times,

---

63   Oliver Goldsmith, 'The Deserted Village'.

Chilliwack High School graduation

the year as a whole was successful. Not what I would call a 'roaring success' but still successful. I am now grateful for that experience, for that opportunity to go to a quality public high school. It is clear to me now that it was there at Chilliwack High School that I took my first few steps on the long road to freedom from religion. However, it was an uneven path and there was still much religion in my veins, in my head, and in my immediate future.

The Fleece Test and the Religious Mind

THROUGHOUT the ages mankind has attempted to gain access to the world of the supernatural to ascertain whether or not some gods, or a god, approves or disapproves of certain courses of contemplated human action. People often, when in the throes of making tough decisions, seek divine guidance in the hope of assuring the right course of action and success therein. Should I, or we, go into battle at this time? And will we win? Will this sacrifice or procedure be a cure for the present malady? Will this marriage be a success and produce an heir? Is this purchase at this price warranted at this time? And so on.

Long before the Greeks consulted the oracle at Delphi, even older kingdoms and nations attempted to unlock the secrets of the gods and be on the safe side of history. This included the Israelites.

As told in Judges 6:36-40, Gideon, son of Josah, a Hebrew judge and prophet, was contemplating war against the Midianites whom the Israelites would have to defeat to procure the promised land. Not knowing whether or not to attack, Gideon asked God for a sign. As the Bible relates it, the Midianites were gathered together to attack the Israelites. Gideon asked God if he should counter-attack and save Israel. The alternative was to surrender. Was it propitious to attack and could they be assured of victory? The 'yes' sign was to be this: if the fleece that Gideon placed on the floor overnight would be wet with dew in the morning but the floor around the fleece dry, then Gideon should attack and be assured of victory. In the morning, the area around the fleece was indeed dry, but from the fleece itself Gideon wrung out a bowl of water.

Though the sign was a 'go', Gideon still was hesitant and demurred. How could he be sure? To get confirmation, he tested God again. This time the sign for the attack was the very opposite of the previous test, that is, if the fleece was dry and the ground wet, that would confirm the previous message. The next morning it was exactly so, dry fleece and wet ground. Now confident, the very next night, Gideon took 300 of his best warriors and attacked an army that vastly outnumbered them and vanquished them with dispatch.

The message from this story seems to be that one can ask God for a sign or signs to determine His will with respect to a course of action to be taken and be assured of success therein. People believe in these signs to this day.

It was so for my father when he contemplated buying homestead land upon immigrating to Canada from Europe:

> *It was difficult to make a decision about the quarter section... [I] knelt down and sought the guidance of the Lord. I thought of Gideon's fleece. I know well that it is not always the right thing to test the Lord in such a way. But in my desperation I weighed the possibilities. 'Lord give me a sign whether I should buy or not. If it should be the right thing then let me be able to buy it for eight dollars per acre.' If it could not be bought at that price then it was not meant to be ours.*[64]

The seller accepted the unusual bid of eight dollars an acre and Dad thought that God's will had been fulfilled. There in the Peace country he dwelled for eighteen years and over time built a (then) modern farm and raised ten children.

My brother Peter reports that he too had a 'fleece test' experience in the determination of his career. He describes the turmoil that he went through trying to decide whether or not to pursue a medical career.

> *Shortly I would have to apply for medical school, if I were to pursue medicine. So after a few weeks of uncertainty, I finally decided to write the dean a letter asking permission to drop chemistry and physics and pick up philosophy and ancient history in their place. For me this was the 'fleece' test. Should permission be granted at this late stage, then it was to be the Lord's will [that I not take up medicine]. I fully realized the momentous decision I was making. It would settle the course of my life's vocation, at least rule out the option of medicine. Without hesitation the dean allowed the change. And that closed the door to medicine.*[65]

---

64 *My Old Home and the New*, p. 53.
65 – *Reflections...* p. 74-75.

Like Dad and like Peter, I too relied on the fleece test. I was raised in a milieu in which we believed not only that God had a plan for each of our lives, but also that He would reveal that plan to us and guide us each step of the way if only we lived good lives, had faith, and sought His guidance. We believed that on really important matters (such as education, career, and marriage) it was acceptable to ask God for a material sign to help us make the decision.

I had already had one or two mini fleece tests. By the time I was in Grade Twelve in 1949/50, I was quite sure I had been 'called' to some form of Christian ministry, the precise nature of which (pastoral, missionary work, or evangelism) still to be determined. I also believed that if I were to do the Lord's work properly, I could not afford to make a mistake choosing a marriage partner. Choosing a mate would certainly be one of the most important decisions I would ever make. I felt that I needed guidance here, guidance from God.

The story of love and sex in our youth as Mennonites was a curious combination of the 'big sin', shame, and guilt on the one hand and a striving for an idealistic made-in-heaven marriage (holy matrimony) on the other. If only we could ascertain what that match was to be. Agreeing with Dad and the church, that the divine will would not be revealed by frivolous sexual attraction, I relied on prayer, introspection, parental advice, and finally on the fleece test to ascertain God's will.

What added to the difficulty of making that choice was the fact that I had already made up my mind to prepare for the ministry by attending Prairie Bible Institute (PBI) for a four year course of Bible study after high school. At PBI the regulations required that over those four years a student was not permitted to date, to get engaged, or to marry. If any of those rules were broken, the student in question would be 'asked' to leave for at least one year. So it was doubly important for me to settle the question of God's will for a mate for me before I entered PBI so I could devote my full attention and energies to my studies and yet still be assured of a mate at the end of my studies.

For some time I had been enamoured of a certain young lady whom I thought was very attractive and would be just right for me, complementing me in my ambitions in the ministry. The question was, would this young lady, who was possibly also interested in me, wait for me during those years? Would she understand those strict PBI rules? Could I trust God to reveal to me His will in this matter? Why not do a fleece test? If God through a sign said "Yes, she is the right one for you and will wait for you", then I had nothing to worry about. The fleece test would give me the answer and confidence I needed.

In the late summer of 1949 it was part of my chores to fetch the cows for milking from the back pasture. The cows were often grazing next to the two or three fenced off acres of low lying hayfield in the southeast corner of our property where the second crop of hay was already ankle high. Some mornings this low lying area was dry, with the grass waving in the gentle breeze. Some mornings the field was motionless, dew sparkling on the grass against the rising sun. On any given day it was either dry, wavy hay or wet, glistening grass. It occurred to me that I could do my fleece test here. Thus I decided that if on the next day the hayfield was dewy and I got my boots wet walking through the grass that would be a sign from God that the young woman in question would be the one for me. There was no indication of a change in the weather and so as far as I could tell there was roughly a 50-50 chance of either dew or dryness. For me, this was entirely a matter of trusting God to give me a sign. This was my fleece test.

In the morning I awoke earlier than usual, anxious to know what the outcome would be. Could I, on this very day, know the answer to my all-important question: was she the one? I hurried to the back pasture. On the slight rise in the centre of our acreage I felt a wind blowing in my face, which likely meant a dry hayfield and a 'no' answer. My heart was heavy because I really did love this young woman, or so I thought. And now my hopes were likely dashed. I began to think that maybe all of this is just a bunch of nonsense, but a little voice in my head said, "Oh ye of little faith!", and that urged me on. "Did I have faith?", I asked myself. "Yes. I will see this through even if it means deep disappointment. I must accept God's will even if it is contrary to my own." So I proceeded to the hayfield in the far corner. As I approached the wind abated and I became joyful again. Perhaps the dew would be there after all. Down in the low lying corner field, there was no wind at all. I hurriedly climbed the fence and in a moment was ankle deep in the moist grass, my boots shining with wetness. "Yes, this is the day which the Lord hath made", I heard myself say, "I will rejoice and be glad in it".[65]

I was so happy that I almost forgot to fetch the cows. It was my duty now to return to mundane activities, but my spirit was on cloud nine. All day (keeping my secret to myself, which I have done up until now) the only thing I could focus on was the fleece test outcome, alternately elated (when I believed in the answer) and despondent (when I doubted it). By the end of the day, my doubts held sway.

Then I thought again about Gideon. He too doubted his sign. What did he do? He asked God to confirm the message by running the test in reverse. So that would be the way I would do it too. If tomorrow morning the hayfield would be dry, that would confirm today's message.

The next morning I again felt the breeze in my face as I walked over the rise but thinking back to the day before that could still mean a moist low-lying hayfield. I approached apprehensively. Very soon I could see the hay waving in the breeze and as I walked through my boots were perfectly dry. I knew that I had received confirmation from on high. Yes, she was the one. I had been silly to doubt God. I now absolutely trusted Him and the sign that He had given.

I knew, of course, that I must do my part in winning the young lady as well. I would need to maintain physical fitness, polish my social skills, and work and study hard to impress her. At least now I knew whom I needed to impress. With God's help I just *knew* that she would eventually be mine. How easy it all seemed if one only trusted in God.

---

66 Psalm 118:24.

Throughout my final year in High School I had many happy conversations and exchanges with my secret love but I never told her of my secret. However as the school year drew to a close I felt compelled to tell her of my love for her and my plans.

The first indication that something was amiss in this whole episode was at graduation time. The practice was to go in pairs to the graduation banquet. Boys and girls had the opportunity to choose their own dates; and those who didn't have dates were paired off randomly by number. I had never had a date and didn't know how to go about arranging one. Of course I had to ask the one reserved for me according to the fleece test. I would then tell her that I had something very important to convey to her at some later time. I plucked up my courage and asked her. She said that I was too late, she had already promised someone else. Not surprisingly, I was very hurt and puzzled. How could this be? If God intended me to be her life-long mate, why would I not get this date? But why blame God? Even He cannot make a date for you. Perhaps she was still the right girl but I had simply been too slow on the draw. There was nothing wrong with God's plan. I just hadn't done my part. Next time I would know better and take the initiative to create the opportunity to meet her, declare my love for her, reveal my plan for us, and ask her to wait for me.

That summer I phoned her and asked for a date to go row-boating on Cultus Lake. To my great relief, this time she agreed to go. On the appointed evening, I, with chores done, car washed, and appropriately apparelled, sped excitedly to fetch her. When I arrived at her home, her mother met me at the front door and told me the young lady was not at home.

"But she agreed to go boating with me", I pleaded.

"Well, that is too bad. I'm sorry, she's not here."

"Will you please tell her I came for her."

"That, I will do."

And with that I was gone. I couldn't believe what had just transpired. In a state of total shock, I slowly drove away. I decided to go to Cultus Lake anyway for a swim in the cold water, hoping to clear the burning in my eyes, to regain some feeling in my numbed body. After the swim, I sat on a huge rock and watched the sun set behind the mountains. I watched the sun set on my hopes and dreams.

I railed against God for having let me down again. Bitterly and reproachfully, I complained about the unfairness of it all and the apparent deception of the fleece test. The phenomenon, which I call one way relationships (A loves B, B loves C, and C loves D and so on) is commonplace amongst young people seeking mates, but that doesn't mean that it doesn't hurt. When unrequited love happens to others we tend to shrug our shoulders, perhaps sympathize a little and forget. When it happens to you, it is overwhelming and earth-shattering. Such was the case for me.

When on top of that, your faith and a direct sign from God are also shattered, the attack on the psyche is devastating. So there I sat on that rock on the shore of Cultus Lake demanding an answer, "Why, God, why? Give me an explanation. Speak to me!" Then, suddenly it came to me, "For whom the Lord loveth, He cleanseth."[67] I began to soften my stance and thought, "Yes, of course. I am just undergoing a trial. It is God testing *me* to see if I can keep the faith in the face of adversity." I thought then that I was being prepared for service to come. I resolved not to doubt Him ever again.

I chose to take the view that my chosen one had not in fact rejected me. Perhaps her mother did not (yet) take kindly to me, or perhaps there were other reasons she could not meet me; perhaps it was all just a misunderstanding. I consoled myself with the fact that there was nothing that could not be overcome with faith and prayer. By the time I got home, I was almost happy again. Everything was going to be all right. God was steeling me for His service. I dare not complain any more. For the next four years while away at Bible School, my faith in God's plan would have to suffice, for I would not be permitted to contact the young lady in question during that time. I would have to take it *entirely* on faith that she would wait for me.

She didn't.

---

67 Hebrews 12:6.

There were indicators during this period of time that pointed to that likelihood. Disturbingly, I heard rumours that she was interested in and dating someone else. That, I rationalized, would only stand to reason but all that would change as long as I kept the faith and kept praying. With prayer, God could work miracles. The really devastating blow was during a heart to heart talk with Dad about my future on one summer evening. He asked me if I was contemplating marriage and I said yes and even mentioned her name. He replied in a matter of fact manner as if he had expected my reply, "She's taken. Whom else do you fancy?" It was a dagger to my heart. "Oh nobody." I replied nonchalantly, trying to conceal my pain. I quickly ended the conversation and headed out to the back pasture to howl privately to heaven in my despair.

I now no longer believed that the plan would materialize. The fleece test had been a horrible mistake. How could I have been so badly deceived? How could God deal with me so harshly when I trusted Him so utterly? I counted on Him, but He let me down. I believed in Him with all my heart, but He made a fool of me. I was in a deep despair not only over losing my 'true love', but also, and equally so, over a loss of faith in the fleece test, in the reliability of God's promises, in God's goodness. I prayed for relief of my agony, for some indication that God still cared and was there for me. He turned a deaf ear. There was no response from on high.

I had lived most of my life with the comfort of believing that God was watching over me and answering my prayers, that God had a purpose for me and that salvation for me was guaranteed. Now suddenly all those beliefs were in doubt and I felt on very shaky ground. I felt a darkness settling over me, with not the tiniest ray of light visible. I felt alone, totally alone, without a ray of hope or happiness. I was completely dejected.

In the midst of my agony I asked, "Is there anybody out there that knows my plight and can help me?" There was only stone cold silence. "Can anyone alleviate my pain?" I asked desperately. There was no response. Still in silence and darkness I contemplated my situation. Had God turned away from me for good? Had I somehow been transported to a place where God is absent, a place of utter loneliness, without hope or comfort? Was this hell? Is this what hell is like? I asked, "God, why have you forsaken me when I trusted you so faithfully?" It dawned on me that these words sounded familiar. Someone else long ago had asked, "My God! My God! Why hast Thou forsaken me?"[68] I realized that Christ had not been forsaken on the cross. It only seemed so. In actuality the apparent abandonment was only a phase in a grand plan and in that story everything was unfolding according to a divine schedule. Perhaps in my case there was also a plan in my apparent abandonment. Maybe this was just *another* phase in my learning to trust Him supremely, so that I could become a *true* believer, necessary to become a dedicated servant of God. Why not accept this whole painful episode as preparation for His service? So instead of rejecting God, I once again surrendered to His will and sang:

> Have thine own way Lord, have thine own way
> Thou art the Potter, I am the clay.
> Mould me and make me after thy will
> While I am waiting yielded and still.[69]

Instead of re-asserting my will and relying on my reason and perception to make a rational decision to reject the fleece test as nonsense and an exercise in self-deception, I, true to the way of the religionist, sank deeper into self-denial and faith in my God. If in fact there were a supernatural being of some sort with the kind of power over us as ascribed to God, namely the power to control and manipulate our lives according to His will and His design, essentially denying us our humanity as independent thinking persons, that would be craven enough. But the fact that we do this to ourselves, with the 'help' of other human power manipulators and indoctrinators, and buy into the 'God delusion'[70] is doubly disturbing, debilitating, and dehumanizing. That is, however, the charac-

---

68 Matthew 27:46.
69 Hymn, 'Have Thine Own Way, Lord".
70 *The God Delusion* is the title of an influential book by Richard Dawkins.

ter of the religious mind. I did what is so typical of the religious believer and that is to contort the actual available evidence in such a way that it bolsters the faith rather than undermines it.

Had I been fully rational I should have drawn some independent conclusions. I should have seen that the fleece test was a bunch of nonsense. The test and it's confirmation were no more than two flips of a coin both coming out the same twice in a row (pretty weak evidence even with a tiny understanding of statistics). I should have realized that it is extremely unlikely that God, if he exists at all, would take an interest and intervene in mundane human affairs. It was utterly naive of me to think that He might somehow reserve a mate for me. To believe that the young lady's rejection of me was God's way of toughening my faith for His service was derivatively arrogant and a dishonest misreading of the evidence to make it suit my wishful thinking. It was rationalization at its worst. I perhaps should have been more aware of this but I had been a victim of delusion my whole life up to that point.

If I had been using reason I would have seen all of that, but in spite of all the evidence to the contrary I doggedly held on to my faith. Despite the darkness and despair, I was not yet ready to walk away from the delusion. I was in good hands with the Almighty. I clung to my faith more feverishly than ever, believing more strongly than ever that I had been picked to serve Him and that the ordeals I was undergoing were just necessary trials in the maturing of my faith.

What I now see as particularly troubling is that I was at that time a graduate of a top-notch Canadian public school with a standard secular curriculum. I was not the dullest of students either. So what was wrong that I couldn't see through all the nonsense? Perhaps it says something about the failure of the public school system to produce independent rational beings. Perhaps it says even more about the power of early and prolonged indoctrination. At any rate it is the nature of the religious mind to reject reason and abandon evidence and plough boldly ahead into ever greater delusion. Instead of siding with Shakespeare, and Antony, that: "the fault, dear Brutus is not in the stars but in ourselves that we are underlings"[71], I sided with the Bible, and with Job, whose faith was sorely tempted by all the scourges that befell him, but who nonetheless proclaimed, "Though He slay me, yet will I trust Him."[72]

In my despair, I made a supreme effort to twist around my fleece test experience to make it enhance my faith instead of undermine it. It occurred to me that if I were angry at God, if I railed against Him, if I blamed Him for not looking after me, if I was insisting on clarification from Him, then I must still be believing in Him. If He let me down, then He was still there to let me down. If something had gone wrong between Him and me, then it could be set right. And so I consoled myself that I still believed and still held the faith. I had found relief from my longest and most serious period of doubt in the belief that my trials were necessary for my preparation for service in God's vineyard. I took comfort in the Biblical verse, "God is faithful; in that He will not allow you to be tempted beyond that which ye are able."[73]

Like Job, I was being tested because God had a plan for me to be His servant, "If ye endure chastening, God dealeth with you as with sons."[74] So that was it; I was being chastened to serve Him. But what precisely was I supposed to be learning through this suffering? Chastened for what? For lack of faith? Yes, for lack of faith. I was, and always had been a believer but I was still of the opinion that reason (and its ally, evidence) and faith could comfortably co-exist. I still had to learn to stop trying to have my faith and reason too. I did not then see that reason and faith are utterly incompatible.

Ultimately religion insists that one must believe in the unreasonable. Faith has no other role. If one wants to hold religious beliefs, one will do so despite the lack of evidence and despite reliable evidence opposing those beliefs. There is very little that will undermine people's religious beliefs if they don't have confi-

---

71 Shakespeare, *Julius Caesar*, I ii 140-141.
72 Job 13:15.
73 Corinthians 10:13.
74 Hebrews 12:7.

dence in the use of their own reason. True believers, the ones who find favour with God, are those who reject reason. Misology, the hatred of reason, is at the very heart of religious faith, hence the intractableness of the religious mind and the never ending battle between faith and reason.[75]

At the time of my fleece-test experience, I was still several years away from coming to these kinds of understandings. Religion was still predominant in my life. Blind faith versus troubling doubt would still provide years of conflict. Eventually I would become more rational, but it took entirely too long. This was a sad period of my life and a needlessly troublesome one. I would wish it on no one. It is difficult and painful now to recall all the details but it too is so revealing of the character of the religious mind.

Leaving Chilliwack

IN THE EVENING of September 25, 1950, a group of young people from our church threw a farewell party for me. I noted in my diary that "I felt humbled and grateful." The next evening I left Chilliwack by train for Prairie Bible Institute in Three Hills, Alberta. I did spend the next spring and summer working for Dad on the farm, but essentially my Chilliwack days had come to an end. Chilliwack had been my home for two months shy of five years. It seemed then, and still seems, a lot longer than that. Why? So much had happened. The struggles of growing up that I experienced there were poignant and stressful.

Our family had moved to Chilliwack primarily because Dad and Mother wanted their flock of children to be 'educated' and nurtured in a Christian environment. This was to be a carefully constructed balance of maintaining our Mennonite faith and heritage on the one hand and assimilation into the wider world on the

---

[75] I return to these matters in Chapter 8 in the section on 'The Embeddedness of Reason'.

other. That was the reason for establishing and operating SMCI and for the overall barrage of church-related activity. An objective analysis might suggest that my Chilliwack experience was one long period of pronounced indoctrination, save for the small amount of interaction with 'the English' public school. Not that we were severely brow beaten, though there was some of that, the methods were much more subtle and insidious, making them that much more effective.

People who are being indoctrinated usually don't know they are and instead think that they are being told important truths. They don't particularly dislike the process and they tend to go along willingly, as I did. The doctrines provided me with a radar for life's direction, with an identity, with camaraderie, and with security. It seems strange to me now, as a free thinking person, how we actually went along with all of that heavy indoctrination so willingly. However, at the time it was so natural, easy, and comfortable.

I remember the power of the crowds, of the skillful speakers and the enchanting messages. There were huge gatherings of young people in Yarrow and Abbotsford to hear and sing en masse and to listen to talented visiting evangelists, Bible teachers, and missionaries. I recall on one occasion a powerful message on "Fight the good fight with all your might and I will give the crown of life" – a beguiling proposition indeed. After the sermon and the altar call, many people came forward to be saved. Since I was already saved, I joined the huge public showing of hands of those who were re-dedicating themselves to continue to fight the good fight. Although I didn't realize it at the time, that fight is essentially a fight against reason, reason being the enemy of faith. All of us Mennonites were brothers and sisters in the Lord and there was great comfort in belonging to such a group. At the same time, however, I felt insignificant, afraid, and unimportant, wondering if I would ever be able to follow the calling to the ministry. Even at moments of affirmation there were seeds of doubt.

Was the indoctrination successful? For the most part, a resounding yes. A few were somehow immune; but many were indeed under the spell of indoctrination at least temporarily and to varying degrees. For most, it was permanent. This lasting effect of early indoctrination was true for most, if not all, of my many siblings. In my case, it took a number of years and much painful soul-searching to escape the enchantment. Having said that, I have to admit that during my Chilliwack years I acquired much useful information and valuable habits that have stood me in good stead for my entire life – habits of focusing on tasks, dedication to hard work, habits of health and cleanliness, habits of sociability and heeding other points of view, self-control and much more. Yes, I think I had a good upbringing; it just wasn't very much fun.

Our life belonged not to us, but to a higher cause, a higher Being. We were being shaped not to enjoy life but to dedicate ourselves to the cause and to fulfill our calling, our duty. Enjoyment could wait for the hereafter. I had a happy childhood, but I cannot say that my teenage years were as a whole happy. The burdens of the world were too heavily laid upon me and I have to admit that I was all too willing to embrace that burden.

Lines from *The Student Prince* come to mind:

> *Golden days, in the sunshine of our happy youth*
> *Golden days, full of gaiety and full of truth*
> *In our hearts we remember them all else above*
> *Golden days, days of youth and love*
> *How we laughed with joy that only love can bring*
> *Looking back through memory's eyes*
> *We will know life has nothing sweeter than its springtime*
> *Golden days when we were young, Golden days*[76]

If that is the hallmark of youth, then I missed mine, at least in large part. Mine was not "full of gaiety and truth" but full of guilt and lies, nor did I laugh with joy that love brought. For me, that came years later. There was for me in my youth a paucity of joy and

---

76 Sigmund Romberg and Dorothy Donnelly, 'Golden Days' from the musical *The Student Prince.*

fun. We had much satisfaction but little genuine *fun*. Most of the satisfaction we experienced was based on relief from farm or school work, success from effort and application, temporary relief from guilt, vague notions of being 'blessed' at church, or approval from the church membership. That is not to say that we didn't have *some* fun. We certainly had some recreational and diversionary activities but they were insufficient to characterize my youth as a happy one. By and large my teenage years were defined by duty.

Our diversionary activities really were diversions more than anything else. They were, in a sense, short but much needed rest periods from the continual onslaught of work and church. The fun things we did do were playing badminton and basketball in the barn, softball in the pastures, or even acrobatics on the chinning bar. One thing for sure is that we were all physically fit, from all that hard work and healthy food. On Sundays or the occasional day off, we often went for bicycle rides or mountain climbing in the towering mountains that surround the Fraser Valley. We also enjoyed swimming at Harrison Hot Springs in winter, and in summer at our favourite swimming holes on Lulu Island and at Cultus Lake. Given the Mennonite traditions of church, work, and duty above all else, such frivolous fun was quite a lot for Dad to allow us, but he did allow some. Dad even took us on trips to places such as Mount Baker (in the USA), Victoria, the Peace Arch and Stanley Park (in Vancouver). Quite unusual for a Mennonite preacher. However, some things remained completely forbidden: organized sports, dancing of any kind, movies, alcohol, dating, and even visiting non-Mennonite homes. The very concept of 'fun' was strictly controlled.

From my present perspective of old age, those youthful years represent an explosion of energy and ambition, a hugely successful acquisition of work habits as well as considerable knowledge and understanding of the wider social and physical environs. Those years also represent lost opportunities and considerable miseducation. Looking back on those years I am appalled at how childish and naive I was then. Despite having graduated from a secular high school and having completed much of my first year of university at the same time, I still actually believed that my doubts and temptations were the work of a real being called Satan. I also believed, as I had been taught, that God actually observed and took into account every thought and deed and punished or rewarded them accordingly. I also fully believed that there was a real hell of fire and brimstone in which we would suffer forever if we didn't get our act together and follow our Christian teachings.

And that's not all. We were also taught that people who didn't believe in our particular brand of Christianity would also burn in hell, as would those who through no fault of their own had never even heard of Christ. And that masturbation was one of the biggest and most punishable of all sins. It seemed obvious too, that God had a plan and a purpose for each of us and that plan would be revealed only if we worked and prayed hard enough. We needed to surrender completely to the will of God. I hadn't yet realized that we are both the potter and the clay.

Of course I am fully aware that many adults still believe all of this and a host of similar doctrines. I also think, however, that that does not make those beliefs any less naive. In any case I left Chilliwack as an adult taking with me the tenets of the faith of my forefathers, having been successfully indoctrinated. I left with the belief that I had been called to promulgate those doctrines. It should have been a case of 'signed, sealed and delivered'. But not quite. Small seeds of doubt had already been planted. Without knowing it, I had already taken the first few tentative steps on the long road back from Damascus.

CHAPTER FOUR

Three Hills (1950-1954)

Prairie Bible Institute

IN CENTRAL ALBERTA, Canada, approximately 125 kilometers north and east of Calgary sits a small town called Three Hills, named after three clearly visible hills to the north and west of the town. It is the centre for a wheat farming community and suitably located near a branch line of the Canadian National Railway. Three Hills was incorporated as a village in 1912. Today, the town stretches over 2.2 square miles (5.6 square kilometers) at the intersection of Hwy 583 and Range Road #240 and boasts a population of some 3,500 souls[77] with all the modern facilities of a thriving small town.

The impetus for this growth, uncharacteristic of many small prairie farming towns, is in large part due to the adjacently located Prairie Bible Institute, or PBI or just 'Prairie' as the locals refer to it. Had it not been for 'Prairie', Three Hills would probably be an unremarkable and almost unknown small town in gradual decline as are so many small farming towns on the prairies. As it is, the name 'Three Hills' is widely known to evangelical Christians across Canada, the United States, and even around the world. This is because

---

77 The 2008 census enumerated 3322 people.

PBI, over the years, became a leading institute for leadership training for those of the evangelical Protestant Christian persuasion. PBI includes over 16,000 pastors, missionaries, and other church ministers in its alumni, spread over 114 countries. It is no wonder that the town of Three Hills survives and thrives to this day.

Back in 1922, ten years after incorporation, Three Hills saw the arrival of a flamboyant, dynamic, and intelligent preacher from the United States in the personage of Leonard E. Maxwell (1895-1984) who stayed and founded PBI. Maxwell, a graduate of the Midland Bible Institute in Kansas City, claimed he had been called by God to Canada to teach the Bible and establish a Bible School. In the fall of 1922, he held his first Bible study class for eight local students. From that humble beginning, Maxwell developed 'Prairie' into a major and complex operation for the training of missionaries, pastors, and for others wanting to study the Bible. By 1948, two years before I arrived there, there were 900 full time students from many parts of the world, representing many countries and many Christian denominations (over 50 if I remember correctly), ranging from Roman Catholic to Pentecostal to high Anglican. In my graduating class of about 125 students, we had students from five Provinces, 22 US states, and from such far flung places as Bolivia, Ireland, Haiti, and Cuba.

Maxwell, until his later years, was wary of outside alliances and outside influences. Thus he tried to run his Institute as a self-sufficient entity. The Institute supplied much of its own food on an adjoining large tract of land. It ran a dairy, raised beef cattle and other farm animals, and grew vegetables. On one fall Saturday, with snow in the forecast, Maxwell called for volunteers to bring in the potatoes which were still in the ground. So there he was himself, alongside dozens and dozens of us, men and women together (as was rarely the case and an occasion to get acquainted) on our knees in the mud, sacking our winter supply of potatoes.

On campus there was also a bakery, a butchery, a huge kitchen, a laundry, a barber shop, workshops of many kinds (electrical, welding, woodwork, auto repair), a radio studio for Christian broadcasting, a 'hospital' (staffed by students who were nurses) and an airstrip. PBI also employed from time to time a volunteer 'bush crew' to provide the lumber for the many building projects. Staff and supervisors worked for low pay or voluntarily in exchange for food, housing, and tuition. A lot of the work was done by student volunteers, some of whom would stay on during the long summer breaks and work the gardens and workshops in exchange for room, board, and/or tuition. As well, every student during the school year was required to do one and a half hours of 'gratis' work daily. Depending on the skills you had, these jobs could be almost anything – teaching, nursing, cutting meat, washing dishes, milking cows, feeding animals, shovelling snow, or running the printing press.

In every way possible, PBI attempted to be self-sufficient. In fact, as much as a Protestant institution can be, for all outward appearances PBI was run along the lines of a Catholic monastery, with a strictly regimented lifestyle and monastic-like rules: strict rising and bedtimes, limited contact and no conversation with the opposite sex, slotted prayer and devotional times twice daily, no smoking, no drinking, no movies, emphasis on neatness and cleanliness, pressure to confess sins however small, and prohibition of 'worldly' activities.

Inwardly and theologically, I would venture to guess, our institution was very different. Catholics arrive at their doctrine through a hierarchical priestly class, hammering out a consistent theology, presumably based on the Bible, but not allowing their initiates a wide range of free thought and discussion, thereby producing a more consistent interpretation. One of the things that Protestants objected to during the Reformation was the idea that Christians needed an intermediary class of priests to interpret the Bible and the message of God, instead wanting to allow a direct reading and interpretation of the Bible, promoting an individual relationship with God. Some Protestant denominations, of course, once established, went ahead and set up their own kind of priestly class. But not all of them did. Some, like the Quakers and Mennonites, felt it was quite possible and even necessary for true Christians to interpret the Bible for themselves, allowing discussion. It was in this spirit of Protestantism that Maxwell set up his Bible study courses at PBI.

However, allowing 'discussion' was not exactly inviting critical thinking never mind dissention. Each of the four years of the program included Bible Study courses, using 'search questions' to guide the study. These core courses were required of all students and they covered the entire Bible. The search questions were meant to guide us to get at the essence of each passage. More guidance was obtained by the provision of cross references to other parts of the Bible. A few such search questions were assigned to us each day. We were to provide written answers after reading *only* the Bible passages. We were advised not to use outside help by reading commentaries and theologies, instead relying on our own understanding. We were graded on our answers. Some students might have an independent insight into God's word and share it with the class, perhaps even spark the imagination of the instructor. Well, that is how it was supposed to work. Surprisingly, or perhaps not, there were not that many student insights.

We quickly learned to guess what kind of answer the instructor wanted and seldom dared to speak our mind, for after we read our answers the instructor would lecture at length on the 'correct' answer to the question at hand. Nor was there much room for actual discussion or debate. On one occasion when there was time for questions, I asked the instructor how Moses, who was said to have written Deuteronomy, could have written about his own death. I got nasty looks from some students and was brushed off by the instructor. Perhaps that was why my grades in Bible Study were lower than in other courses. I just couldn't seem to do as well in Bible Study where the 'search question' methodology was used. I guess I actually thought of them as genuine questions allowing various answers and in turn I asked genuine questions, but I quickly learned that that wasn't really what was expected. Ironically it was the idea of the search question, along with their ecumenical stance and favourable reports from two of my brothers-in-law, that attracted me to PBI in the first place.

First Year

ON FRIDAY MORNING, September 29, 1950 I boarded a train in Edmonton, where I had overnighted in a cheap hotel, en route to Three Hills and PBI. As I got on, I felt a strange sense of foreboding and a flood of questions entered my mind. What would the crowds in the train think of me, carrying my one old suitcase and my violin? How would I fit in and compete with all the serious religious people I was soon to meet? How would I find my place in the flock? Who would be my roommate? Would I be allowed to take singing and violin lessons? When I stepped inside the coach, I immediately felt better, seeing other young people shoving even smaller suitcases under their seat and others placing their treasured instruments on the racks above.

In short order I was being introduced to this 'brother' or that 'sister'. I realized then that most of the passengers were 'Prairie' students, the majority of them veteran students returning for another year to continue their studies. They were all very kind and friendly and I was soon at ease, though rather taken aback when someone asked me if I had been called to a specific mission. Many of them were already sure of where they were going as missionaries: China, Nigeria, Bolivia, etc. Upon arrival at Three Hills station, we were met by a PBI truck, which took us and our luggage to the campus. I was relieved to learn that Walter Sawatzky, my old friend and fellow high school graduate, was to be my roommate.

Classes began on Monday, October 2. The courses I enrolled in that first year were Bible I, Bible Atlas I, Ancient History, Personal Work I, Homiletics I, Word Study II, English I, Music Theory I, Voice I, Large Chorus, Public Speaking I, Violin and Private Voice. Out of a total of 19 hours of instruction per week, seven were in the field of music. That ratio continued more or less for the following three years as well. If Bible Study was my major, as it was for everybody, then Music was certainly my minor. In the following years I also took Psalms I & II, Leviticus, Acts, Christian Evidences, Doctrine I & II, Theme Writing I & II, Orchestra, Radio Choir, Advanced Conducting, Advanced Harmony, and Bible II, III and IV.

The first few weeks and months were periods of uncertainty and adjustment. I was uncertain about the status of my faith and what would be required of me in terms of public expression thereof. I also needed to adjust to the pressure of constantly having to be prepared to be called upon to pray before the whole assembly or to read to the whole class my responses to the Bible search questions. The following entries in my diary record some of my early PBI experiences:

> *Oct. 1, Sun. – Maxwell spoke on the theme of 'analyzing scriptures'. I thought that my problem of doubt stemmed from my over-analysis of the Bible. I will not have peace until I stop demanding that I understand everything.*[78]

> *Oct. 8, Sun. – I know something is wrong in my heart.*

> *Oct. 17, Tue. – As usual, no deep fellowship with God yet. But I long for it.*

> *Dec. 1, Fri. – Felt the Lord's help all round.*

> *Jan. 23, Tue. – I am enjoying myself immensely. Got many letters from home. The music office sent me notice granting practice hours in the studios. I thanked God for help in getting 100% on several tests. Was really happy. Thought perhaps Walter S. just pretended to like me, but didn't really.*

> *Mar. 23, Fri. – Still no peace in my heart. Feel torn apart inside.*

> *May 31, Thur. – Had serious religious doubts and thought of giving up PBI and going to University instead.*

---

78 To me, some of the hallmarks of a rational mind are to search for clarity and non-contradiction. The Bible does not pass these tests. My rational mind refused to be bullied into submission, causing much inner conflict.

Three Hills (1950-1954)

We men were from time to time called upon to do the 'night watch'. Usually two of us, one leaving ten minutes later than the first, would start at the kitchen and follow a prescribed route and sign in at ten to twelve checkpoints and return to the kitchen, where hot cocoa awaited us. After a brief rest, we repeated the rounds. The purpose of the watch was ostensibly for regular security concerns, such as fire and theft, but in reality it included making sure all of the 'flock' were inside the fences. I enjoyed this work, to do something out of the routine, not to mention that knowing the route would come in handy later when I myself had an occasion to step out. One evening my friend Harry Hiebert and I snuck out at midnight to meet with two female students in the radio studio to listen to Handel's Messiah as performed by the Huddersfield Choral Society. Had we been detected we all most assuredly would have been expelled.

We freshmen students were required to take several sessions of etiquette lessons and demonstrations upon first arriving. These took place in the kitchen on Saturday mornings and were presided over by an English lady who specialized in Emily Post. The idea behind that was that no servant of the Lord should ever be an affront or an offense to a potential Christian convert because of bad manners. So we learned how to properly set a table, make introductions, greet

Name	Corney Hamm		19 51
Subject		Periods per Week	Credits in Percentage
Ancient History		2	97
Personal Work I		1	96
Homiletics I		1	97
Bible I		3	87
Bible Atlas I		1	92
Word Study II		1	96
English I		3	94
Music Theory & S. S. I		2	99
Voice I		1	88
Large Chorus		1	90
Public Speaking I		1	90
Instruments		1	90
Private Voice		1	89
P. T.			97
Gratis			97
Conduct			95

Prairie Bible Institute (PBI), final grades, year 1

newcomers, apologize or beg forgiveness a la Emily Post's strict social rules. To this day, I feel uncomfortable when diners do not return their chair to the original position when leaving the table.

After my first year of classes and after the Missionary Conference that immediately followed, I journeyed back to the family farm in Chilliwack for a rest and a visit. After having driven with a friend all night to avoid the expense of a hotel, I arrived back home at 10:30 a.m. on April 22. I was immediately put to work hoeing weeds in the berry patches and helping Frank with the dairy farming. Nothing had changed. I wanted to talk with my family about the huge blessings I had received, the possibility of my being called to the ministry, and about my struggles of faith, but nobody wanted to hear about any of that. There was plenty of work to be done, as always; so I kept quiet.

The pattern of oscillation between faith and doubt, between surrender and self-assertion, which I was experiencing at this time, set the stage and tone for the remaining three years at PBI. This internal conflict continued right until the end of my time there.

Witnessing with the Chilliwack Gospel Gang

WE HAD BEEN warned upon leaving PBI about returning home and languishing in our spirituality and being tempted to fall back into our old ways. Ironically for me, our 'old ways' were quite religious. Even so, I felt a need to fulfill my responsibility to 'witness' to the public. So I formed a witnessing group with my old high school and Sunday school friends, Jake, George, and David, all fellow church members. We called ourselves the 'Chilliwack Gospel Gang'.

Some people who call themselves Christians are ever so reluctant to proclaim that plainly and publicly, while others relish any opportunity to announce their beliefs loudly and flamboyantly. Through measures such as singing hymns, handing out Bible messages on street corners, and asking strangers if they are 'saved' and prepared to die, these Christians are 'witnessing'. Witnessing is much encouraged in evangelical circles and thought of as a duty for anyone who would hope to become a minister or missionary, as I did. However, I always felt embarrassed doing so and often wondered why.

Was my reluctance and embarrassment an indication of lack of faith? Or was it something else? If I was to be a true Christian, I would have to overcome this reservation and not be tempted by the Devil to be silent. Was my desire to fulfill my duty to witness motivated by an attempt to compensate for any lack of Christian behaviour on my part, to compensate for my sins? Was it that the less I led the good life, the more I needed to proclaim to be a true Christian? Or was my reluctance an early premonition of my lack of fully trusting those beliefs and practices? As it turned out, it was the latter.

Even with the increased comfort of working in a group, I still was hesitant in this important duty. On one occasion I hurried to get the job over with by placing stacks of tracts in public places like washrooms and theatre lobbies, hoping that I wouldn't be seen by people I knew. Later I would feel guilty about having cheated in this way and go back again, hoping to find that they had all been taken by eager seekers of salvation. They weren't. As far as I could tell, not a single one had been taken. So again, I would reluctantly hit the streets of Chilliwack to distribute my literature until after dark when I would meet up with the rest of the gang and report my good work. Later I would be able to tell my colleagues back at PBI in somewhat clear conscience of my witnessing.

Looking back on this behaviour now from my present perspective, I am less embarrassed about it now than I was then. That behaviour was, after all, consistent with what I then believed. I have long held the view that if one truly believes something, as distinct from what one merely espouses, then one needs to take action according to those beliefs. In this way, one learns quickly either to validate or discredit that belief. In my case, I was liberated from what I now consider to be an irrational belief system, in part, because I took action according to it.

My experiment with witnessing by forming the Gospel Gang and distributing tracts culminated in a change of mind and attitude for me even by the end of that summer. I came to believe that distributing gospel tracts is not a very effective mode of proselytizing. I also realized that most of the people who received the tracts were probably Christians already. Furthermore, I felt that truncating the salvation story to a line or two or just vaguely alluding to it significantly cheapened the message through over-simplification and distortion. Perhaps most significantly, I began seriously to doubt the existence of a literal hell. Wasn't it our main purpose in witnessing to save people from hell in the first place? By putting my beliefs to the 'action test', deciding to act in accordance with my beliefs, I found that I either had to change my beliefs or change my method of witnessing. In my second summer break I would therefore use a different mode of witnessing as we shall see.

In the meantime, before returning to PBI for my second year, some changes would have to be made to the farm. Peter was on his own now, teaching and studying in the summer. Frank was about to get married and soon he too would be leaving the farm. Walter, my younger brother, capable as he was (and is) with only one hand was not the best bet for a long term dairy farm operator. Nor was he interested. He did, however, dutifully run the farm, together with Dad, for the next fall and winter season. Dad and Frank then entered into discussion for Frank to take over the farm entirely. Dad really wanted me to come back to the farm for at least another year, but I insisted that I needed to work for myself in order to earn some money to live on, being tired of my shoe-string existence. After long hours and days of hard negotiating, Dad finally told me that I was free to do as I pleased. It could have had something to do with the fact that I also wanted to do some itinerant trial preaching the next summer. I thanked him for letting me have my leave and I was so happy I almost cried. It felt as though a huge burden had been lifted from my shoulders. I was, at long last, a free man.

Of course that didn't mean that the work stopped. I agreed to work on the farm until the berries had been picked, the weeds hoed, the haying completed, the new plantings prepared, and until

Walter had a chance to learn how to operate the milking machines properly. This was all accomplished by the end of July, 1951. On July 21, I received a letter from Dad, who was away at a Mennonite Conference, letting me know he had found me a job harvesting grain for the Penner family in Grassy Lake, Alberta. This Mr. Penner was a very rich man. He and his family were the owners of vast productive farm lands and wielded great power and influence in the Mennonite community in southern Alberta. I was to arrive there some time before Aug 15, when the harvesting would begin in earnest. Perhaps Dad was as happy as I was for this job for he would now not have to pay for my next year's tuition.

In mid-August I took my battered suitcase and violin and boarded a Greyhound bus in Chilliwack and headed to Coaldale, Alberta, where, as was pre-arranged, I would overnight at my brother John's place before catching a ride to Grassy Lake the next morning with a certain Mr. Pankratz. John dropped me off at Pankratz' place at 6:00 a.m. on the Monday morning, and we were off. Pankratz, likely as sleepy as I was, hardly said a word during the trip but suddenly came alive upon arrival at the Penner's. This Mr. Pankratz was the very man that came to La Glace years earlier as an itinerant lay preacher so I had already met him. Little did I realize it at the time, but I was about to have breakfast with two of the leading power brokers of the Mennonite Brethren Church in Western Canada.

Old Mr. Penner, a huge man, sitting at the head of the large kitchen table greeted us without getting up and introduced me to his many family members and pointed to where Pankratz and I were to sit. I was seated beside John Dyck, who had married into the Penner family, and who was to be my boss. He had come to fetch me. He lived several miles distant from the Penners, whom I never met again except once briefly at church. John was courteous and seemed fair-minded but not particularly affable; but we would get along just fine. John and his wife Mary, with their four year old son, Dennis, and a sister of John's had just moved into their brand new house, and I was happy to find out that I would be the sole occupant of their old one. There in the evenings I could play violin or read alone in peace.

My main job was to be the driver of the tractor that pulled the combine, operated by John himself. Other tractor jobs included some swathing and fall cultivation. When the fields were too wet to work, I did other farm jobs such as fencing and general repairs, but mostly building granaries. I also did the chores morning and evening, milking the cows and tending other animals as I had done so often throughout my life.

There was a matter of wages to be settled. John offered me $10 per day when combining and $5 per day on other days. Combining (threshing) days would be long and intense, beginning as early and ending as late as the weather would allow. Non-combining days would be a more leisurely 8 hours per day, plus chores. Thus if I got in say, 25 days of threshing @ $10 per day and 15 other days at $5 per day I would be able to make $325. On the other hand, if it rained the whole time and we got in no harvesting days at all, I would earn only $200. I figured out that I needed $210 for PBI tuition, $10 for pocket money, $5 for work boots, and $12.50 for the train fare from Grassy Lake to Three Hills for a total of $237.50. I proposed to John that that was all I needed and if he would pay me that exact amount I would ask for no more even if we combined every day of the available 40 days. Thus if it rained a lot and we didn't do much threshing, I would benefit and if the weather was good and we got the crop in, John would benefit. He agreed, and since we were both believers, we left it in the hands of God.

The next day it started raining, and the next and the next. I built a lot of granaries; maybe I should have been building an ark. Finally, the rain let up enough to get some harvesting done but only for a few days. The entire time at Grassy Lake, between mid-August and the end of September we only got in two more days of threshing. I did, however, get a lot of violin practice and reading done.

One day at dinner, John turned to me and said, "Do you know what day it is tomorrow?"

"I sure do."

"I'll take you to the train station first thing."

Grassy Lake summer employment, 1951

That was all that was said and the next morning we were on the road at the crack of dawn. I tried to make conversation during the trip to hint that I had not been paid.

"I sure hope the weather improves and you can still get your crop in", I said, hoping he would take the hint.

"Me too."

"I still owe you that $5 for the boots", trying a new tactic this time.

"That's right."

And that was that. There was no way that I was going to ask him directly for my pay and he was not going to show his hand either. I started to think that if my pay was late or if it didn't come at all, I would have to ask my father for a loan for tuition. We drove on in silence.

When we got to the station he said, "You can wait in the truck while I get your ticket."

He was back in no time and simply said, "Here's your ticket. The train is coming."

"John, I enjoyed working with you. Here's to better weather." I said as the train pulled in.

"And I enjoyed having you. Good luck with your studies."

We shook hands and I stepped towards the train, still with no pay.

"Oh, just one more thing", he said as he handed me a cheque, a very slight smile on his lips, "You really are just as stubborn as I am."

I boarded the train and was off for my second year at PBI.

I had forgotten one thing. Cash. I had no pocket money at all. I had missed breakfast, was hungry, and couldn't buy anything. It wasn't until I got to Calgary that I could go to a bank to cash my cheque. My cheque! I hadn't even looked at it (had he honored our deal?) but when I did, there was the full amount of $237.50. He hadn't even deducted the $5 for my boots as agreed and he had purchased my train ticket as well. When I tried to cash the cheque in Calgary, I was told that they couldn't cash it and would have to send it back to Grassy Lake to have it certified. Banks! More hungry than annoyed, I returned to the station and climbed back aboard the train that was to take us to Three Hills. There, with the same tattered suitcase and violin and with the same sense of foreboding I had had a year ago, I met the same friendly student faces returning to PBI. We were met at the station by the same old PBI truck which took us to the campus once again. With some trepidation I approached the comptroller's wicket to pay my tuition armed only with a cheque that the bank in Calgary wouldn't take. When I handed Mr. Muddle the cheque he just said, "Sign here. Welcome back to Prairie."

Year Two

MY SECOND YEAR at PBI started much the same way my first year ended, in a state of inner turmoil. I was still struggling with my inferiority complex which I was told was really a matter of inflated pride, of wanting to appear better than we really are. And pride was a deadly sin against God which needed to be confessed and conquered. Then, too, I was still wavering in my attempt to fully surrender to the Lord. I just didn't seem to know how to do that or really what exactly that meant. Wasn't I already diligently preparing for the ministry? For His service? Wasn't that enough? I still had doubts of many kinds, including the literal truth of the Bible, about the reality of hell for the innocent, and about the creation story. However, I was dedicated to working these things out by studying the Bible even more. These two little 'pockets of disbelief'⁷⁹ I kept to myself.

What was becoming clearer to me was that my calling was not to be a missionary, which was the emphasis of PBI, but to pastoral service or even teaching theology. Not believing in hell for the ignorant and innocent really does take the sting out of missions. All the while I was trying hard to comply with the expectations set by PBI to be the ideal Christian servant of the Lord: living a pure life, having a close relationship with God, communicating through prayer, trusting in and surrendering to God completely, reading the Bible faithfully, and sharing my faith with believers and non-believers alike. Though I was trying, I was not really succeeding in these matters. I was still vacillating on many issues. I discussed some of these issues with my brother Peter who was my roommate for that term. He had come to study at PBI for only one term before returning to teaching and completing his degree at the University of British Columbia (UBC). Though Peter and I got along well, we did not see eye-to-eye on matters of Bible interpretation and theology.

On one occasion, as I recall, we were required to express our differences openly. It so happened that Peter and I were both enrolled in the same class, Doctrine I, taught by Miss Ruth Dearing. Here, too, we used the renowned search questions to find out what the Bible had to say on certain items of doctrine. We were trying to find a clear answer to the tricky question of the role of women in the church. This was a particularly sensitive issue at PBI because so many missionaries, at least for a while, were single women preaching the gospel and teaching the Bible, as was our instructor for this course, Miss Dearing. I was hoping that she wouldn't pick me to speak on this issue because I knew that I had a controversial answer prepared. I was relieved when she called on Peter to read his answer on this issue. Peter's answer was in line with the prevailing view of the church and PBI, including Miss Dearing, as was expected from us, namely that the Bible support-

---

79 'Pockets of disbelief' is explained more later in Chapter 8, 'The Road Back'.

ed the position that women could minister, that they could spread the word of the Lord, but clearly had a lesser role than men.

It was very rare for an instructor to call on roommates to answer the same question but much to my surprise and dismay she immediately called on me to read my prepared response to the same question. This was not likely just a coincidence. Was she testing our integrity? She needn't have; we would never plagiarize. Did she suspect that my answer would be different and was setting up a debate? In any case, out came my answer and it was that the Bible was vague on this issue and that there was a potential or genuine contradiction on the matter. Therefore there could be no definitive answer other than by arbitrary fiat. This was not the expected answer and it bordered on an unacceptable attack on the clarity of His word. I was publically expressing doubts about the literal veracity of the Bible.

So what does the Bible itself have to say about it? Does it support the position that women should be allowed to play a significant role in the Christian church (praying, proselytizing, preaching, teaching, and ministering) or does it support the position that women should not be allowed to play these roles and be silent and subservient. I contended that the Bible supports *both* positions.

Trumpeting the equality of men and women, Paul says:

> *For as many of you as have been baptized into Christ have put on Christ. There is neither Jew nor Greek, there is neither bond nor free, there is neither male nor female, for ye are all one in Christ Jesus.*[80]

Paul also sent his greetings to various members of the church he had established.[81] Among these were the following women: Phoebe, a deacon; Preisca, a missionary; Tryphaena, Tryphosa, and Persus, Paul's co-workers; and Junia whom Paul calls the 'foremost among the apostles'.

---

80 Galatians 3:27-28.
81 Romans 16.

In his ground breaking work, Bart D. Ehrman, a Bible scholar, writes:

> *The Pauline letters of the New Testament provide ample evidence that women held a prominent place in the emerging Christian communities from the earliest of times... ...women appear to have been actively involved in the weekly fellowship meetings, participating for example by praying and proselytizing much as the men did.*[82]

However, Paul (apparently) also says:

> *For God is not the author of confusion, but of peace, as in all churches of the saints.*
> *Let your women keep silence in the churches: for it is not permitted unto them to speak; but they are commanded to be under obedience as also saith the law.*
> *And if they will learn anything; let them ask their husbands at home: for it is a shame for women to speak in the church.*[83]

Another similar passage, also apparently written by Paul, says:

> *Let the woman learn in silence with all subjection.*
> *But I suffer not a woman to teach, nor to usurp authority over the man, but to be in silence.*[84]

For me, studying the Bible at that time, it was not merely a question of whether Paul was consistent in his thinking, but whether *the Bible* itself was consistent in its message. If the Bible was not

---

[82] Bart D. Ehrman, *Misquoting Jesus: the Story Behind Who Changed the Bible and Why*, Harper San Francisco, 2005, p 180-181.
[83] Corinthians 14:33-35.
[84] Timothy 2:11-15.

consistent about its view on the role of women in the Christian church then it cast doubt on the literal veracity of the Bible itself. Miss Dearing, did not, perhaps *could not*, give me a satisfactory response to my request for consistency. From then on, I could no longer in all honesty accept the Bible as a reliable scholarly work, let alone the literally faultless word of God.

This was not a happy conclusion. Instead of triumphant, I felt quite isolated and sad. Shortly after the Dearing incident and over the Christmas holidays of 1951, I fell into a mild depression. By all accounts I should have been happy. I had received Christmas cards from many friends. My family had sent me a package of sweets, presents, and even extra pocket money. I, too, received assurances that I was indeed saved and that I was indeed called to serve in the Lord's vineyard. I should have been a happy man; but I wasn't. I was lonely, sad, and conflicted. Peter had gone to visit our brother John in Coaldale. Most of the students had gone home for Christmas, but I stayed there at PBI, doing some extra 'gratis' to earn my keep and to try to clear my mind.

Not only was my weakening faith depressing me but the events of the world paralleled my feelings and it all weighed heavily on me. The horrible Second World War was just barely over and we were now sending troops to the killing fields of Korea. It should have been a happy time of peace and prosperity for me and for the rest of the world too; but it wasn't to be. I went to the library to try to dispel my gloomy mood by listening to music. I thought that Tchaikovsky's 'Pathetique' would do it; but no, it just made me even sadder. This music reflected the story of humanity struggling against all odds to find happiness amidst a scene of self-inflicted misery. My shocking discovery that the Bible could no longer be trusted had shaken my faith and brought me despair:

> The Sea of Faith
> Was once, too, at the full, and round earth's shore
> Lay like the folds of a bright girdle furled.
> But now I only hear
> Its melancholy, long, withdrawing roar,

> Retreating, to the breath
> Of the night wind, down the vast edges drear
> And naked shingles of the world.[85]

Had I had the wherewithal and courage, I would have up and quit PBI right then and there. But I didn't. I hung on for a few more days, and then a few more. Peter soon returned and so too did my classmates. Classes resumed and my melancholy dissipated as I fell back into the comfort of routine. I felt as if I had emerged from a terrible nightmare and all was well again. I resumed my role as a prospering PBI student and my calling to the ministry. Doubts were put on the back burner.

The winter passed.

In no time at all our classes were over and the PBI sponsored Missionary Conference began. There I met Alf Bayne, head of the West Coast Children's Mission (WCCM). He was there to represent his mission and to recruit both for his Mission and pastoral posts available in small villages up and down the coast of BC. The centre-piece of his Mission was a summer Bible camp on Quadra Island. The Mission owned a 40-50 foot boat used to ferry children to and from the camp and to access various small villages. A number of PBI students worked for the mission during the summer break to earn their tuition for the next term: building and repairing the camp, teaching and supervising children, and performing at religious services. Others, usually in pairs, were sent to outpost sawmills, logging camps, and fishing villages to work but also to spread the word of God, even if there were no churches.

This was just the opportunity that I was looking for to try my hand at pastoral work and preaching. It also appealed to my old friend, Jake, now also a PBI student. We teamed up and signed up for a posting at a Crown Zellerbach logging camp at Beaver Cove on the east coast of Vancouver Island just opposite Alert Bay. It was arranged that we would meet Alf Bayne in late April, in Vancouver, where his boat was being serviced. From there he would

---

85   Mathew Arnold, 'Dover Beach'.

ferry us up the coast to the Mission, where we would work for a week in exchange for the transport and then head on up to Beaver Cove, to which there was no road or land access.

After visiting the Crown Zellerbach office in Vancouver, where Jake and I were fitted for logging boots (on credit, or so we thought), the three of us set sail up the Strait of Georgia heading north to Quadra Island. It was a beautiful sunny morning with only a whiff of breeze skimming the sea surface and weaving it into a shimmering lace of gold. It was such a joy to have a job, to have a chance to advance my calling, to have this close comradeship, and to have this first ever sea voyage thrown in on top of it all! Quite a thrill for us prairie boys! I felt both lucky and grateful.

As island after island slipped by at cruising speed, Alf suddenly pulled back the throttle and announced "fishing time". I took the wheel as he and Jake went below to set up the fishing gear. Soon Jake and I, on either side of the boat, were trying our luck with rod and reel. Alf meanwhile maneuvered the boat to a shallower bay where he thought there might be some 'blue backs' (coho salmon). We were not disappointed. Very quickly we filled our limits with foot-long shiny 'blue backs'. Filleted, coated with flour and spices, and fried in butter, they made a fantastic lunch. There were plenty left for the folks back at camp.

The week of work that Jake and I put in, building a walk-way to the beach, was tough and I felt my aching muscles each morning. It was, however, excellent training for the even harder lumberjack work to come. The week at the mission camp vanished quickly and soon we were on the boat again en route to the logging camp at Beaver Cove. Alf explained to us that our timing through Seymour Narrows would have to be perfect in order to have enough tide water to clear 'ripple rock'[86], a major navigational hazard at the southern end of the channel and known to be a graveyard for unwary ships, and to have enough time to get

---

86   Ripple Rock was removed in 1958 by one of the largest non-nuclear explosions the world has ever seen, using some 1,270 metric tons of dynamite. It was a Canadian national historic event.

through the narrows before a strong rip tide could perhaps force us back again. At the given time, save for the hum of the engine, we silently slid over the ominous 'ripple rock' with enough water in-between and were moving against the increasing current in the middle of the narrows.

We had made it. Or so we thought. I was at the helm while Alf and Jake were below cooking dinner. Steadily I watched both coastlines to gauge our speed as the current became faster and faster and we moved more and more slowly. As long as we kept on moving forward we would be in good shape. We were nearly out of the pass with a few dozen or so feet to go when I noticed that we were not moving at all. I pushed the throttle forward but it was no use; it was already at full. I yelled down to Alf that we were in trouble. He quickly grabbed a wrench and proceeded to the engine compartment where he worked some alchemy to squeeze just a little more power out of the engine. Ever so slowly we started to move again. Alf then took the helm and said nothing as he gazed ahead, white knuckles pasted to the wheel. Finally we reached a point where Alf veered the boat to the right to get us out of the rip tide. Only then did he look at us, smile, and say, "Thank God we made it. Perhaps we did leave it too late."

Once out of the danger zone and away from the vicious tide, we dropped anchor near an island and had our dinner. After dinner we continued our voyage, this time into the darkness, with only beacon lights to guide us, the islands all around us barely visible to straining eyes. Only when we approached one beacon light, did the next one become visible in the distance which would then become our new target. Thus we zigzagged our way through the islands. Since we had to be at work in Beaver Cove the next morning, it was necessary to sail on through most of the night. If we each took three hour shifts at the helm, we could easily arrive at camp just in time for an early logger's breakfast. The only thing that could stop us would be fog. We agreed that the person at the helm would wake the others from their sleep should the fog roll in and obscure our guiding beacon lights. With that agreement in place, we pulled straws for the helm and bunk rotation. I was first at the helm.

With Alf and Jake fast asleep in their bunks below, I set the throttle and headed for the next beacon, and then the next. Perhaps an hour into my shift, I noticed a cloud or two of fog drift into my line of sight. I was just about to throttle back when the fog lifted again. I breathed a sigh of relief and let my thoughts wander when another fog patch obliterated my view. Then I saw the light again, and then not. The intervals of being blanketed in fog became more and more frequent. Suddenly we were completely surrounded with thick fog. I pulled back the throttle, and like a shot Alf was at my side, and then Jake too. Alf killed the engine to find out if we could hear other vessels in the area. We heard nothing but the faint lapping of the water on the hull. Then with flashlights and fog lamps we peered into the pea soup to try to detect light or land or anything. For quite a number of minutes we held our breath and kept our posts in silence. Then Alf from the fore deck said "I feel a light breeze coming; the wind will help." As quickly as the fog descended, it vanished again. We could then see the beacons again. With Alf at the wheel and Jake and I on either side we began to sing an old hymn, which until then had only been a cliché but now had great poignancy:

> *Let the lower lights be burning!*
> *Send a gleam across the wave!*
> *Some poor fainting struggling seaman,*
> *You may rescue, you may save.*[87]

Beaver Cove was a typical logging camp operation of its day. The location was chosen because the sheltered waters of the cove permitted 'boomers' to create huge log booms to be tugged for miles and miles along waterways to sawmills in the region. The camp itself consisted of a company store, a few portable houses for the management and married workers, a huge kitchen and dining hall, a portable school, and rows and rows of bunk houses.

---

87 Hymm "Let the Lower Lights be Burning", Philip P. Bliss, 1871.

Now the work would begin in earnest. The first and most dangerous job in the forestry industry was felling the trees. 'Fellers' sometimes also bucked the trees, that is, removed the branches and cut them into manageable lengths. From then on they are called 'logs'. Usually, however, 'bucking' was a specialized job, done, not too surprisingly, by 'buckers' who followed the 'fellers'. After that it was the 'loggers' who moved the logs into a huge pile at the base of a 'spar' tree, where a specialized tractor called the 'loader', loaded the logs onto the huge logging trucks, which then would carry the logs, often along steep and rough mountain roads to the waters' edge and dump them into the water. The boomers took over after that.

The loggers themselves had specialized jobs too. A crew of loggers would typically consist of a 'riggin-slinger', who was usually the foreman of the crew, a 'loader', a 'whistle punk', and two or more 'chokermen'. The first job of the riggin-slinger was to set up the log collection equipment. A 'spar' tree, a centrally located, tall, topped tree, left standing by the fellers, standing alone in a sea of clear-cut, was put to use. From the top of the spar, support or 'guy' cables were placed in all directions to keep it stable. At the base of the spar was the 'donkey', a huge diesel engine that powered the 'riggin' operated by none other than the riggin-slinger. The rigging itself was a set of cables and pulleys attached to a large metal block. The 1-1/2" thick cables, called 'chokers' were about 25 feet long with a bell and a knob at the end for snaring the logs. The chokers were attached to long thick cables running through pulleys, one at the top of the spar, the other on a stump, often high up a mountainside hundreds of yards away.

When all was ready, the riggin-slinger dropped the rigging near where the logs lay. After the cables stopped moving he would signal to the whistle punk to send in the chokermen. When the whistle punk, situated in a safe place near the action, where he could survey the scene, blew the whistle, the chokermen dashed into the danger zone amidst loose branches, churned up ground, rocks, mud and undergrowth and as quickly as possible grabbed the cable end and bell, attached it to the log and then scrambled back to safety, whereupon the whistle punk signalled to the riggin-slinger to pull in the logs. Often the huge logs dangled many feet in the air, depending on the terrain, as they raced to the log pile at the base of the spar tree. By the time the chokermen caught their breath and dusted themselves off, the rigging was back, the whistle punk blew, and into the fray they dashed again. It was a tough and dangerous profession. Jake and I were chokermen for the duration of our time at Beaver Cove, the toughest and most dangerous job in the logging crew. We were a well coordinated team though and we worked hard. If the company didn't make any money, it wasn't our fault. The company actually did very well.

Much less successful than our logging work was our attempt to set up religious services and a Sunday school at camp. We did however manage to attract a small gathering of kids to the local portable school where we met each Sunday at 10:00 a.m. The children, five or six of them, were the camp superintendant's kids and from one other family. We sang and taught the usual curriculum of evangelical Christian Sunday School. Jake and I also advertised for church services but the vast majority of the loggers much preferred to sleep in on Sundays after drinking and carousing on Saturday nights. And those who didn't drink were generally not interested. Once or twice a few adults came along, so we just chatted rather than preached.

Near the end of June we were laid off because of dry weather and fire hazards. But, as always, good ol' Alf was a step ahead of us. He had found out about this through the grapevine and had arranged another job for us at the nearby fishing village of Sointula on Malcolm Island. After collecting our substantial pay, not having spent any of it on partying, nor even paying the expected deduction for the logging boots (the superintendant insisted), we took a water taxi over to Alert Bay and there caught the public ferry to its next stop on the coastal milk-run to Sointula.

Sointula (meaning 'place of harmony') began in 1901 as a Finnish utopian socialist society, operating on principles of equality and sharing. The 'Sointula Cooperative Store Association', which began in 1909, is the oldest functioning cooperative in BC. Some of the early ideals are still extant in the population of today which stands at about 800 permanent residents. Another of Sointula's claims to fame, is the reputation of being the highest per capita consumers of alcohol on the entire North American Pacific coast, and that takes some doing. On one occasion when I went to an address to fetch something, I, after prolonged, very prolonged, rapping at the door, heard someone opening a window above. And even that took an amazingly long time. Finally the head of a man poked out of a window from above and in a gravelly voice slowly muttered, "What month is it?"

When Jake and I arrived there in late June, 1951 we were met by one of Alf's 'Christian' contacts. I will call her 'Mrs. Paul' because Paul was her husband and I can't recall her name. Paul and Mrs. Paul ran the local Post Office, above which they lived with their children. Mrs. Paul drove us to see a certain Mr. Butchart, another of Alf's contacts who, being a carpenter, had contracted to build a house for an unmarried school teacher. While the school teacher was away at summer school at UBC for July and August, Jake and I were to build him a new house ostensibly under the supervision of Mr. Butchart. Butchart just handed us the blueprints and told us to get going and left. If we didn't know how to proceed we were to call him. It was a good thing that Jake and I were both farm boys and handy with hammer and saw. Occasionally we did call him and he probably showed up an average of a couple hours per week. By the time we left Sointula in late August, we had the house roughed up to the lock-up stage.

Sointula summer employment, 1952

Mrs. Paul and her children also took leave for Vancouver for a good part of the summer. In her absence, Jake and I stayed at their house, presumably for free but in reality to look after and cook for Paul and help him with the mail sorting. Paul, along with quite a few of his fellow islanders, was a heavy drinker. One evening after supper, I made a round of brief visits as I often did to get to know the neighborhood and offer spiritual guidance. This was another opportunity to witness for Christ and I wanted to take advantage of it. Jake and I also ran a Sunday school in the local public school. This time we also actually held regular Sunday services for which we prepared and delivered sermons.

On this particular evening, I was running past my usual bed time engaged in discussion with a splendid chap about communist and socialist notions in the Bible. I learned as much from this fellow as he did from me. It was nearly midnight when I returned home. When I opened the door, smoke hit me in the face. I jumped inside, closed the door, and ran to Paul's bedroom. There beneath his bed was a clump of glowing mattress and a burning hole through his bed from whence it came. I raced for a pail of water from the kitchen to douse the fire and only then did I open the doors and windows to let out the thick smoke. Both Paul and Jake had slept through it all. Paul, not too surprisingly, was stupefied with liquor. I don't know what Jake's excuse was. Apparently Paul had fallen asleep while smoking in bed. I pulled him off the bed, stuffed a pillow in the gaping hole in the mattress, re-made the bed, and then placed him back in the bed. At breakfast the next morning, I casually asked him how he had slept. "I slept very sound, very sound" he replied.

Near the end of August, Jake and I, mission accomplished, boarded a ferry back to Vancouver. From there we hitch-hiked to Chilliwack where our parents still lived. With nearly three weeks remaining before my third year at PBI, and seeing no point in wasting the time, I took a job as a miner in the construction of a BC Hydro project, a conduit through a small mountain between Jones Lake and Hwy 1 near Hope, BC. In late September, I returned to Three Hills, catching a ride with Reg Bennet from Vancouver. It had been a memorable summer, full of adventure and well-paid work. And I had witnessed for Christ too, as we were expected to do. Now I could return to PBI, and if not boast, at least report on my service to the Lord. I had stories to tell and also I had earned more money than I had expected, more than enough for my expenses. It was a real pleasure for me to send a small donation to Alf Bayne's West Coast Children's Mission.

Year Three

MY JUNIOR YEAR at PBI began as usual, with apprehension of what lay ahead. Again it resolved itself rather quickly through association with like minded Prairie folk, returning students, and expectations from new students struggling with their own anxieties, seeing me as a victorious Christian believer and successful servant of the Lord. This time it was easier for me to push aside my lingering doubts for later resolution, my pockets of disbelief and my heretical secrets. In fact, I was becoming, if not a model student, at least a most acceptable one, by both students and faculty. This became increasingly evident to me both in class and elections to various committees.

At Prairie it was the practice for the juniors to plan and produce the annual Junior-Senior banquet and design a program in honour of the senior class, the climax of the school year. Shortly after New Year's, 1953, the junior class met one Saturday evening to elect their officers. I was both surprised and honoured to be one of several nominated for class president. On the first ballot, another person and I were tied for first place, much ahead of the other candidates, so there was a two-way run-off. I lost on the second ballot but the winner was a deserving one. Later I was elected to chair the important Program Committee. The Program was usually designed around a Bible verse which became the motto, the central theme of class thinking and energy. Our class motto was 'servants unto all'[88], which I was proud to have a hand in choosing. To this day I think that public service, including politics, when done in the spirit of actually serving the public, is laudable, giving both personal satisfaction and making life better for everyone. In my tenure as a PBI student as well as later in my teaching career, in fact throughout my life, I have tried to do just that.

In this third year at PBI, my curriculum focused heavily on music. I took courses in Advanced Harmony, Advanced Conducting, Voice and Violin. In addition to the coursework, I also played in the Orchestra and sang in the Radio Choir. Sometimes too, I sang solos or duets with my brother Walter, he with a beautiful natural tenor voice and me a baritone. Walter was my roommate for my Junior and Senior years.

PBI radio choir (C. is front row r.), 1953

Overall, I was quite a visible student for many reasons, and approved of by faculty. I was frequently asked to be an usher in the big tabernacle for Sunday services. I knew just how to behave. I was quick in spotting seats, courteous and friendly in greeting arrivals, and at ease with people without being overweening. When I seated the young women whom I had my eye on during the week my heart would beat much faster but I was good at keeping my rac-

---

88 Corinthians 9:19.

ing emotions in check. I was also asked to be the supervisor of huge dishwashing operations as my gratis work in my last two years.

The Prairie dining hall, a vast place, seated upwards of 1200 people at a time, women and girls on one side, men and boys on the other. To try to provide a friendlier, homier atmosphere, diners were seated at an appointed place at tables of eight. Usually at the head was a staff member or senior student. Every week or two the seating assignments were changed by drawing numbers. We men always thought it good luck if we drew a table near the women's side of the hall. Meals were served three times daily, and after each meal an enormous number of dishes had to be washed. At the centre of the hall was a huge, homemade dish washing machine which ran on the same principles as a modern home dishwasher. Right after the meal, the closing prayer, and the hasty exit of the diners, a crew of mostly High School boys, would grab trolley carriers to pick up the already neatly stacked dishes from the tables, bussing them to the dishwasher, where another crew stacked the huge trays and pushed them through the washer. At the other end of the washer-dryer a bevy of beautiful high school girls examined the dishes, dried them further if still a bit wet, and stacked them on empty trolleys ready to be distributed again by table setters. The whole procedure took about half an hour. My job was to supervise and coordinate the operation, which, to my delight, meant that I had the rare opportunity to talk to and observe the young women and their supervisors. Thus it was that over the weeks and months I got to know a certain very pretty and shapely young lady, though I tried and probably succeeded to hide my attraction.

I believed, and later confirmed, that the attraction was mutual. She was not only attractive but I also learned through the grapevine that she was popular with her classmates and a person of excellent reputation. While on tour for PBI in the summer of 1954 I met her at Winona Lake at a Youth For Christ Conference. At this time, I also met her mother, who approved of me and thought that we were a good match. For the next year and a half, much letter writing ensued while I attended Normal School and became a public school teacher. At Christmas into my first year of teaching, I bought a ring on credit, hopped on a Greyhound, and headed south to Atlanta, Georgia where she then lived. She accepted the ring and we were engaged, our mutual attraction running ahead of our good judgement, for we had some serious unresolved religious and philosophical differences. She thought of me as a future minister and possible missionary. She herself had ambitions to be a missionary. I, on the other hand, was in the process of shifting my interests and ambitions away from church life to secular public education.

Months later, when I wrote her and revealed my growing pockets of disbelief, she wrote back to say that the marriage would never work. I sadly agreed. When she sent back the ring, I took it back to People's Credit Jewelers. They only charged me one month's interest. I was despondent and yet somehow relieved at the same time. My hopes were dashed, with much energy wasted and much pent up passion dissipated. It was, however, I believe the right decision. I have to wonder how many disappointments of imaginary relationships, broken engagements, or bad marriages were the result of PBI's severe restrictions on interacting with the other sex.

By the end of my third year at Prairie, I had accumulated several more pockets of disbelief. I still however believed in miracles, namely the cessation of the laws of nature at the will and whim of God. I therefore still believed in some of the more fanciful stories of the Old Testament, such as Jonah and the whale, Daniel in the lion's den and Shadrach, Meshach and Abednego being spared in the fiery furnace. But now I would pick and choose what I believed literally and what I would take metaphorically. I suppose I thought that the Bible *contained* the word of God but wasn't entirely and literally so. I particularly balked at Revelations where I was expected to believe in mythical creatures like dragons:

> *And there appeared another wonder in heaven,*
> *And behold a great red dragon, having*
> *Seven heads and ten horns and seven crowns*
> *Upon his heads*[89]

---

89 Revelations 12:3.

I still took quite a lot on faith, but I drew the line at dragons. In fact, there were a lot of things about that inane book that I couldn't make heads or tails of. I nearly flunked an assignment to make a pictorial chart of the end times based on Revelations. That was the reason for one of the lowest marks (75%) that I ever received for an assignment at Prairie. Curiously, one of the highest final grades that I ever received (98%) was in a course called 'Christian Evidences', a sort of apologetics course, having to do with the defense and proofs of Christianity. I found it relatively easy to build a more or less coherent and consistent set of doctrines to flesh out Christian theology, but I couldn't get that from reading the Bible without contortion and distortion. The Bible, I was steadily realizing, was fraught with disturbing discrepancies, contradictions, and errors, some of it wide open to interpretation and some of it just plain nonsense.

Clerics and theologians, I now believe, in their attempts to defend the Bible cheat by trying to make bizarre Biblical claims *sound* reasonable. Discrepancies are merely pushed aside, not taken seriously, and outright inanities are construed as mysteries beyond our human comprehension. At the time though, I was mostly mystified by the Bible and thought that I simply had a lot more to learn before I was ready to proclaim the Word. In the summer break following my third year, I did not have the gall nor the certainty to try my hand at pastoral or Sunday school work again. Instead, this time I returned to greater Vancouver to take a 'normal' job to earn next year's tuition.

Having had some experience as a carpenter, both at Grassy Lake and Sointula, I answered an ad in the Vancouver Sun newspaper calling for a carpenter's helper. A curt response to my phone inquiry told me to show up at 6:30 a.m. Monday morning with my tools at a certain address on 41st Street. I had no tools, but decided to show up anyway. At 6:15 a.m. or so I arrived at the address only to find that this was no construction site but a quiet residence with no signs of life at this early hour. At exactly 6:30 a.m. I knocked on the front door and waited. About 5 minutes later, a voice from the back porch asked me what I wanted. When I told him why I was there, the voice said "I didn't think anyone would show up at this ridiculous hour." That is how I met Mike Pisesky, owner/manager of a small construction company, building mostly detached houses in the Vancouver area.

He didn't seem to mind that I had no tools, telling me not to buy any just yet, "Not until I can see if you can use a tool." On that first day he lent me his hammer, goose neck, pliers, and snips and told me to remove and stack the boards from the frame of a concrete house basement. As he dropped me off, he asked me to call him that evening for instructions for the following day. It turned out to be quite a big job and so I worked very hard, all day without lunch, until nearly 7:00 p.m. before I finally finished. I took the bus home and called him as I was requested to do.

"Go back to the same place and continue the job", were the instructions.

"I finished the job."

"No, you didn't. You obviously didn't understand what I wanted you to do," he snarled, "Go back and pull all the nails, pile the lumber, and cut the wires."

"But I already did that!"

"Come back here at 7:00 tomorrow morning and we'll go over there and have a look."

The next morning, this time lunch in hand, I was taken back to the site. Mike could hardly believe what he saw. Not wanting to betray his obvious surprise, all he said was "Where are the tools?" I went to fetch them from under a pile of boards. "Never leave tools out like that; they'll just rust. Or get stolen," he chastised. Then he took me to West Vancouver, where he and his crew were roughing up a house. He gave me the use of his tools for the entire summer and made me a regular. Mike was a bit rough and gruff but we got along well and I worked for him for several summers.

One evening in early July, while working for Pisesky, I got a phone call from Chilliwack to say that Mother was seriously ill as a result of a cerebral hemorrhage, and was in Chilliwack Hospital. She was not expected to live. Peter, Walter, and I, all in Vancouver at that time, rushed back to Chilliwack to be at her side, as did all of my siblings. When we got there it was already too late to converse; in fact, I don't think that she even recognized us. Back at work in Vancouver, I got word that she died on July 13, 1953. The last time I spoke to her was on the July 1st weekend, two weeks earlier. My last words to her were "*Vielen Dank, Aufwiedersehn*" (thank-you, goodbye), the thanks due to her kind habit of giving us bachelors borscht and other goodies to take along. Fittingly, we six sons were the pallbearers, carrying her to her final resting place, Grave 55, Row L, Little Mountain, Chilliwack, BC. I miss her now more than I missed her then, wishing I had gotten to know her better, lamenting that I had not been more thoughtful and kind.

Had Mother known what I was up to that summer she would not have been happy with me. Possibly she wouldn't have minded too much that I went on a double date but she certainly would have disapproved of my going to see a movie. Our church as well as our parents strictly forbade us from going to a movie theatre or any non-religious public performance for that matter. Only twice in my life up to that point had I even set foot in a theatre, once to see Hamlet (ironically recommended by our SMCI teachers) and once for our high school graduation ceremony. To go voluntarily to see a Hollywood movie was a grave offence that could get you expelled from church membership. In fact, one of my brothers did get expelled for precisely that reason. Dating and movie-going were also prohibited by PBI, even while on summer vacation, either of which would have resulted in my expulsion if anybody had found out. I had to be cautious.

My good friend from high school, BD Johnson, who at the time chased around town in a convertible Volkswagen, persuaded me to join him to see "a really clean, sinless movie". Knowing the risk I was taking, he suggested waiting until it was showing at a drive-in so that no one could see us or recognize us at the theatre. As we approached the ticket stand, I slouched really low and looked aside as he bought the tickets. Once at our stall and as darkness set in, we folded down the roof and sat back to enjoy my first ever real movie, 'Goodbye Mr. Chips', featuring Robert Donat as the likeable Mr. Chips. I was totally enthralled by this wholesome and innocent experience and couldn't understand what was so evil about the movie industry. So many damaging senseless rules are born of ignorance! At the time, however, and for obvious reasons, I dared not discuss this experience with anyone at home, church, or at PBI.

My summer job as a carpenter went well and my earnings mounted. Having saved more than enough for my final year at PBI, I decided that it was time to undergo some much needed plastic surgery on my nose to help me breathe better and to improve my appearance somewhat. The surgeon, a Dr. Cowan, charged me a special reduced fee because he viewed my ambition to be a minister favourably. Towards the end of September I checked into St. Paul's Hospital in Vancouver for the procedure. When the anaesthetic wore off I realized that I had undergone no small operation. I hardly recognized myself as I looked into a mirror; and the pain in my hip was atrocious. Yes, my hip. The surgeons had taken a slice of bone from my hip and placed it in my nose. To this day the tip of my nose is as hard as, well, bone. The recovery took longer than expected, so I arrived back in Three Hills with black eyes and a swollen face, days late for opening classes.

Senior Sermon and Higher Education

ONCE AGAIN I was apprehensive about returning to PBI. This time not having done much witnessing, having gone to the movies and found nothing salacious, and having dated a woman, all in direct contravention of PBI rules. I returned late with guilt and misgivings but once again that was alleviated by the embracing camaraderie and positive energy of my fellow students. With some catching up to do, I set to work and soon I had settled in to the PBI routine again. I felt accepted, even popular. I, despite my failures at witnessing and my nagging doubts, still felt myself to be a soldier of the cross, seeking to uphold the values of the church. Despite my conviction that the Bible wasn't in its entirety to be taken literally, I still believed that there was much good in it. I approached this, my last year at PBI, with the view that being a good servant of the Lord was to "fight the good fight with all of your might". There was to be no end to the Devil tempting me with doubt to undermine my faith, but I would soldier on.

Christian service, even in the capacity of minister (which I was still thinking was my calling), was for me to suppress one's personal doubts, keeping silent on items of disbelief, keeping to the common ground of central doctrines, and promulgating the positive messages of Christianity. And there were plenty of positive messages in which I still strongly believed: loving one's neighbor as oneself; caring for the sick and poor; considering others, including women, as your equals; seeking peace by turning the other cheek; forgiving those who harm you as you seek forgiveness for the harm you have done; bringing out and advancing the best that is within you; being truthful and sincere in all your dealings; and not imposing your will on others, allowing them to be free to decide what is God's will for them. With these, what I thought were the core Christian principles, I had moved away from the evangelical persuasions of my earlier years.

In mid-winter I received an enticing invitation to join a tour of the USA for the next summer to advertise PBI and its evangelical message. This was a challenge to my new way of thinking about Christianity. I thought long and hard about it and concluded that my theological stance, though somewhat unorthodox, was not sufficiently divergent from the PBI position to warrant refusal.

My studies went along smoothly and I felt well accepted and well considered in the PBI fellowship, though underneath that smooth veneer I felt somewhat hypocritical, not really worthy of that respect. But, I repeat, this was the way I was beginning to to think that the good fight had to be fought, refusing to admit one's doubts and hanging on to faith despite all the contrary evidence. How easy it was just to be one of the regulars, one of the flock. Faculty and fellow students trusted me, believed in me, accepted me. Underneath were they all partial hypocrites? Were they all just playing the same game of outwardly adhering to the faith which they espoused publicly but inwardly doubting it as I did? Was this attitude perhaps the very nature of being loyal and faithful, bolstering each other in common expression of prayers, thoughts, and observances, and thus not allowing doubts or misgivings to take hold?

In the spring term of 1954, my turn came up to deliver a 15 minute sermon for the entire student body and faculty during the daily morning devotional. It was the custom for seniors in their final year to make a trial run at preaching, which they were presumably now trained to do. When I was asked to take my turn, I knew immediately what my sermon would be and it didn't take me long to prepare it.

Prairie had the reputation of a missionary finishing school, with emphasis on *finishing*. The staff, and many students too, took a dim view of advanced theological studies and perhaps even a negative view of general arts and science studies at secular Universities. The generally held view was that too much intellectual probing and use of reason undermined faith. At that time, however, I was of the minority opinion that advanced theological and secular studies could actually support faith, particularly with respect to scriptural inaccuracies, discrepancies, and contradictions. These, I argued, needed to be addressed to show that they were only *apparent* contradictions. What *was* needed, I felt, was further general studies in the humanities and science, particularly Christian apologetics. These preparations would be of particular importance to those of us who were not called to be missionaries but were called to minister at home to well-educated and sophisticated parishioners.

For my Bible text I chose:

> *Beware lest any man spoil you through philosophy and vain deceit, after the tradition of men, after the rudiments of the world, and not after Christ.*
> *For in Him dwelleth all the fullness of the Godhead bodily.*[90]

---

90   Colossians 2:8,9.

And:

> *Beware of false prophets, which come to you in sheep's clothing, but inwardly they are ravening wolves.*[91]

My sermon went something like this: though the warning against false prophets and false philosophy are duly warranted (and we have been trained to recognize them), it is nevertheless the case that there are good prophets and good philosophers whom we are fully justified and morally bound to seek out and learn from. With the warning not to follow false prophets and fake philosophers, we can be assured of gaining much understanding of our faith and of the Bible if we do further studies with theologians and academic scholars. In particular it is our duty, I continued to argue, to probe into those questions that linger in our mind, those unresolved issues that still give us cause to doubt. Only in this way can we eradicate all doubt and cleanse Christian theology from all its discrepancies.

At this point in my offering, I quoted Wordsworth:

> *The thought of our past years in me doth breed*
> *Perpetual benediction: not indeed*
> *For that which is most worthy to be blest –*
> *Delight and liberty, the simple creed*
> *Of childhood...*
> *Not for these I raise*
> *The song of thanks and praise*
> *But for those obstinate questionings*
> *Of sense and outward things*
> *Those shadowy recollections*
> *Which, be they what they may,*
> *Are yet the fountain light of all our day,*
> *Are yet a master light of all our seeing.*[92]

---

91 Mathew 7:15.
92 From Wordsworth's. 'Ode to Intimations of Immortality'.

And with that my fifteen minutes were nearly up. I quickly rounded off what I had to say, but essentially I ended my sermon not with a Bible verse but quoting poetry, a bit unorthodox to say the least.

Later I was upbraided by a faculty member for quoting 'Godless' poetry. Weren't there enough passages in the Bible to support my arguments? Fellow students complimented me on my ability to speak but very few indeed complimented me on the content. I don't think it went over well. Though I had received an excellent grade in my course in Homiletics (the art of constructing and delivering sermons), this particular sermon was greeted with silence, a sure sign that it fell flat.

Today I can see why. Careful study of history, about the actual origins of the Bible; Biblical scrutiny, about the coherence and reliability of the scriptures; philosophical study regarding the proofs of the existence of God, any god; and scientific study about cosmological events, the origins of the Earth and Universe, all undermine traditional Christian beliefs and religion. My own experience is testimony to this, as is the experience of many former believers.

The Bible simply does not stand up to close intellectual study, to logic and reason. Anyone who reads it carefully and with a truly open mind, without prejudice or outside influence, will quickly realize that it is full of discrepancies, historical errors, distortions, contradictions and, yes, even vulgarities. That is not to say that there are not also some historically accurate, morally sound and even poetic passages, but that is not the point.

If the Bible as a whole is to be taken literally, as a flawless revelation of God's clear message to mankind, laying out the history of the Earth, how we are to conduct ourselves and setting forth a plan of salvation, it fails miserably. It is fairly easy to compile quite a long list of contradictions and inconsistencies in it and point to early tampering with the scriptures, with many inclusions and omissions based on very human political motives and personal prejudice. As well, many theologians have tried to smooth over apparent inconsistencies, only making matters worse with more human tampering. Many books have been written on the subject, showing that there are hundreds if not thousands of such Biblical infelicities.

To show a few of these, I will use Dan Barker's method[93] by asking simple questions and then citing contradictory answers from the Bible followed by chapter and verse:

1) Q – Are we saved by works?
   A – No. Ephesians 2:8,9. Yes. James 2:24
2) Q – Should we keep the Sabbath?
   A – Yes. Exodus 20:8, 31:15. No. John 5:16, Col 2:16
3) Q – Does God change His mind?
   A – No. Malachi 3:6. Yes. Exodus 32:14, Jonah 3:10
4) Q – How old was Ahaziah when he began to reign?
   A – Twenty-two. II Kings 8:26. Forty-two. II Chron 22:10
5) Q – How many pairs of clean beasts of each type were on the ark?
   A – One pair. Gen 7:8,9. Seven pairs. Gen 7:2.
6) Q – How many children did Michal, daughter of Saul have?
   A – None. II Samuel 6:23. Five. II Samuel 21:8.
7) Q – What time of day was Jesus crucified?
   A – Third hour. Mark 15:25. Sixth hour. John 19:14,15.
8) Q – Did Paul's men hear a voice on the road to Damascus?
   A – Yes. Acts 9:7. No. Acts 22:9.
9) Q – How many stalls of horses did Solomon have?
   A – 40,000. Kings 4:26. 4,000. II Chronicles 9:25.
10) Q – Who was Joseph, husband of Mary's, father?
    A – Jacob. Mathew 1:16. Heli. Luke 3:23.

---

[93] Dan Barker, *Losing Faith in Faith*, Freedom from Religion Foundation, Madison, Wisconsin, 2006, p. 165.

The list could go on and on and on. Ruth Hurmence Green cites hundreds more. She in fact says:

> *The mass of baffling contradictions that go to make up 'God's Plan' as conceived by Christian theology is staggering...*
>
> *The many contradictions in the contents of the Bible both as to 'fact' and as to concept gradually impose upon the reader the uneasy realization that ideas do not evolve logically in the pages of the Holy Book. 'That just doesn't make sense' is the reaction that even an avid proselytizer must feel at times and that some religious philosophers must have voiced.*
>
> *It has been noted that most members of religious communities prefer to have their spiritual manna spoon-fed to them than to try to gather it for themselves. To try to gather it from the Bible is admittedly a time-consuming, mind-boggling, frustrating, and finally a faith-shaking enterprise...*[94]

She points out at least a dozen cases of contradiction with respect to the crucifixion, burial, and resurrection of Christ alone. Of these she says:

> *These contradictions along with numerous others understandably kept under wraps, would seem to argue, except for the most ardent apologist that the persons, unknown, who wrote the gospels were not present at the happenings described or that they were very careless about the facts. Less important events might not make an impression great enough to produce accuracy, but surely the crucifixion, resurrection and ascension of the Saviour of the World does not fit into that category...*[95]

---

94   R.H. Green, *The Born Again Skeptic's Guide to the Bible*, Freedom of Religion Foundation, Madison Wisconsin, 1979.
95   Ibid. p. 152.

It should however not be that surprising that the New Testament is full of error. Biblical scholars, and here I don't mean theologians, have pointed out repeatedly that what we read in the modern translations of the New Testament must not and cannot be thought to be exact copies of Jesus' sayings, St. Paul's writings, or the texts of unknown writers of the gospels. The originals, against which any good historian must check, just are not extant. These writings have simply been copied too many times and gone through far too many translations to be deemed anywhere near accurate by historiography.

World class Biblical scholar Bart Ehrman says:

> *Not only do we not have the originals, we don't even have the first copies of the originals. We don't even have the copies of the copies of the originals, or the copies of the copies of the copies of the originals. What we have are copies made much later. In most instances, they are copies made many centuries later. And these copies are all different from one another, in many of thousands of places... These copies differ from one another in so many places that we don't even know how many differences there are. Possibly it is easiest to put in comparative terms: There are more differences among our manuscripts than there are words in the New Testament.*[96]

These differences were not just errors made by scribes, though there were undoubtedly some made by error despite efforts to copy faithfully, but also deliberate additions and deletions made in an adversarial manner to reflect changing political, social, and religious positions taken on controversial matters.

As quoted in Ehrman, a church father living in the 3rd Century complains about the scribes as follows:

---

96 Bart Ehrman, *Misquoting Jesus: the Story Behind Who Changed the Bible and Why*, HarperCollins, San Francisco, 2005, p. 10.

> *The differences among the manuscripts have become great, either through the negligence of some copyists or through the perverse audacity of others; they either neglect to check over what they have transcribed, or, in the process of checking, they make additions or deletions as they please.*[97]

One can only imagine how many more accidental and/or scurrilous changes happened between the third century and the seventeenth century when the King James Version (also known as the 'Authorized Version'), the benchmark for 'consistency' in English language Bibles, was written. Intense secular scholarship should and indeed does undermine a simple faith and discredit the belief that the Bible is literally true.

Bible study, under the guidance of the committed (as at PBI), not theology or philosophy, is the main and proper study for the Christian believer. Secular education, for the Christian, is often just pretence and self-aggrandizement. Courageous, unbiased, open-minded, let-the-chips-fall-where-they-may investigation into history, science, literature, and other 'liberal arts' are indeed truly liberating. They free one from the psychological and social necessity to assert as true and to propound as given, highly suspect matters of faith and dogma. In short, these studies undermine faith and free one from the pressure to believe what evidence does not support.

Academic study can add good window dressing to a believer's house of belief but if pursued honestly and ardently it can only bring the house crashing down and so Christian 'scholarship' is mostly highly selective and done with great prejudice. Some Christians, especially in positions of power or influence, like to add the letters 'PhD' beside their names, trying to insinuate that their beliefs are on par with other academic disciplines. However this will not and cannot add one whit to the credibility, validity, or veracity

---

97 Ibid, p.52.

of Christian faith because that faith is not based on evidence, on academic rigour and scrutiny, open mindedness, or willingness to be proved wrong, namely all that characterizes any real academic study. Those Christians who claim, as I did in my trial sermon, that scholarship strengthens faith are under delusion.

On Tour

WHAT STICKS in my memory about my final year at Prairie is the heavy work load. In addition to the make-up studies because of my late arrival, frequent musical practices and performances – on top of an already full course of study – there was now also the matter of making preparations to go on tour in the summer. Several such Gospel teams travelled across the US and Canada to spread the Word and recruit for PBI. The first task was to form well rounded groups who fit together both musically and personally, for we would be in very close contact with each other for quite a while.

The team I ended up with consisted of: Will Bruce, a faculty member from Public Relations, our itinerant preacher and leader of the group; Harding Braaten, pianist; Gary Graber, Vern Hutchinson, and Herb Zimmerman, trombone trio and vocal quartet members; and me, quartet member, vocal soloist, and master of ceremonies. Once the group was formed, we practised and practised during every available spare hour. At times we also went on short junkets to surrounding locales as a dress rehearsal for our planned preaching and musical tour of the US later that summer. The most intense practicing period followed cessation of classes, a two or three week period in April before we headed out on the road for the real thing in May.

During this time, a fellow graduate of Gary's and mine, asked our group to perform at his wedding in Edmonton. We jumped at the opportunity. So one frosty Saturday morning in mid-April the five of us (excluding Will Bruce) motored north to Edmonton to sing and play at his wedding. I was in the back seat going over

On tour with PBI (C. is far r.), 1954

some song lyrics when I looked up and noticed our steep descent into one of those deep-cut, meandering prairie creeks. We were half way down to the bridge when we hit black ice and in a flash found ourselves heading for the ditch. In another few seconds we rolled over completely such that we were back on four wheels, in the ditch, with the motor still running. "Is anybody hurt?", I enquired. Only Harding reported that his shoulder was a bit sore. Everyone else seemed just fine.

With that good news, we simply drove the car out of the ditch and back onto the road to get a better look at the damage. Luckily, there were only a few dents and everything else seemed fine, so we continued on to our destination. Before long though, Harding, our pianist, reported that his shoulder was seizing up and he wasn't sure if he would be able to play at the ceremony that afternoon. We happened to know a fellow PBI student, a junior named Ernie, who lived in Edmonton and was a gifted pianist and a resilient kind of guy. If only we could get hold of him. We took Harding to the hospital where he was diagnosed with a broken collar bone, and was certainly not fit to play. We then set to work looking for our unsuspecting replacement pianist.

We found him in greasy overalls at work in a garage.

After we explained our dilemma to Ernie and his boss, it was agreed that Ernie would indeed substitute for Harding. By then, time was pressing and there was not enough time for Ernie to go home and change clothes so we simply provided him with a choir gown and hoped nobody would notice. On our way to the church we handed him our music sheets and books, thankfully most of which he was familiar with already. He even said that he could ad lib a number or two as a prelude before the wedding march. It was agreed that when the wedding party arrived at the front door, one of the party would press a buzzer which would alert the minister and the performing team to enter the church from a foyer near the front and take their positions, the minister at the pulpit and the rest of us in the front pews. At this point, Ernie, on the organ, would quickly wind up his prelude pieces and start the wedding march, ushering in the happy couple and entourage. That was the plan.

At the appointed time, we and the minister stood at the ready waiting for the signal. Ernie, still in his greasy overalls under the fine white choir gown, without any rehearsal or even any notice, played his ad lib pieces, and then played them again, and again stretching them out as long as he could. He must have been sweating more than just a little. I figured that something was wrong so I volunteered to run outside to find out what the problem was. At the front of the church I found a frustrated wedding party, wondering why the wedding march had not begun. The buzzer had failed. I quickly suggested that in exactly two minutes we, the performing group, would open the door and go to our designated seats whereupon the march would begin. And that's what happened.

It also happened that I was seated on the front pew, not three feet behind the groom. The couple had just exchanged rather lengthy marriage vows and were standing in front of the minister. Upon completion of the vows, the minister had us all rise for prayers, as evangelicals are wont to do. True to form, their zealous cleric took this opportunity to pray for the well-being of the couple, for the parents, for the faithful in attendance, for the sinners present, for the church missionaries, for the soldiers off in Korea, and for a whole lot more things. During prayer, I usually closed my eyes but for some strange reason I opened them just for a moment to see an anxious bride beside a severely teetering groom, about to fall.

I quickly stepped forward and caught him just before he fell. "What now!" I thought to myself. I sat him down on the pew beside me, put his head between his knees and whispered to him to breathe deeply. Meanwhile the minister droned on, finding even more things to pray for. When the groom had recovered, I helped him back up and he took his place again next to his bride, now clinging to him feverishly. I had just stepped back to my place at the pew when the minister finally said "Amen". Nobody appeared to have noticed what had just happened.

After the ceremony, the couple and the bridal party received the guests in the church dining hall. There was quite a crowd of guests and well-wishers waiting to partake of the food and drink. Being an evangelical crowd, of course there was no alcohol served and so coffee and tea were the main event. However, someone had made the grave error of getting decaffeinated coffee and so it had to be sent back in exchange for something with more kick. Meanwhile there was tea. While the coffee drinkers were waiting for their real coffee, the tea drinkers happily ate up all the sandwiches. When the coffee arrived, there were no sandwiches left and so more had to be ordered. After the bride threw her bouquet and the couple left for their honeymoon, the crowd thinned and by the time the sandwiches arrived, there were no eaters left. We, the performers, were the beneficiaries of the chaos, heading back home with a carload of freshly made sandwiches. They were delicious.

Just days after our eventful and educational junket to Edmonton, we headed south into Idaho and Washington states for our real tour. For the first week or so, while waiting for Harding's shoulder to fully recover, we did what we had done in Edmonton, namely search for a local pianist and limit ourselves to well-known pieces. Even so we had some dicey moments. In Bremerton, Washington we were lucky enough to engage another PBI student to play piano for us. He was a huge man with long flexible fingers which tickled the ivories with quite some flair. During our rehearsing for that evening's program, I asked him if he was familiar with the solo piece that I was slated to sing. "Oh yes", he said "I've played that a lot". When the time came for my number, he ripped into a fanciful introduction which was nice but seemed unlike anything I had heard before. When I came in, we both immediately knew that we were thinking of different tunes. So I just sang the piece my way and left him to figure it out. When I signalled to him to do just one verse, he eagerly nodded back in acknowledgement. We got through it somehow and whether the audience were just gracious or whether they thought that Prairie had gone modern and wild, I never did find out. It was a bit tense on stage but we had a good laugh in the car on the way back to our billets.

The work load was less stressful and more enjoyable once we settled into our routine. Usually members of the church in which we performed took one or two of us in as billets. Often we would chat about PBI well into the night, this being prime time for recruiting, our main reason for being there. There would be no time for sleeping in though because we had to keep on the move. After beginning the day with brief morning devotions and offering to help with household chores we would gather at the local church and move on to the next stop. Our departure time would vary with the length of the drive ahead. In the state of Washington, for example, we visited churches in Mount Vernon, Bremerton, Tacoma, Centralia and then on to Portland Oregon.

We would aim to arrive by mid-afternoon and usually the pastor or a senior church member would greet us, show us the ropes, and allow us to do a quick rehearsal for that evening's performance. Just before dinner, our host family would pick us up and take us back to their homes where we would have a meal and don our uniforms of white permanent press nylon shirts (easy to wash and didn't need ironing) ties, trousers, and blazers. Then we would be driven back to church in plenty of time before the service started. The service usually consisted of congregational singing (which I led), several music numbers by our team, Bible reading, a testimony by one or two of the team members, some information about PBI, a sermon from Will Bruce and an altar call of some kind after that. The service ended with more singing and a closing prayer. Then it was back to the billeting family for tea and cocoa and more visiting and chatting about PBI well into the night. It made for long days but it was also quite enjoyable.

This routine went on every day from Tuesday to Saturday. On Saturdays we sometimes had two performances, an afternoon service and then Youth for Christ rallies in the evening as well. I recall the trombone trio blaring out 'True Hearted, Whole Hearted' and me singing 'How Great Thou Art' in the famous Los Angeles Palladium for a YFC rally, where Will Bruce delivered one of his best 'hell fire' sermons and many came forward. On Sundays we usually conducted two services, the more typical formal service in the morning and our routine musical Prairie style service in the evening. Monday was our one day off.

On our off day, we tried to work in some physical activity, to relax, and to do some sight-seeing. This is how I got to see Crater Lake, Mount Shasta, Yosemite, Fisherman's Wharf (San Francisco), Long Beach, the San Diego zoo and more. While visiting with a farm family outside of Fresno, CA, we also were introduced to a new sport: water-skiing without a boat. We took turns shooting up and down concrete irrigation canals, being pulled at a considerable speed by a car travelling on the narrow dykes. I guess our prayers for safety kept us from smashing our helmetless heads wide open. Nobody got so much as a scratch but we all got a bawling out later from our leader Will Bruce.

Thus we made our way from Idaho all the way south to Los Angeles and San Diego, east through the southern Midwest to the Atlantic coast, north to New York, back west through to Chicago and Minnesota, and then on to Montana and back up to Three Hills, Alberta. At times, as when we headed east from LA through Death Valley on to our next appointment several states away, we would drive all day and all night. Only seldom did we take a motel, mostly because we lived off the meagre offerings of church service collections. We did, however, treat ourselves to at least one hot meal a day in a restaurant. We would always scout out a potential restaurant to see if they served liquor before we would enter. If they did we would explain that we didn't patronize restaurants that served liquor, which we thought was unchristian. Once, I think it was in Palm Springs, we couldn't find a liquor-free restaurant and so we had to return to one that we had already been to and dine on humble pie, but of course we drank no liquor.

Very seldom did any of us become ill, but I recall on one occasion, I think it was in Virginia or West Virginia, I suffered from sun stroke. We were visiting and performing at a youth Bible camp. I had spent much of the day under the hot sun, swimming and playing games with the local young people. That night and the next day I spent under a thin sheet in a dark tent recovering from delirium.

Several days before that, perhaps somewhere in Kansas or Missouri, I had a traumatic experience of another kind. We were slated to do one of our slick Prairie performances when it so happened that our fiery preacher, Will Bruce, was plagued with severe laryngitis and lost his voice. So he called on me to give the sermon that evening. We had anticipated this possibility and I was prepared with a sermon up my sleeve.[98]

In evangelical circles at that time, it was not considered good form to applaud or compliment a preacher for a good sermon, but it was acceptable to say to him that they had received a blessing. I received many such comments. In fact at the back of the church I noticed several church elders (this church was without a pastor at the time) discussing something with Will Bruce. It turned out that they were sizing me up as a potential pastor and Bruce had favourable things to say about me. Just before going out for a milkshake with some of the younger congregation, one of the elders approached me and asked me to a breakfast meeting the following morning for the purpose of interviewing me for the vacant pastor position. I agreed to meet them. Almost in a state

---

98   With Exodus 12: 7-13 as my text, backed up by Revelation 7:14- 15, I delivered a message about being spared damnation because of the cleansing blood of Christ, the Lamb of God. It seemed to go over quite well.

of shock I made my way to the restaurant where the young people of the church had saved a place for me. Despite being surrounded by pretty young ladies, who I would otherwise be quite interested in, my mind was elsewhere. I was about to be faced with a momentous decision.

Many questions raced through my flabbergasted mind as I tossed and turned through the night weighing up the pros and cons. Would I accept the pastorship if it were offered? After all those years of preparing for just this moment and feeling all the while that I was being called to this kind of work, was I now *actually* being called by the Lord? At age 22, was I not too young to lead a church? Would I, not being married, be able to guide and advise church members about marriage? Was I prepared to leave Canada for the USA? What did I know about this particular community? Would I be able to honestly subscribe to the credo of the Southern Baptist Church? Could I really pass up this opportunity to get experience in what I believed to be my calling, even if I wanted to take up more study? What about my many religious doubts, my 'pockets of disbelief'? Could I honestly present the Bible as the word of God when I saw so many faults and confusion in it? Even if I could hold the post with skill and aplomb, preaching and teaching the parts that I believed in, wouldn't I be a hypocrite and be exposed as such? Could I live with myself in good conscience, knowing full well that my congregation would think that I believed what they believed? Or is it even necessary that we have exactly the same beliefs? Could we not worship together even though we interpreted the Bible differently? How important is the unity of worship? Isn't it the minister's job to build this unity of mind and worship? Could I do all of this and still be honest about my doubts? After struggling with these questions for a good long time I decided that I could not take the position. I would simply tell the elders the next morning that I wasn't ready to be ordained and that I needed to continue my studies.

I almost fell asleep, having made this difficult choice, but then I was startled back awake doubting my own belief that further study would resolve my doubts and confusion. I suspected that doubts

Three Hills (1950-1954)

would always be part of the fight to keep the faith. What if my decision to turn down the offer, if presented, was just a trick of the Devil tempting me to evade my duty, to avoid my calling? Would it not be true to form for the Evil One to tempt me with a rationalizing excuse not to heed the Lord's calling at the very moment when it was about to come to fruition? Yes, of course; I must not let the Devil tempt me to avoid taking this post. But wait a minute; wasn't I hesitating because of very real doubts? So where did those doubts come from? The Devil of course. But was the Devil tempting me to take the job despite my doubts (thus positioning myself to become a hypocrite) or tempting me at the same time to decline the job despite my sense of duty? How could I decide this? I was back to square one.

The dawn was peeking in through the curtains when I finally made up my mind. I must be clear and rational about his, I said to myself. It would be tempting to adopt a full time prestigious vocation so early in my adulthood. However, a higher priority was the truth. I must resolve the issues of my doubts that I had put on the back burner before I could proceed with whatever aspect of the ministry my calling was to be. I harkened back to my own advice in my senior sermon, namely to pursue further education, particularly in theology and apologetics, in order to gain a clearer and fuller understanding of the Bible and from that to build a coherent, justified body of Christian doctrine that I could stand on. I needed to keep digging until I found my bedrock of Truth. At breakfast I told the elders about my struggle and my decision. They understood and didn't proceed with the interview. I never did find out if they were actually prepared to offer me the position.

Sometimes a little decision turns out in retrospect to be a huge one. That decision that night was one of those. In order to earn the money to attend college or seminary, I would later that fall attend Normal School to become a teacher, with the view to teach for a few years to earn enough money to go to seminary. As it turned out, public education became my profession, and with the further erosion instead of validation of my faith over the next few years, I never again entertained Christian ministry.

The Road Not Taken

Two roads diverged in a yellow wood,
And sorry I could not travel both
And be one traveler, long I stood
And looked down one as far as I could
To where it bent in the undergrowth;

Then took the other, as just as fair,
And having perhaps the better claim,
Because it was grassy and wanted wear;
Though as for that the passing there
Had worn them really about the same,

And both that morning equally lay
In leaves no step had trodden black.
Oh, I kept the first for another day!
Yet knowing how way leads on to way,
I doubted if I should ever come back.
I shall be telling this with a sigh
Somewhere ages and ages hence:
Two roads diverged in a wood, and I –
I took the one less traveled by,
And that has made all the difference.

Robert Frost

As our Prairie touring team made its way up the Atlantic coast, we stopped at Atlantic City to see the famous Boardwalk and have a swim in the Atlantic, the water noticeably warmer than the Pacific. Then it was on to New York City, a destination we all looked forward to a great deal. After our Saturday and Sunday duties, preaching, proselytizing, and making music in churches and at YFC rallies, we were free on Monday to do some sightseeing before heading off to Pennsylvania. We saw the usual sights, including the Statue of Liberty, Wall Street, Fifth Avenue, the Brooklyn Bridge, and, of course, the Empire State Building (then, the highest building in the world). Harding, the quiet wit from a farm in northern Alberta, put his thumbs in his side belt loops, bent his knees outward and drawled, "Gee, wouldn't that buildin' hold a lot of hay."

Once we left NYC, heading west, we felt like we were on our way home, even though we still had weeks of hard touring left to do. We were all getting a bit tired of the road but seeing new places and unique people, helped to keep our spirits up. On Pennsylvania backroads we noticed a number of cars with bumpers painted black and others painted red. After enquiring about this at a stop, we were informed that we were now in Mennonite country and the colour of the bumper indicated the degree of worldliness permitted. Chrome bumpers, which were standard for everyone else, indicated the most worldliness, and black the least and therefore the most pious. Mennonite congregations had actually split over this issue, thus there were chrome bumper Mennonites, red bumper Mennonites and black bumper Mennonites (and then there were the Amish, a sub-group of Mennonites, who didn't use cars at all, preferring to use horse and buggy and still do to this day).

Another memorable stop on the tour was Winona Lake, Indiana. Here, beside a beautiful lake, after which the town was named, we attended a YFC conference at which groups from all over the US and Canada performed, including us. There we set up a display advertising PBI. It was here that I first heard a huge choir sing 'The Battle Hymn of the Republic'. The tune was familiar to me, but not the lyrics; so I was quite surprised, even shocked, by the militaristic bent to what I thought of as a gospel of peace and love. At Winona Lake too, I met again the young lady from PBI, already mentioned, that I would later be engaged to. She was there with her Mother to attend the conference and, of course, also to meet me.

We parted ways with Herb Zimmerman in Moline, Illinois, his home town. As we pushed on, we missed him, not only because he left a hole in the trombone trio and the vocal quartet but because we just missed him. We hadn't realized how much of a family we had become. Then we dropped off Verne Hutchinson at his home town in North Dakota. Same thing. It felt as though we were leaving our brothers behind. Next to go was Gary Graber, who returned to Washington State by bus from somewhere in Montana. Each time we lost a group member the rest of us had to pick up the slack because we were still preaching and performing. We became wearier and wearier. The last couple of days, after finishing our last evening meeting, I became totally exhausted and hoarse, and slept in the back of the car as Will Bruce and Harding took turns driving through the night back to Three Hills.

After resting for a few days at PBI, I had to make a decision about what to do next. One option was to stay on at Prairie and join Will Bruce in his department and continue on with the kind of work I had just been doing. It didn't take long to decline that offer. That would not help resolve the problem of my continuing and ever increasing religious doubt. As a faculty member I would have been given the fare to go home to rest and see my family, but having turned that down, I was still just a student and would have to find my own way home. I had almost no money and so I decided to hitch-hike all the way back to Chilliwack, BC.

For a day or two more at PBI, while waiting for a ride to Calgary, I tried to sum up my situation. I had rejected the ministry as a profession for the time being and had also rejected to stay on at PBI as a staff member. So what would I do? I was no longer sure of what in the Bible I *did* believe in or even what I definitely didn't. My faith was ebbing and flowing like the tide, beyond my control. I wasn't ready to give up on Christianity entirely, for there were plenty of good bits in the Bible and positive doctrines of the church that I embraced. I still sincerely believed, or at least hoped, that advanced studies in theology and further Bible study would help to resolve my doubt and strengthen my faith to the point where I could surrender to Christ completely. What I really needed to do next was to earn enough money to proceed with further religious study, perhaps at Wheaton College in Illinois or the Fuller Seminary in California.

The best prospects for work, for me, were in Vancouver and so that is where I decided I needed to go next. I had arranged a ride as far as Calgary with our PBI dairyman. He was glad to drive me

Three Hills (1950-1954)

as we had been quite friendly over my four years at PBI. After a pleasant drive and a nice visit, we parted ways in Calgary, my last contact with PBI.

Alternately sad and happy, but mostly just exhausted, I sat on my suitcase beside Highway #2 on the southern outskirts of Calgary waiting for a ride. I had plenty of time to ponder my situation and to explore the source of my wild mood oscillations. I mourned the faltering of my faith, my love that was leaving me. The anguish of the loss brought dry tears to my eyes. Then suddenly I became elated, rejoicing in the prospect of a lifting of the burden of a love gone sour. My jubilation brought on silent laughter. Back and forth I dithered, from agony to ecstasy, much like the main character in *By Grand Central Station I Sat Down and Wept*.[99]

Not only was I alternately sad and happy, I was also apprehensive and anxious. I was now leaving the safe haven of PBI and the comfort and camaraderie of the church. I was heading home. But 'home' was in name only, for there really was no home for me to go to. Our family had more or less dispersed. The house and one or two siblings were still there in Chilliwack, but after a brief visit it would be on to Vancouver to seek work. I was truly heading into unknown territory and I recalled what the Psalmist had asked, "How shall [I] sing the Lord's song in a strange land?"[100]

Lost deep in thought, I was startled out of my reverie by an approaching car, in fact a limousine, which pulled up beside me. As I stood up, the back window opened and a man in a dark suit and clerical collar called out to enquire after my destination and reason for being there. The moment he discovered that I was from PBI, he asked the chauffeur to stow my suitcase and violin in the trunk and asked me to join him in the back seat. After introductions, we immediately dived into deep discussion. He, a defrocked minister of the Congregational Church, was itching for a good theological debate, and knowing that I had just graduated from a highly regarded evan-

---

[99] Elizabeth Smart, *By Grand Central Station I Sat Down and Wept*, Flamingo (Harper and Collins) 1945.
[100] Psalms 137:4.

gelical institution, I would suffice. Here we were, two individuals who had read the Bible from cover to cover, had given our attention to problematic passages and had a thorough understanding of Christian doctrine. We had much to discuss. We argued about various interpretations of Bible verses and ferreted out each other's views on difficult and arcane doctrine. He was surprised that I was not at all as straight-laced as he might have assumed I would be, coming from conservative PBI, about which he knew a lot. I found his forthright declaration of somewhat heretical views refreshing, as I suspect he did mine.

We got along royally and chatted for hours on end. Most of our discussion centered around three core questions: (1) to what extent could and should the Bible and the Christian story be taken symbolically. My position was roughly that we should be selective about that, letting our intuition (Holy Spirit?) be our guide. His position was that we should take the entirety of the Christian message metaphorically. There was, for example, for him, no real heaven, only heaven on Earth (the kingdom of God is at hand); no real hell, only hell on Earth and in one's conscience; no real resurrection, only renewal of intention and commitment, and so on. (2) To what extent could University or Seminary studies strengthen one's faith and resolve doubts about the Bible and Christian doctrine? My answer was: considerably. His answer: not at all, in fact the opposite. (3) Can one be morally good without believing in God? My reply: probably. His reply: absolutely.

We had plenty of time to discuss all of this and we did, for my interlocutor was on his way home to a town in Washington State, perhaps Brewster. For dinner that evening, the three of us went to their favourite Chilli House restaurant in Spokane. The chauffer asked me how I would like my chilli con carne:

"I don't know." I replied, "I've never had it before."

"Interesting," the cleric interrupted, "You'll want it hot, of course..."

"Oh, yes!"

Whereupon he briefly disappeared to put in our order. After a while, the waiter appeared with our meals and plenty of ice-water. I put one spoonful of the chilli into my mouth, but couldn't chew or swallow, immediately realizing that 'hot' didn't mean temperature as I had intended. The two of them laughed hilariously as they handed me a dish to spit it out. The waiter, also laughing, was standing by with some cold water and a dish of 'mild' chilli, which was in fact delicious. After dinner we continued on until dusk. At my host's insistence, I agreed to let him put me up for the night in a motel which I couldn't have afforded on my own. I slept like a cat. The next day he also insisted that he drive me to the BC border at Osooyos, all the while discussing religion.

I somehow felt very much at ease in the company of this intelligent, knowledgeable man who had been thrown out of his ministry for his heretical views. When I revealed to him some of my secret pockets of disbelief he was not surprised, elated, nor condemnatory. When, for example, I told him that I didn't literally believe in hell, he simply said, "nor do I". This was the first time I had ever openly and freely conveyed to anyone my doubts and disbeliefs; and he seemed to think that it was all obvious and natural. It would still take me a few years to arrive at a religious position similar to his; and a few more after that to be free of religion altogether. But on this fortuitous, timely journey, I was taking huge strides in that direction, admitting to myself and for the first time someone else, that I was not a run-of-the-mill ordinary evangelical Christian as indeed was my upbringing and training but instead very much on the periphery of orthodoxy. I consider myself very lucky to have met this kind man at a very important time in my life. Then, I might have thought it was a Godsend but now I just think it was blind luck. We shook hands warmly as he dropped me off opposite Osooyos, BC. Unfortunately, even though he had a profound influence on my life, I never saw him or heard from him again.

From Osooyos I hitch-hiked home to Chilliwack, where I arrived late that evening. I remember very little about that segment of my journey except that my head was swimming with new ideas and new possibilities. I was tired, very tired, but at the same time elated. Deep down there was also apprehension. That I needed to go to work right away was obvious. I was broke and had a grand total of 25 cents to my name. For a day or two I rested in Chilliwack and pondered. I knew that soon I would be hitching a ride to Vancouver to seek work, but what kind of work and where would I go for my next round of schooling? I was now leaning more towards a secular education anyway and since I would need to keep working in order to pay for it, why not then, go to Normal School, to get teaching credentials and have a professional job to fall back on whenever needed? I thought that if I could still get accepted (for I was already way late in applying and classes were underway) and if I could get the tuition money somehow, then that is what I would do. I dashed off a letter to my brother-in-law, Nick Siebert, a successful farmer, still living back in La Glace, to ask if I could borrow the needed money (about $200). Believing that he would say yes, I decided to go ahead with my plan. Little did I realize at the time that this was a pivotal decision.

CHAPTER 5

Vancouver (1954-1963)

Normal School

ON AN EARLY Monday morning in late September, 1954, I hitched a ride into Vancouver from Chilliwack with a UBC student. He dropped me off at Cambie and 12th, then the site of the Vancouver Provincial Normal School, where I would test my luck at obtaining late admission. Shortly after 9 a.m. I entered the office of Tad Boyes, the principal, seeking admission one month after the application deadline had passed and indeed two weeks after classes had begun. I explained my situation. He then asked me if I was related to Peter and Martin who had both successfully completed their teacher training there a few years earlier. They, of course, were my brothers. Much to my relief, Mr. Boyes informed me that he would admit me, but there were four conditions I would have to meet: I had to submit a character reference; I had to get a part-time job to sustain myself; I had to come up with the tuition fees; and, finally, I had to obtain nearby accommodation to obviate the need for travel. None of that was going to be easy, but I had my foot in the door.

On the southeast corner of Cambie and 12th, kitty corner from the Normal School, stood an Esso gas station; beside that to the south was an Aristocratic drive-in restaurant. Hungry and anxious about how I was going to fulfill all four of those entry conditions in a short time, I took a seat in the restaurant and looked at the menu to see what I could afford to eat. There was a special on pancakes for 25 cents and so that's what I ordered, knowing full well that that was my last penny. The waitress offered me some coffee with the pancakes for only a nickel more. When I told her that I didn't have any more money, she just gave me the coffee anyway. There was nobody else in the restaurant and she seemed lonely and bored. In any case she wanted to chat. I asked her if she liked working there. She said she did because she had a very friendly boss and good work mates, except for one of the car hops who was messy and lazy. With that, I perked up and asked her if her boss was in and could I speak to him.

Thereupon I was ushered into the basement where 'Bud', the boss, was doing the books. I explained my situation and asked if he had a job for me. "As a matter of fact I do", he said. (Later I discovered that he had just fired the lazy car hop). He offered me 76 cents an hour and one free meal per shift, during slack time. Perfect, I thought, I wouldn't even have to buy groceries or cook. My working hours were to be 6:00 p.m. to midnight Monday to Thursday and 6:00 p.m. to 2:00 a.m. on Fridays and Saturdays with Sundays off. I then asked Bud if I might use his phone for a local call. I called up a certain Mr. Klassen, father of a fellow student of mine from PBI and minister of the local Mennonite church. Yes, he remembered me, and yes, he would be delighted to write me a character reference. He would send it along with his son who happened to be attending Normal School as well. Two conditions were now met; I was elated.

Without any money at all now, but at least with a full stomach, I made my way to the front door of a large two-storey house across the street from Vancouver City Hall. Not seeing any 'for rent' signs, it was rather audacious of me to expect there to be any lodging available in this prime location. But try I did. I rang with not much hope. A very pleasant man opened the door and invited me in. Once again, I explained my situation, telling him that I was a Bible school graduate, now hoping to become a teacher. I also told him that I had a job. He said that he didn't have any vacancies right now but he would at the end of the month. Excellent! I could improvise a place to stay for a week or so. He showed me the room, a small gable studio suite. It was perfect for me. So I decided that I would take it. He asked for a deposit to reserve the room. I told him that I had no money but that my word was enough. Apparently it was. Not only did he take my promise as a deposit, he said that his daughter could sleep on the couch for a week and that I could take her room immediately. What extraordinary luck!

I left my much travelled suitcase and violin at the house and headed back to Normal School. It was only 10:30 a.m. and I had already met three of the four conditions, all but the tuition money. I went in to see Mr. Boyes again to tell him the good news. I argued that I was quite sure that I would get the loan from Nick Siebert and failing that I would come up with the tuition one way or another, coming from a large family as I did. At that point Boyes shook his head and smiled, "Come with me, I'll take you to your class." That night, I learned how to balance two four foot long and six inch wide food trays, one on my shoulder and one by my side, loaded with freshly prepared food, to carry out to the cars. That evening I also had a double cheese burger, fries, and a strawberry milkshake for my supper and collected nearly two dollars in tips. I was on top of the world.

I was not exactly wealthy but I was managing quite well. The cheeseburger, fries, and milkshake combo would come to be known as the 'Sunday Special'. Because I didn't work on Sundays, I didn't get the free meal. And on some weekends I just didn't have enough money to buy food. The back garden of the house I lived in was contiguous with the parking lot of the restaurant at the corners. I could position myself in the garden corner such that I could signal the cook and have the on-duty car hop bring me my free 'Sunday Special' without anybody the wiser. We were all very friendly and helped each other out and word never got back to Bud, the boss. After doing this for a while, conscience got the better of me and I had to tell Bud that I owed him for about eight meals. He just laughed it off and said "If you work in a restaurant and go hungry, you've got to be quite stupid." In fact he gave me a raise so that I could afford to pay for my Sunday Specials. It wasn't likely just pity though, as I worked very hard for him, and he knew it.

Relatively speaking, the academic workload at Normal School was not all that demanding. As a rule, I could do the required homework between 4:00 and 6:00 p.m., after which I went to work at the Aristocratic. Not having to travel any distance sure helped. Getting up at 8:00 a.m., after seven hours of sleep, left me with little time for anything else but my job and my studies. I couldn't even squeeze in my daily half hour of devotional time, prayer, and Bible reading, as had been my typical practice. The only free time I had was on Saturday and Sunday afternoon, using that time to catch up on sleep, housework, homework, and on occasion recreation.

Normal School was intended to prepare us for teaching all subjects in an elementary school, although one could specialize in one of the three 'platooning' subjects of art, music, and physical education. I chose to emphasize the teaching of music, having already studied much of that at PBI. It was while participating in musical events that I met my good friend, David Janzen. Even though I knew that he had declared himself a non-believer and had been repudiated by the church (he had come from a similar background) and even though he knew that I had just graduated from PBI, that didn't seem to matter to either of us. We just clicked. Even though we were constantly together, we very seldom talked about religion or the church. We often went to symphony concerts together on Sunday afternoons, he sitting near the front with the ticket holders, I in the vacant seats at the back or on the steps as a reward for ushering for the MacMillan Club. We went to movies together, seeing the 'Student Prince', still one of my favourite movies, at least four or five times until we had the lines memorized. We experimented with smoking and drinking. We walked the streets and later in the year we became roommates. We have been close friends ever since.

David was also my partner for the spring major practicum at Florence Nightingale School, where he and I took over the class of Mr. Mahr, who once he saw us in action, disappeared from the scene for almost the entire six weeks. We also taught music to the grade 4 to 6 classes. Half the time we were teaching and half the time we observed and criticized each other. We made a good team.

Besides music, we also taught other subjects. I remember the time when I was teaching a Grade 6 boys Social Studies class and I discovered that the students became very interested in the crusades about which I was teaching them. Perhaps that was because I myself had found a good book on the subject and was myself very interested. I used lots of pictures, maps, and medieval gadgets to supplement the lesson. I put a review of the previous day's lesson on one blackboard and an overview of today's on another. When I walked to the front of the classroom, the boys immediately stopped their chatter, eager to learn. I began with some review questions about the previous lesson and just as the boys' arms shot up, in walked Mr. Truax, my supervisor from Normal School, to observe the class and write a report on my teaching. Even though I was nervous about that, I put on the cool, as I had done so many times before in public appearances, pretending that Mr. Truax wasn't there. The lesson came off with vigour and panache.

As David took over the next class, I was summoned by Mr. Truax to a quiet corner of the school for a verbal assessment of my teaching performance. I recall three things that he said: "Well organized material. Don't overdo the enthusiasm or you will burn out too quickly. Aren't you glad that you have found your profession?". I was overwhelmed. Was it really true that my talent and my 'calling' was teaching rather than the ministry? Was teaching my end game rather than my transition strategy? These serious questions immediately stared me in the face. A few simple off-the-cuff remarks often have deep implications. The words, "Aren't you glad you found your profession" kept ringing in my head for days and weeks to come.

One facet of my Normal School experience foreshadowed my later interest in moral education, which turned out to be both the focus of my PhD dissertation and my research in University. Our PE instructor, Lorne Brown, asked us to write a paper on a choice of topics, one of which was, "The character of viceroys of the Empire was developed on the playing fields of Eton" (echoing Wellington who said that "Waterloo was won on the playing fields of Eton"). The idea is that attributes of character such as honesty, co-operation, perseverance, and equality could be fostered by playing games and sports. I agreed that this was the case and that PE was not just a peripheral subject for the purpose of 'blowing off steam', but was part of a well-rounded curriculum. Even early on in my secular teaching career I was interested in moral development as separate from religion.

This reorientation from preaching to teaching was part of a huge ground shift that took place during that year at Normal School. If teaching indeed was going to be my profession then my further education would need to be centred on a secular university rather than a seminary or Bible college. I hadn't even thought about further theological studies for months. In fact, it had been many months since I had given up regular prayer, Bible reading, church-going and other church-related activity. And I didn't even feel guilty. The world hadn't collapsed because I didn't go to church anymore; I wasn't at a loss psychologically or spiritually because I didn't pray anymore; I didn't lose inspiration and love of literature because I didn't read the Bible anymore; and I didn't walk around with a guilt complex because I tried drinking alcohol, smoking, and going to movies. In fact, I enjoyed those things.

I did perhaps feel a bit guilty for being a hypocrite in that occasionally I would attend IVCF (Inter Varsity Christian Fellowship) meetings at noon on Fridays and conduct the choir. But I gave that up too. When at Easter the IVCF was to put on an Easter program (including the singing of 'The Church's One Foundation'), I bowed out at the last minute and asked my old friend, Jake, to take over instead. Never again did I attend IVCF meetings. I felt wonderfully liberated. The burden of religion was lifting like a disappearing morning fog. I still had my struggles with religious doubts and 'pockets of disbelief' were still there but it didn't really matter anymore. Overnight, well actually over a period of about six months, religion had become more or less irrelevant. Being so busy that I didn't have time to commit to my devotions or go to church regularly ended up being fortuitous. Away from the flock, I was free to see the world and think for myself. Being preoccupied with my new vocation, teaching, and having a good friend to share new experiences with helped me to escape the clutches of the church. Quickly the year came to a close. Having more or less dropped religion for the time being and focusing entirely on my new-found profession, I eagerly signed up for more courses at UBC Summer School and prepared to send out applications for a teaching position. I was brimming with confidence, having successfully completed my year at Normal School and ready to face the world.

Elementary School Teaching

IN THE MID-SUMMER of 1955 I got my grades from Normal School. I received a 'most promising' notation, the highest assessment given. I then immediately applied to West Vancouver district for a job as an elementary school teacher with a specialty in music education. At that time North and West Vancouver were one district. I was called to an interview with a Mr. Lucas, superintendent of the combined districts. The job in question was teaching music in West Vancouver. Mr. Lucas asked me how I could teach music without being able to play the piano. I told him that children copying singing, which I *could* do, was a better teaching device. I then demonstrated my point by having him sing a new song by copying me. He saw my point and hired me on the spot. I was to report to John Allen at Hollyburn Elementary School in West Van. Mr. Allen, a stern disciplinarian, was happy to have on board another male teacher to mitigate the preponderance of female teachers in his and indeed most elementary schools.

Since the majority of the teachers at this school, including me, had only temporary teaching certificates, becoming permanent only after two years of successful teaching, we were all worried about random inspections by senior administrators. Even as I got nicely settled into my new classroom, there was always the possibility of

My first class as teacher in elementary school

an unexpected intrusion. At any time a principal, superintendent, district teaching supervisor or any of a number of senior bureaucrats could come into the classroom uninvited and without warning and do an assessment. What the inspector sees is recorded and reported to the board who hired you, no matter if it is a good day or a bad one. Let me add that there really are good days and bad days, even for the very best teachers. In one or two 40 minute periods, your dreams of a happy successful career in teaching could be made or broken. Even if the review process exists for good reason, beginning teachers, good or bad, confident in their skills or not, are understandably terrified of the inspection process. Our staff talked of the 'Lucas terror'. Mr. Lucas, it turned out, was actually quite a fine, kind, and intelligent man, worthy of respect, but that made no difference. We were terrified.

Yet, I do not think I fared all that badly with the inspectors. In fact their reports stood me in good stead and actually helped me in promotions and scholarships. However, still, the experience was entirely too stressful. It is unfortunate that these random inspections have to be done in such a psychologically damaging manner. Why couldn't the inspector make an appointment and let the teacher prepare both physically and emotionally, allowing the teacher to perform at his or her best, rather than potentially having that all important assessment on a misfortunate Monday morning misfire? I'm not suggesting that I know the exact answer of how to do a reliable, accurate, and fair assessment of a teacher's quality. However I would like to suggest that administrators, frequently make important judgments of a teacher's performance based on inadequate information and/or the wrong criteria.

In fact, what principals and inspectors like to do is grade teachers on criteria that are not central to the achievement of education. Schooling is not really about teaching, but about the achievement of education, the improvement of the mind through the acquisition of knowledge and understanding. It is a long and subtle process. Too often, inspectors (principals, supervisors, superintendants, and other adjudicators) focus on more tangible peripherals such as classroom control, student interest, parental satisfaction, staff cohesion, student socialization, student neatness and work habits, all of which are somewhat important but only as aids to helping with mastering the content, the real goal in education, not just the appearance of it. It is of no small consequence that in my ten years of public school teaching, having taught at just about every level (Grades 3 to 12) and every subject (save Home Economics, Latin, Typing and Industrial Education), I was never ever asked about or criticized for the *content* of what I was teaching, the most significant feature of the entire enterprise.

Westcot School staff, 1957

Just as stressful and full of tension were parent-teacher interviews. What do you say to caring enquiring parents whose children are of only moderate ability and capacity and are performing only at a mediocre level despite good work habits and effort?

I had given my best in that first four months of my teaching career. Feeling somewhat spent, I was eager for the Christmas break. Because my parents and siblings had been so generous to me over the years spent at PBI and because this was the first time in a long while that I actually had some extra money, I decided to give everyone in the family, including nieces and nephews, a Christmas present. At that time I was sharing an upstairs suite with Bev Johnson at 1325 W 13th Ave in Vancouver. The wrapping and mailing was a huge job, for mine was a big family. Bev had already gone home to Chilliwack for Christmas. Down the hall from us lived a pretty nurse named Jean who, when she saw me carry in my huge pile of presents, offered to help me. So there we were, late into the night singing Christmas carols, wrapping gifts and writing notes and addresses. The next day, after mailing the presents, I boarded a bus for the very long journey via LA to Atlanta, Georgia to visit the young lady with whom I became engaged. We already know how that turned out.

On the long return trip from Atlanta I was troubled with misgivings about what I had done. It was easy to fake allegiance to my former faith and to share in her family worship in church. I even sang a solo on Christmas Eve. The truth is that I didn't know where I stood or what I believed after a year or so of not participating in religious practices at all. I was puzzled and restless. On the trip home from Atlanta, I composed the poem, 'Discontent', which represents the state of mind I was in at the time.

Discontent (1956)

Tranquil sleeps the winter earth;
No hint as yet the spring's rebirth.
The grass is brown and dead;
From trees the leaves are shed;

And fallowed fields lie silently at rest
While man roves anxiously in quest
Of myriad mysterious somethings
Surging violent in his breast.

The shrubs are bare and brown;
Their strength is gone, the sap is down.
Bent branches groan, but do not moan
That oft they're blown
By winter's wind.
They clamour not for unseasonable green;
Patient, they wait by the frozen stream.

The motionless river moves along
Croaking its icy winter song;
Winding its way where it is led
By meaningless twists of the riverbed.

Proudly beside the roads and streams
Long telephone poles reach from the ground
High up and beyond
Where the only faint sound
Is the empty echo of men's spent dreams.
They yearn not for branches when they are dead
Nor sigh for leaves to crown their head,
The earth beneath, though trodden down
By restless man, still does not frown.

Nature does not fret and plan;
Striving troubles only man,
Depletes his joy
And shrinks his span.

Content is nature to be nature,
To be none other than it is –
A tree, a tree; a field a field;

Back from Damascus: Leaving Religion Behind

Cloud, cloud,
Sod, sod,
But man, not man;
He wants to be a God.

In late summer of 1956, before beginning my second year of teaching at Wescot, I responded to an ad offering reduced room and board in exchange for gardening help and house chores. I was accepted. That is how I got a plum position in a big house and garden on the corner of 33rd and Arbutus, a very nice area of the city, where Miss Jean Storey and her aging father lived. By saving on rent, in a very short time I was able to afford a car which increased my sense of freedom and allowed me to explore my surroundings and engage in more '*verboten*' activities, such as dancing, dating, and drive-in movies.

In one of my journals of that time, an entry for Monday, May 21, 1957, reads:

My first car (1952 Chev), 1957

> On this May Day holiday, I am studying poetry and composition for an upcoming Sr. Matric English exam (I was taking English 100 at night school). Yesterday, after not having attended church for several

months,[101] I suddenly felt a strong urge to attend. Perhaps this urge was just for more social contact, but I wanted to find that in a church setting. (Nostalgia? Camaraderie of brotherhood?) So yesterday I went to Trinity Baptist Church (on Granville and 49th) with Jean Storey and Mr. Storey. The morning service was very inspiring. The message was "Peter and the waves; steadily through the storm". I decided that I had been in a storm, but needn't be any longer.

In the afternoon I took Walter (brother) for a drive in my newly acquired grey '51 Chevrolet two-door.

In the evening, I went back to church, this time to a young people's meeting. I met many fine young people including Harley Harris and John Gunnell. I liked the pastor a lot for his humanity, affability, and humour. He drove me home after the service and offered to listen to my problems and personal convictions. My ambitions, I told him, was to teach theology.

I was falling back on what was known and comfortable.

In any case I continued attending Trinity and before long was asked to join the choir. Eventually I became the leading bass, also singing in small groups and performing solos. A number of the solos were the same ones that I had sung on tour with PBI, numbers such as 'I Walked Today where Jesus Walked', 'How Great Thou Art', and 'So This is Life'. I recall on one occasion when singing 'Let us Break Bread Together' that my mind wandered and I sang "When I fall on my face..." (instead of knees) "With my knees (instead of face) to the rising sun..." I had hoped that nobody had noticed the embarrassing gaffe. It appeared for a while that I had gotten away with it, for I got no strange looks and I didn't observe any unusual stirring, but later when I shook hands with the pastor, he whispered "I noticed" and we had a good laugh.

---

101   It was, in fact, except for a bit of experimentation with Anglican, Presbyterian and Unitarian church services, not since September, 1954 that I had attended regularly.

I soon joined Trinity Baptist Church as a regular member, simply by transferring my membership from the Mennonite Church, where I had been baptised as required. I was accepted into the congregation on the pastor's recommendation even though he knew that I was no longer an orthodox believer. He seemed to suggest that we all have our areas of doubt and disbelief and that was not something to overly worry about. I sure went along with that and began to enjoy the social outlet that the church provided. For a year, I even formed and conducted a children's choir, which performed in the church from time to time. I gave up regular church attendance and participation a few years later when my UBC studies became more demanding.

UBC – Discovering Philosophy

WITH THE COMPLETION of English 100, taken as a night school course at King Edward High School, I completed in June of 1956 what was then called Senior Matriculation, the equivalent of first year University. Eventually I would go on to earn my BA degree in 1960. Courses for my second and third years were taken at more night school and Summer School sessions. Each summer, for the years 1956 through 1959, I took two courses in Summer School (July and August) and one course in the evening while teaching (September to June). In my final year I resigned from full time teaching, taking a half-time position as the principal's aide, so that I could take full time day courses on campus.

It was a very busy time for me. On Monday, Wednesday, and Friday mornings, and Tuesday and Thursday afternoons I was teaching the principal's class at Glenmore School in West Vancouver. That meant that for each of those days I had to race by car from UBC across town to West Vancouver or vice versa during noon hour, typically eating my lunch in the car en route. After all that running around, when I finished my final exam to earn my Bachelor's degree in May of 1960, I swore that I would never darken another University door again. However, that resolve soon weakened and by late June I was enrolled in a Master's degree program at the University of Washington in Seattle.

I had always been enamored by the word 'philosophy', literally meaning 'love of wisdom', but it wasn't until I started into my second year of coursework at UBC that I started to study it formally. That would change my life. How I stumbled into taking Philosophy 100, I'm not sure but as soon as I heard my instructor, B. Savery, speak I knew I had come upon a winner of a subject. I was enthralled. Savery's lectures were simply excellent. Every word that he said seemed to be brilliant, truly filled with wisdom. It was as if he had planned the course just for me. I absorbed everything he said, writing copious notes at first and then abandoning that lest I miss a word. I wasn't worried about the exam results; should I fail it wouldn't matter as this was all too good to miss. It seemed futile in any case to write it all down. Surely I could remember the priceless things said about the autonomy of ethics, the nature of metaphysics, and the distinction between knowledge and belief. It was a wonderful relief to know that a recognized philosopher could be so clearly articulating out loud ideas that I myself had been struggling with. Now these same ideas came out of the fog in brilliant clarity. My experience with Philosophy 100 must have been much like Emerson's when he wrote:

> *In every work of genius we recognize our own rejected thoughts; they come back to us with a certain alienated majesty.*[102]

Not only did this fine philosophy course help me to clarify what I already believed but it also stimulated me to study the subject further and to help me change my mind on a number of nagging issues, particularly those surrounding religion and ethics. For example, I received much insight from Plato where he inquires whether holiness is holy because the gods loved it or whether the gods loved holiness because

---

102   R.W. Emmerson, 'Self Reliance'.

it was holy.[103] I came away with the conviction that we didn't need God and religion in order to be good, and if one can be good without religion, why even bother with the rest of all the confusing dogma? Such thoughts thrilled me, and to think that I had almost come to that conclusion on my own through my own personal struggle with religion. I say 'almost', for I had repressed that thought because I didn't have enough confidence in my own mental ability. A fellow student also taking the course, with whom I became friends, had a similar eye-opening experience. He and I, after class ended at noon, often grabbed a sandwich and headed down to the beach, near campus, to discuss the lectures. We didn't even bother doing all the reading but spent hours and hours on those beaches discussing philosophy, sometimes agreeing with our professor and each other and sometimes not.

When exam time came, it wasn't at all certain that we were ready. We didn't care. That in itself was liberating. Discovering philosophy in this way made it a delight. We felt that our money and effort were well spent no matter what the outcome on the exam. When I finally saw the exam questions, it all seemed too easy. Maybe we had misunderstood something or missed the point. The results were that both my new friend and I were awarded a 'first class'. We had not missed the point. That summer, I had not only made a new friend but found a new subject that would come to dominate my educational and professional life, a subject that I would eventually come to teach.

Secondary School Teaching in Vancouver

MY PATTERN of studies at UBC at this time, namely one evening course during the school year and two more during the summer, continued for the next two years. Because I needed at least one major and one minor in teachable subjects to teach at the High School

---

103   Plato, from the dialogue 'Euthyphro', sections 9-11, from *The Dialogues of Plato*, Random House, New York 1892 and 1920.

level, which I had in mind to try at some point, I decided to major in English and minor in German. However, I also pursued a major in my new favourite subject, philosophy. I had no idea at the time, but that turned out to be a very good career move. Musically, my interest in singing and teaching children to sing was waning, while my interest in orchestral music was increasing. I was still singing in the Trinity Church Choir and the Vancouver Bach Choir, but I would give up both of those over the course of the next two years. I also gave up my position, and tenure, in West Vancouver. Not only was my interest in teaching music waning, I also wanted to work in Vancouver to be closer to UBC (all that frantic commuting was getting to me), not to mention that I wanted to distance myself from the stress of working in that tense environment with that principal back in West Vancouver. He had a knack for making a stressful job even more stressful by keeping his entire staff on edge. When I informed him of my resignation, he snarled "You can't do that!" I told him that I had already done so.

"I don't mean that; it's just a shame that you are chasing philosophy and all that and not carrying on with your God given talent to teach music to children." It didn't matter what he thought; the die was already cast.

I got a position at Southlands School in Vancouver as a regular Grade 6 teacher, which did not include the teaching of music, and was actually less stressful, even though I somehow got on the wrong side of the principal there as well. I think it had something to do with giving Terry the strap. Back then public education still used corporal punishment and the prescribed method was 'the strap'. Even before I had met the class for the first time, I was warned by the principal that there was a boy in my class named Terry who was a problem from a behavioral standpoint. I told him that I typically had no problems with classroom control and not to worry about it. Well, we were not ten days into the new school year when the showdown with Terry inevitably came.

We had just finished a spelling lesson and the class was at work on an assignment while I, at my desk, had the children come up one by one with their spelling scribbler for me to mark. When I called on Terry, he got up from his back seat in the middle row, walked half way up the aisle, and then, looking me square in the eye, elbowed another student in the head. After marking his scribbler, I told Terry that that kind of bullying was intolerable and strictly forbidden. Adding "Do you understand!" for emphasis. "Yes, sir!" said Terry. He then walked back to his desk on the other aisle, stopped halfway and elbowed poor Munro in the other ear. I, of course, was watching carefully and in a flash was beside Terry, took hold of his shirt, and said "Come with me." I took him to the principal's office, sat him down, and told him to wait. I then went to look for the principal. When I found him, I asked him to come back to the office to witness a strapping. An observer was a legal requirement. As we walked back to the office, he warned me that I would have to deal with Terry's father, which, seemingly unlike the principal, I was prepared to do.

I gave Terry a strapping, three lashes (not the maximum allowable) on the palm of each hand. I then escorted him back to the classroom, tears still in his eyes. The hush in the classroom was palpable. We went back to work and not too surprisingly the whole class was well behaved from then on. A week or so later I met Terry's father. He had volunteered to drive part of the boys' softball team, which I happened to coach, to an interschool competition.

When I met him, he said "So, you had a run-in with my son?"

"Yes, I gave him three of my finest on each hand."

"It was about time," is all he said.

From then on, Terry was a model student and his grades even improved. At the end of the school year, I got my standard principal's evaluation which was perfect save for 'discipline' (classroom control). When I challenged him on this, suggesting that I had rather good discipline in my class, he said "But you achieved it by using the strap. That suggests you are not a perfect disciplinarian." Hmm, perhaps he had a point.

Terry's was the only case where I used corporeal punishment in all my many years of teaching. Am I proud of what I did? Not really. Do I feel guilty about it? No. The use of the strap for severe cases of misbehaviour was the practice at that time whether or not one deems it effective or ethical. In any case as long as it is done within that cultural context and that there is no lasting damage, physical or otherwise, it is allowable. For punishment to be effective, it has to be predictable, consistent, and fair. I wouldn't even consider using physical punishment today, not only because it is now illegal but also because I think of it as reprehensible. In just one generation, the *zeitgeist* on punishment has shifted dramatically. I believe it is for the better.

After two years of teaching at Southlands, and as my University credits started to pile up, I asked for and got a transfer to Prince of Wales Secondary school. There I found that administrators can be very affable, non-threatening, and sometimes even helpful. I found teaching at the secondary school level to be altogether more enjoyable and rewarding than at the elementary level. Part of that was a better camaraderie amongst the staff owing to a more balanced gender split and part of it was a more sophisticated level of subject matter. Even though philosophy wasn't a regular course subject, I was able to start an extra-curricular Philosophy Club, using A. Stroll's *Philosophy Made Simple* as a text. It was a great joy to see these young minds grasping really profound ideas.

Not only did I find teaching and studying more enjoyable, but my social life also took on new dimensions. At UBC, in a German course, I met and immediately liked a young lady who was also a teacher working on her degree.[104] I was attracted to her for her carefree manner, her intelligence, her great shape, her sparkling eyes, and her pleasant smile. She was of Mennonite background and so we understood each other in many ways. We dated on and off for a year or two, and while we never openly discussed it, I suspect that we were both considering marriage. I liked her enough to ask her to be my date at my UBC graduation dinner and dance at the Commodore on Granville. However, shortly after that I stopped seeing her, for we so often ended up quarreling over religion and philosophy.

---

104 At that time, one could become a public school teacher at the Elementary level with only Normal School teacher training and without having a full degree. Now, both are required before one can teach in either Elementary or Secondary School.

Graduation, B.A., UBC, 1960

I was beginning to think that I would never meet a woman suitable for me. In an attempt to widen my contact with women outside of the church, I had for several years in my early teaching career, taken up dancing. After having taken lessons at the Arthur Murray Studio, I regularly danced on Saturday nights at the YWCA. Sometimes I took a date, but more often I just went on my own and danced with other singles. I quickly learned that the women who showed up to dance didn't show up to talk philosophy. That was quite alright though, for I also learned that there is exquisite joy in well coordinated movement to the rhythm of music.

Dating, dancing, doing dinners, and driving a car all cost money. So does going to university and church. Despite my reasonable teaching salary, I found that I was often short so I took the opportunity to earn a little bit here and there with odd jobs and to apply for scholarships. I did gratefully get some scholarship money, two from the Vancouver Elementary School Teacher's Association to attend Summer School, and a Walter Gage (Dean of Men) scholarship, but they didn't amount to much. In addition to my summer school attendance, I sometimes worked at the PNE (Pacific

National Exhibition) during the last two weeks of August. So for holidays, I only got the usual statutory holidays and one week each at Christmas and Easter.

In early July, 1959, I came across an ad placed by the West Point United Church inviting applications for a singing quartet to replace the regular choir during the summer holidays. The church was offering something like $25 per week for only one rehearsal and two performances, Sunday morning and evening. I applied for and got the job as the bass singer, with Jerry from the Vancouver opera chorus singing tenor, Marjory, later to sing in the Sadler Wells opera company in the UK (and fellow Normal School graduate) took the alto role and I can't remember who sang soprano. The work was easy, the pay was good, and it was very enjoyable. We sang well known hymns but also such numbers as Haydn's 'The Heavens are Telling', Mendelssohn's 'How Lovely are the Dwellings Fair' and pieces by Mozart. We also all took turns singing solos. In fact, it didn't seem like work at all. I would have done it for free, as I had so many times in the past, if I hadn't needed the extra cash.

Later in the summer after a morning service in which I had sung a solo, a lady approached me to compliment me on my singing and to remark "I can tell that you really mean it when you sing". I thanked her and quickly removed myself from the scene. However, those words stayed with me. I sat in my car, numb, for a few moments before driving off. The truth of it was that I couldn't even remember what I had just sung; it was all so mechanical, just a stage act done for pay and for fun. Yet here, I was unintentionally involved in the process of religious indoctrination, a religion I didn't really believe in anymore and a process that I was beginning to dislike. It occurred to me that this was just as hypocritical as being a fake pastor, preaching the gospel without really believing it. Why did I not then refuse to sing about Christ as I had previously refused to be a professional preacher? I realized that I now was doing it primarily for the aesthetics rather than the religious message so I decided that in the future if I were to perform these numbers again, it would be in a concert hall where the music was meant to be enjoyed for its own sake rather than in a church where the words were actually meant to be believed.

I carried through with that decision. After my contract with West Point United had run out a few weeks later, I never again sang for pay in a church. I also quit singing in the choir at Trinity Baptist. As a matter of fact, I quit going to church on a regular basis altogether. Except for weddings, funerals and special celebratory services I have not attended church for the sake of church since the fall of 1959. The time had come for me to declare myself a non-believer, a non-theist. It was also time to stop lending support in many subtle ways to an institution that I believed did more harm than good. It was time for me to lend my support and action to those institutions such as secular schools and universities and humanitarian organizations that could alleviate the damage done by religion.

Not only did I sever ties with Trinity Church but also with the Storey's fine house, not having time for gardening anymore. After finishing up my stint as half-time principal's relief in West Van, I moved around a bit, including a summer stint at the University of Washington in Seattle, working towards a Masters of Education. I took some counselling and administration courses along with some philosophy and psychology of education, only to find out that counselling or administration weren't for me. In the fall of 1960, I returned to a pleasant suite at 4407 Puget Drive in Vancouver and to teaching high school at Prince of Wales.

I now had a permanent secondary teaching certificate, tenure with the Vancouver school board, and felt very comfortable and successful in my profession. Without all of my other distractions, I now had both a little bit of leisure time on my hands and some money to spend, both of which were quite new to me. I enjoyed my new found free time by resting, reading, listening to music, and taking trips in my car down to the beautiful Oregon coast or up to the warm and sunny Okanagan. I purchased a fine Saba, German made stereo system, and records to go with it. I bought a number of books, including Hutchinson's, major collection of 'Great Books of the Western World'. Just before Thanksgiving, I also bought a new car, this time a Buick.

Immediately after school closed for the Thanksgiving holiday, I drove off to Penticton, BC, to visit my friend David, getting there late Friday evening. Early Saturday morning David and I drove on to

Pullman, Washington to visit Glen Franklin, who was studying German and Russian at the so-called 'Cow College' (Washington State University, Pullman). I had become friends with Glen earlier that summer in Seattle, where we were roommates in the University of Washington dorm. In Pullman we listened to music, chased girls, and true to Cow College form, drank lots of beer. We also drove across the Idaho border to Moscow to see a typical game of American College Football in a huge bowl, complete with pep band, cheerleaders, junk food, more beer (of course), team hats, banners – the works. On Sunday, David and I returned to Penticton, and I left Monday morning to drive back to Vancouver. On my way through Manning Park, high in the southern BC mountains, it began to snow heavily. The roads became treacherous. Numerous cars were stuck or in the ditches. Several times I stopped to assist hapless drivers put chains on their tires. I myself had no chains, nor even snow tires. I warily weaved my way through the mess, relying on good ol' prairie know how – it wasn't the first time that I had to deal with snow. I had a heavy car, which meant traction. At 8 a.m. on Tuesday morning when I arrived at school for work, the salesman from Brown Brothers, from whom I had bought the car, was pacing about in the school parking lot eager to intercept me before my entering the school. He told me that he had let me drive off the lot without signing the papers and that the Buick was not technically mine until I did. Apparently I had done that whole trip in a 'stolen car'. Good thing I didn't smash it up or have any dealings with the police stateside.

Getting Married

MORE THAN ONCE I had been told by my siblings and friends that I had set the bar too high when it came to standards for a marriage partner. I didn't think so. I told myself that I would rather stay single than marry the wrong person and I was actually beginning to think that single life wasn't all that bad anyway, though my real preference was to get married. The person I hoped to meet and marry would have to be physically attractive; but that was not enough. I also wanted someone who was intelligent, well educated, artistic, and generally sophisticated in the ways of the world. She would have to come from a good family. I was hoping that this person would also have interests similar to mine: perhaps a talent and ability in music, in books, ideas, conversation, and in other arts. I was looking for friendship in addition to attraction. She would also have to have similar political, social, and moral values. Maybe my siblings and friends were right after all, but I would settle for nothing less.

And then I found her. It was shortly before Christmas 1960, when my roommate at the time, Harley Harris, asked me to go on a blind date with him and his girlfriend Mary Babcock. Mary's friend, also Mary, had just returned for Christmas holidays from London, where she was attending the prestigious London School of Economics. I had been on a few blind dates before and had found them to be rather disappointing. I almost said no. But then I thought that it might be interesting to talk about and learn something about London; at least an LSE student would likely be intelligent and well spoken. I reluctantly agreed to go and that is how I met Mary Hamilton, who would, the following year, among other things, agree to drop the last two syllables of her name in exchange for an extra 'm'.

Mary lived with her Aunt and Uncle, Sue and Ron McKinnon, in a large house in the West Point Grey area of Vancouver, her own parents having died tragically in a plane crash years before. Mary and I clicked immediately and she had me over to the McKinnon's house several times during that holiday season. We saw each other almost every day. Mary did indeed come from a fine home and she did indeed have all of those qualities that I was looking for. She even played the piano, and played well, and we made music together. Those were intense days of getting to know each other. We were falling in love. The big question for me now was whether I should propose marriage or not. Surely a few weeks is not enough time in which to get to know a person, but what more did I really need to know? Would our love endure? Nobody knows the answer to that. All I knew was that she would soon be going back to school and

I would have to act if I wanted our love to continue. Being apart would test the strength of our commitment but we could write to each other and if our nascent love survived we could get married in the summer. As I pondered these matters, the libretto from 'Some Enchanted Evening' kept forcing itself upon my consciousness:

> *And somehow you know / you know even then.*
> *That somewhere you'll see her / again and again.*
>
> *Then fly to her side / and make her your own.*
> *Or all through your life you / may dream all alone.*
>
> *Once you have found her / never let her go.*
> *Once you have found her / never let her go!*[105]

So the night before Mary flew back to London, on January 10th 1961, I did propose and she accepted.

Then began a furious six month period of air mail correspondence, with a few phone calls too. We discussed anything and everything under the sun from art to literature to politics, from ethics and economics to birth control and religion. And, of course, we made wedding plans. We also planned a honeymoon tour in continental Europe. On February 19, I wrote the following in a letter to Mary:

> *I am overjoyed that our communication has by all appearances been successful and that we are in agreement on so many subjects and that we are understanding each other better. Not at any time since our last evening together here (i.e. Vancouver) have I been so delightfully content that we will be a very happy couple and that we were extremely wise in taking advantage of a good thing when we saw and experienced it.*

---

105 "Some Enchanted Evening" is a show tune from the 1949 Rodgers and Hammerstein musical *South Pacific*.

Cornel and Mary, July 22, 1961

On Saturday morning, July 22 1961, we were married in an Anglican church in Hampstead, London, with a very traditional ceremony. Mary even promised to "obey" me, although she verbally stumbled when actually saying the word. After a reception, hosted by Mary's landlords, we took a train to Dover, arriving early enough to check in to our hotel and visit Dover Castle before it closed. Wanting to squeeze out every minute there, we almost got locked in the castle when closing time arrived. The key was already in the door when the gatekeeper noticed us.

The next morning we ferried to Calais, where we rented a Renault Dauphine car and began our month long tour of Europe, visiting many interesting places in France, Germany, Austria, and Italy. Not only did we see the typical tourist sites including cities with great architecture, monuments, museums, and galleries but also many unusual places in more remote areas. We even took in a Strauss performance on the shores of the Bodensee at the foot of the Alps in Germany. The performance however didn't live up to the amazing setting and we, in fact, walked out. We took to the practice of scouring the backroads for 'pensions' or '*Gasthäuser*' (bed and breakfast style lodging) which worked out very well for us, allowing us to meet and interact with the locals who would drop by these kinds of places for their evening beer. The fact that I was fluent in German didn't hurt any. In the mornings we would drive back into the bigger cities to view what they had to offer and to discover each place's unique claim to fame. One of the highlights of this tour was the Salzburg Festival, for which we had planned long in advance and managed to get tickets to important orchestral and operatic performances. I still to this day get chills when I recall George Szell conducting the Vienna Philharmonic Orchestra, performing Beethoven's Fifth Symphony. He had loaded up the double bass section (to 14, I believe) to fully explore the vibrancy and majesty of the third movement. Amazing!

Married life was going smoothly so far. I was having a wonderful time. In fact, I had been on cloud nine since the previous Christmas when I had first met Mary. It seemed that life had come together beautifully and I had at last found bliss, contentment, and great hope for the future. Dream had become reality. It seemed as if it was all too good to be true. Of course it was all too good to be true as no marriage can keep up with its initial rapture, its idealized form. The first dark cloud appeared on the horizon in the small town of Feldkirch, near Bregenz, Austria.

Mary had for a few days been suffering from a stomach ailment despite taking medicine prescribed by a doctor. Because we had prepaid for our seats at a performance and at her insistence, we pushed on until we got to Bregenz. After Bregenz, with no appointments looming, we decided to take some time off just to rest. We checked in at a hotel in Feldkirch, rested in the afternoon, and then went out for the evening meal. We found a restaurant with a nice outdoor garden seating. Mary requested that I, since she didn't speak German, ask the waiter to omit any fat in her meal, owing to her upset stomach. I thought I had done so, but when our meals arrived, apparently there was still too much fat present in the food. In retrospect, I suppose that I should have refused the food and reordered; but having been brought up to eat whatever is set before one, and not having ever rejected food before, I began to eat my meal. Mary started on hers too; but after only having nibbled at it, she suddenly dropped her utensils, got up, and ran away into the garden. I was very worried.

Not knowing what to do, I was about to follow her when I realized that I didn't want to run out on our bill, so I decided to pay up before going after my skittish new bride. It took some time to pay the bill and when I was finally free to pursue her, I dashed off in the direction that Mary had gone. She had vanished and I was terrified. I ran back to the hotel. She wasn't there. I ran back to the restaurant and found her back at the table crying. I tried to console her and eventually did persuade her to eat something at another restaurant. We made our way back to the hotel, where she took a good warm bath, a rub-down, and her medicine, and went straight to sleep.

I stayed up for hours pondering over what had happened. I do not recall whether I begged forgiveness for not turning the food back or if she had for running away. We probably both did. I of course forgave her and she probably forgave me too; but it wasn't really about forgiveness. It was the loss of innocence, the breaking of the illusion of perfection, the death of the dream that marriage would solve everything. It was the first time that we had to face up to the fact that things weren't perfect and that love and marriage couldn't make it so. Our romance would continue and reason and commitment would prevail. We would move forward together according to our and other's expectations. However, the spell had been broken.

I had wanted not to travel across Europe as an ordinary married couple; I wanted ours to be a truly special dream of a honeymoon. But there we were, faced with the reality that we were indeed just another couple coping with what all couples do, namely putting up with minor irritations, misunderstandings, insignificant disagreements, and petty annoyances. We were learning of each other's' shortcomings to be filed away in the back of our minds as problems to be faced at a later time. The resilience of youth allowed us to dismiss and forget these stresses and we as maturing adults could and did overcome these minor marital problems.

Before long we were back in London to complete the clean-up of Mary's business there. Then after a delightful visit with friends in New York, the B. & B. Johnsons, we arrived back in Vancouver at the end of August. The McKinnons, Mary's guardians, put on another huge reception for us. At this reception, Mary and my family met for the first time. My family was very impressed and I was very proud. We then moved into our first nest, a beautifully designed house on Chancellor Boulevard, near UBC. Mary enrolled at UBC to continue her graduate studies while I resumed secondary school teaching at Prince of Wales. Life was good.

A Year at Columbia

BACK IN FEBRUARY, before we were married and while Mary and I were in the middle of furious letter writing, I was asked by Howie McAllister, acting principal of Prince of Wales School, to give a demonstration lesson in teaching poetry to a Grade 8 class of boys. I couldn't think of a more difficult teaching assignment, so I uncharacteristically refused. I knew McAllister well from the time when I worked with him on a Philosophy of Education Committee for the BC Teachers Federation. He had treated me very well and I rather owed him a favour. So when he asked me again and lured me with a small stipend, I relented and agreed. The poem I selected was 'The Fighting Temeraire' by Sir Henry Newbolt. Not only was I relying on the hope that the imagery of naval warfare would spark the boys' interest, I was also actually able to get hold of some physical artifacts of naval warfare as well as a huge print of Turner's famous painting by the same name, depicting Nelson's glorious ship being towed to her last berth. I placed the painting front and centre, wrote some key words on the board and distributed the items around the classroom before I started the lesson so that the boys could see and interact with the physical objects. When the buzzer sounded for the class to begin, the learning aids had their desired effect and the boys were soon abuzz with excitement. I briefly explained to the class that the twenty or so young men and women at the back of the classroom were teachers in training here to observe how well Grade eights could learn and behave.

I began the lesson by giving a short historical context to the poem, Nelson and the battle of Trafalgar, discussed the 'new' words that were on the blackboard, and then read the poem out loud. The boys were captured by the subject and rolling rhythm. We then discussed the technical elements of the poem – meter, rhyme, repetition – and the themes. We even waxed philosophical, branching out into such questions as: "Was war really that glorious?" and "How can heroism be expressed apart from war?" We even had time to discuss Turner's impressionistic painting, its artistry, and the meaning he intended to convey. All in all, the lesson went very well. In fact, it went so well that primarily on the basis of that one lesson, McAllister nominated me for a Provincial 'Teacher of the Year' award.

I was thrilled to be one of the three winners, and with that honor came a scholarship for advanced study anywhere in the world. Not only that, but also, to my surprise, I found out that Mary was pregnant. I wasn't ready to be a father and this pregnancy was not planned but when our son arrived we were thrilled. Martin Winslow Hamm was born on July 21st, 1962. Although I was apprehensive beforehand, it felt right, as though he had always been with us. So with my scholarship money, a bit of savings, and an allowance from Mary's deceased parents' estate, we, all three of us now, were able to spend a year in New York where I did an MA degree in 'Social and Philosophical Foundations of Education' at Teacher's College, Columbia University. Because I was able to transfer graduate credits from courses I had already done at the University of Washington in Seattle, and with a lot of hard work, I was able to complete my Master's Degree in only 10 months. Instead of a major thesis, I chose the option of doing extended in depth papers for each of my courses.

The courses that interested me most were philosophy and arts courses rather than education courses. In particular E. Nagel, Sidorsky and Taylor's courses stood out, respectively in Philosophy of Science, Aristotle, and Ethics. Also noteworthy was a course in 'American Social Thought' from the sociology department. Another course that stands out for me was a course on 'The Law and the School' from Teachers College for which I wrote a paper entitled 'What Constitutes Teacher Incompetence in the Eyes of the Law?' The answer? Almost nothing, save for gross indecencies, for which there are extant laws already in place. I was quite disappointed with my philosophy of education courses. Dewey was too woolly and unstructured for me to be of any help in understanding the central concepts of education. My advisor and philosophy teacher was also no fan of Dewey's, so he had us read from his area of interest some avant-garde religious writers such as Martin Buber and Paul Tillich. That didn't do it for me either. In fact, I came away from Columbia thinking that there was no strong discipline called philosophy of education to be found *anywhere*. I had already applied for and was accepted into Columbia's PhD program, but instead decided to return to Vancouver to teach in a high school again.

Despite my disappointment in exploring the field of philosophy of education, my year at Columbia was a very rich experience nonetheless. Apart from the academic exposure there was so much more. This was New York City after all, and there were so many world class events to see and things to do both on and off campus. I didn't really have time for much sightseeing but we did attend quite a few concerts, operas, and plays.

Once when our good friends Bev and Betty Johnson were over for a visit, we were chatting over our pre-dinner drinks, when, as planned, I asked Bev if he had read Bertrand Russell's *Skeptical Essays*. He said he hadn't. I told him that I would like to point out a passage that I was really fond of. Little Martin, who was now about 10 months old and just beginning to walk, was at our feet playing. I casually said to him "Marty, would you go and get Russell's *Skeptical Essays*?" He immediately wobbled on two feet to the paperback bookshelf, pulled out the very book and brought it to me. The Johnson's couldn't believe what they just saw. "You have a genius on your hands," they muttered. "Well, he does take after his parents," I proclaimed. Martin was and indeed is very clever but we had set the whole thing up. Russell's book was the only one that he could recognize.

As soon as I had finished my Master's degree at the end of June, I was eager to get back to Vancouver and find a new home. Mary, now pregnant with our second child, and Marty flew back to stay with her Aunt and Uncle McKinnon, while I cleaned up and lumbered home via Winnipeg driving our old Dodge that we had bought after our honeymoon[106] filled with our meagre possessions. During the summer of 1963, Mary and I looked around for a suitable house to buy, wanting to be settled in before I started teaching again and before the new arrival. We settled on a newly constructed four bedroom house with a full walk-in basement in the new neighborhood of Westlynn Terrace in Lynn Valley, North Vancouver. The house cost $26,000 and our mortgage rate was 6-1/2%. I thought that that was horrendous and that I had sold my soul to an everlasting mortgage; Mary thought that we could afford it. And she was right. Now, about 50 years later, houses in that neighborhood sell for close to a million dollars. In any case, on September 1st, 1963, the landscaping now done and the house finished and furnished, we moved in. I wouldn't live in the actual city of Vancouver again until 2007.

Our Family Home, N. Vancouver

---

106 I sold my Buick as soon as I had become engaged to save money and to stay in shape by walking.

CHAPTER 6

North Vancouver (1963 – 1984) (Also London, Dawson Creek & Langley)

A Year at Van Tech

MY LEAVE of absence from the Vancouver School Board to attend Columbia guaranteed me a teaching position upon my return but not my choice of position or school. I had just completed my MA and had hoped to obtain a position teaching senior high English, but such a position wasn't available. I was offered a post as a home-room teacher for an advanced Grade 8 boy's class at Vancouver Technical High School (Van Tech). I was now in the working class 'east side' of Vancouver rather than the affluent 'west side' where I had previously worked and lived. Though initially somewhat disappointed, I soon learned to enjoy these precocious somewhat hardened lads. They kept me hopping. It was hard work just to keep up with all the questions and at times they pushed me to use my imagination to keep them gainfully at work after they had mastered the regular curriculum. One project we undertook, to increase their skills both manually and in research, was to construct a miniature of Fort Langley. They were responsible for budgeting, purchasing materials, providing tools, obtaining accurate measurements (for which we took several trips to the actual Fort about 20 miles away) and putting it all together. When completed, this replica, along with other school projects and trophies, was displayed for years at the entrance to the school. We must have done something right.

I had taught most of the Grade 8 curriculum before and so even with the challenges that this particular group presented, the work load was relatively light. I already had tenure and a permanent teaching certificate, not to mention 'Teacher of the Year' honors and now a Master's Degree, so I didn't have to worry about inspections and the principal more or less gave me free rein. The commute was easy too, just over the bridge from our new house in North Vancouver. In retrospect, in terms of work, that year at Van Tech was in fact the easiest and lightest of my entire working career and relatively stress free.

Life at home was very comfortable too. Mary and I were settling nicely into family life, establishing a routine that would prevail for many years. At that time I was quite content with a joint bank account with Mary, who with her own income from her parents' estate, did the shopping, paid the bills, managed the money, and set the tone for our standard of living. In my spare time, the first I had in many years, I gardened (including planting many trees on the embankment behind our house), finished the basement, did the odd carpentry job in the basement workshop, and helped with some of the heavier chores around the house. Hobbies that I started around that time, and would continue to do for many years, were playing bridge and chess, and forming a musical trio, with David Williams on piano, my good friend David Janzen on cello, and me on the violin. We played some simplified classical pieces but mostly we played pieces written for us by David the pianist who even composed them in line with the low level of our skills, in the few keys we could manage. David J. was just beginning his cello playing at the time. We weren't world class performers but we did have a lot of fun, occasionally playing for house guests but mostly just for ourselves. Our biggest problem was finding an audience.

Our urge to get settled in our own home was partially motivated by the expectation of our second child in late September. On the 23rd, my own birthday, our long standing friends Bernie and Mary Bowker were over visiting to celebrate. We had just sat down to dinner and taken our first bites of our T-bone steaks when Mary announced that she had to go to the hospital "right now!" Before rushing off to Grace Hospital, I asked the Bowkers to look after young Martin and to finish their meal without us. Within the hour, Colin, our second son, had opened his eyes to the world. I congratulated Mary on a job done well and done so quickly, rubbed her back and promised to return as soon as I could. After we named him, held him and wrapped our newborn in a blanket to go to sleep, I was back at home in no time finishing my steak and toasting Colin and Mary.

Shortly after Colin's birth, Mary and I engaged a German *au pair* (maid) on weekdays to help with the two little boys. We found a very good one. Hildegard not only helped Mary out a lot but also grew very fond of our two little blonde-headed tykes and for years afterword would write to us from back home in Germany to enquire about their and our well being.

My year at Tech passed by quickly, and despite all the good things that I experienced there (and some not so good – Kennedy was assassinated during school hours) I was growing restless and felt a bit underused professionally. I really wanted to try my hand at teaching English literature, reliving all of those masterful works I had enjoyed so much while majoring in English at UBC. I made my wishes known to the school board, who responded by offering me the position of Assistant English Department Head at Lord Byng Secondary School, back on the west side of town, provided I obtained the approval of the Department Head, Don McLean. Don asked me down to his office one day after classes for a chat. We saw eye to eye on so many issues that in short order he assured me that I would be transferred to Byng for the fall of 1964. So I was set to put forth all my energy and abilities for the next two years to try to become the best English teacher I could possibly be.

Two Years at Lord Byng Secondary

THE TWO YEARS I taught Grade 11 and 12 English at Lord Byng High School represent my best years as a public school teacher. Once again everything seemed to come together at just the right time and under ideal circumstances. The students in this preferred area of the city, Point Grey, were capable and motivated; and the staff, particularly Don McLean, was a joy to work with. The administration was both efficient and helpful[107] and any experienced teacher knows that this is not always the case. The facilities were more than adequate and the material I was teaching, a broad range of English literature, was of great interest to me as I studied it along with my students, giving me great energy and enthusiasm. I was at my peak as a teacher.

At Lord Byng Secondary School, Vancouver, 1966

In addition to regular classroom contact with students, I got to know a number of them quite well by sponsoring the school annual, *The Aristocrat*, and a school literary publication, 'The Scarlet and

---

107 An extraordinary example is that when I wanted to teach Golding's *Lord of the Flies* to my advanced Grade 11 class as an additional text, the administration provided extra funds to buy a class set of the book. I was one of the first teachers in BC to use this novel for class study.

Grey'. As well, I started a philosophy club. Staff and students alike were appreciative of my efforts. The principal, Mr. L. Meadows, gave me a glowing report in which I scored top evaluations in all categories. He also wrote me in the summer following my departure from Byng personally to thank me for my contribution. Students also showed their gratitude. The last issue of 'The Scarlet and Grey' called 'Omega' in the summer of 1966 was dedicated to me. The editor of the Annual, with whom I worked very closely, also wrote a thank-you note to me after classes ended, one of her sentences being, "Thank-you for treating us like the adults we weren't but will be someday." That was a very kind and astute observation. It reminded me of an adage I had heard at Normal School to the effect that 'good teachers put education within the reach of their pupils, but make them stand on tip toes to get it.'

I was not aware that that was what I was doing. I certainly wasn't doing so consciously. In fact I had puzzled for a long time why it was that, by all accounts, I was successful as a teacher at all. I always felt like I didn't fully understand what I was doing or why. Was I popular because I was using indoctrination to lead the students where I wanted? I didn't think I was, but at the time I didn't really understand the important difference between education and indoctrination. Was I successful because I was popular or was I popular because I was successful? Why was it that not one of the observers or administrators ever commented on the content of what I taught? I was teaching all this (to me) wonderful prose and poetry, without giving the students the slightest choice in the matter. How indeed does one justify the choices one makes in the selection of works in the curriculum? These and many more questions relating to the philosophy of education kept rising up again and again. These were important questions that were being ignored by educational philosophers, or so I thought at the time.

So here I was on solid ground, successfully teaching English, finding my niche in the Secondary School, but deep down I was still a bit unsure of myself. I felt like a bit of a fraud[108]. I had already complet-

---

108 Apparently the majority of professionals of all kinds, even with proper creden-

ed an advanced degree in 'Social and Philosophical Foundations of Education' at a prestigious University (Columbia) and had come to the conclusion that genuine philosophy of education was relatively rare or perhaps even non-existent. I had more or less decided that I would make my career teaching instead of pursuing an academic life, but I was starting to feel uneasy with that decision. My restlessness, born of inquisitiveness, had returned.

I became active in the Vancouver Secondary School teachers Association (VSSTA) and was elected vice-president in 1965/66. While in that position, I chaired a sub-committee, formed at my suggestion, to address the question of how teachers could opt out of Bible reading and daily recitation of the Lord's Prayer in class, as was still the practice then and in fact required by law in the School Act. Under the law, teachers could opt out of the practice on grounds of conscientious objection. Few, however, did so because of fear of reprisal and associated stigma. To make it easier for the growing number of teachers who objected to Bible reading and forced prayer in public schools to opt out, the committee recommended to make available a standardised letter with the provision for individual signatures to be sent out en masse to the board office, such that anyone wishing to opt out need only to ask for and sign the letter. In our school alone, about ten or twelve teachers signed on. I was one. In my home room it was arranged that one of the students would read the Bible and lead the prayer while I left the room. It actually worked out quite well; those who wanted it got their Bible reading in, and I felt no stigma or reprisals for opting out in this manner. I am glad to say that the practice of Bible reading and prayer in public schools in BC has since been abandoned completely. I may have helped that.

It was fairly routine at that time for VSSTA presidents to work their way into administrative positions. Looking ahead, if all went well, I would likely become the VSSTA president for the following year and possibly have the option at a later time of an administrative job. Alternatively, I probably could have become an English De-

---

tials and experience, feel like a 'fraud' at some point in their career.

partment Head if I wanted to continue teaching. Had those options come to be, I probably would have remained a classroom teacher, for I could not see myself spending the rest of my career doing administrative duties, even though I would have been capable and competent in doing so. However, I never had to make that choice. Before the school year was out, I had applied for and received another leave of absence to do further academic study. As it turned out, I would not teach in public schools again.

As mentioned already, sometimes what appears to be a trivial incident turns out to be a hugely important, life changing event. This time, the 'trivial' happening came in the shape of a relatively short and unassuming book, a Christmas present from my wife Mary, which I began to read in late 1965. It was R.S. Peters' *Authority, Responsibility and Education*. Mary knew about my disappointment at not finding satisfaction in philosophy of education at Columbia and about my lingering interest in the subject. When she, an avid reader and bibliophile herself, came upon this book while browsing in the UBC book store she thought I might like it. Did I ever! Because I was a very busy person that second year at Byng, it took me a while to read this career shifting book, reading it piecemeal, a chapter here, a chapter there, not finishing until Easter. With each new chapter I got more and more excited. Here was an author who did careful analysis of educational concepts such as authority, responsibility, education, freedom, restraint, and so on. Here was a scholar who convinced me that there was after all a real philosophy of education, and I most certainly wanted to learn more even if it was centred in London, England.

I rushed off to UBC to make enquiries. I discovered that one of the professors there, Dr. Murray Elliot, was a recent graduate of the London Institute of Education. I applied for and was accepted to do a Doctorate in the Faculty of Education at UBC under Dr. Elliot's supervision. Another professor there, Dr. Ken Argue, who at the time was head of the Foundations Department, had the uncanny ability to seek out and find the best books and professors in our field even though he himself did not write and publish a great deal. Thus it was that he had invited Richard Peters himself from

London to give a seminar in 'Ethics and Education' (also the title of Peters' latest book at the time which we used as a text) at UBC summer school in 1966. What good luck!

Peters was about 10 days late coming over because of previous commitments. During Peters' absence, B. Savery, my first philosophy professor who back in 1955 had lit the spark for me, and was now the Philosophy Department Head, started off the seminar. Savery was an ardent relativist in ethics, whereas Peters was staunchly a non-relativist. It was an ever so delicate and demanding task for Savery to be true to his own point of view without stepping on his esteemed guest's academic toes. He did a superb job of setting up both points of view and letting us, the participants decide where we stood. Very ethical.

My Best Ever Golf Game

MY RUN OF good luck continued. One afternoon following the morning seminar, I ran across Peters at the University golf course where he was teeing off with Savery. We were all delighted with our common interest and Savery suggested that I take Peters for a round of golf at Seymour Golf Club over in North Vancouver, where I was a member. It was thus arranged that the following week Peters would come by for lunch at our home in Lynn Valley to be followed by a game of golf at Seymour. By this time I had already written and delivered several papers for the seminar, which Peters had thought were quite good. As we two made our way from flag to flag we discussed the nature of philosophy of education. He wanted to know what Columbia was like with respect to this subject. I told him of my disappointment there and my delight in discovering his work. He then suggested that I come to London to work with him on moral education. I was overjoyed with this idea, but I told him that I had already registered and started at UBC. He didn't think that it would be much of a problem to finish my year at UBC and then transfer to London, using the year to fill in a few gaps in my philosophical background. If I wanted it he would talk to Ken Argue and sort it out. If I could afford it, why not consider coming to London? I said I would consider it.

For the next several weeks Mary and I discussed the possibility. Mary, having already lived there, was quite happy to return to London, and I calculated that if we cashed in my pension fund, leased out our big house and got a Canada Council grant we could not only afford it but be quite comfortable for the duration. By the time summer school was over I had made arrangements with Peters to make it all happen. He then advised me in the selection of courses to take during the winter semester, which ended up being 'The Logic of Teaching' (J. Coombs), 'History of Educational Thought' (K. Argue), 'John Dewey' (C. Brauner) all from the Faculty of Education and 'Advanced Seminar in Ethics' (B. Savery) and 'Theory of Action' (Faculty) from the Philosophy Department. During that year my thoughts on the foundation of ethics matured considerably.

Having flirted with ethical relativity early on under Savery's influence, I now saw more than ever that there had to be some universal principles underlying even relative ethics. I rejected the Deweyan 'science of ethics'. Utilitarianism, it seemed to me, had some merits, for surely there must be some connection between the 'desired' (a descriptive concept) and the 'desirable' (a prescriptive concept). However, universalism in ethics comes about through the requirement of universalism in reason; and here Kant (and Peters) were, at least for me, almost totally persuasive. In the end, my position on the foundation of ethics is a combined position between Utilitarianism and Kantianism, with heavy emphasis on Kant. That is the ethical position that I took to London and upon which I built a theory of moral education. My position is fairly well summed up by this passage from a text that I wrote much later:

> *If one considers the point and purpose of morality, together with the logically necessary conditions presupposed for moral discourse to be possible, one is able to provide a fairly complete set of constitutive moral principles acceptable to, and widely accepted*

> *by, any rational person, such principles being both formal enough to catch the essence of the unique character of moral discourse and rich enough in substance to provide guidance in practical inter-personal behaviour and judgement.*[109]

In my text I then go on to state the principles, which are: justice as fairness, non-maleficence, minimal beneficence, freedom, and truthfulness. To find and articulate an exhaustive list of fundamental principles of morality was one of the things I struggled with that winter at UBC and continued to struggle with in London.

In the summer of 1967, Argue brought to UBC another member of the London School of Philosophy of Education, Paul Hirst, who offered a seminar in 'Epistemology and Education'. It was another eye-opener. Meanwhile, I was also in correspondence with Robert Dearden of the Institute in London who read and commented on some of my papers on 'moral education without religion'. I had now interacted with three faculty members of the London University Institute of Education and was extremely anxious to get to London to begin my studies there. The plans, finances, and preparatory course work were all done, and that August our little family happily made their way to London. Great things can happen on a golf course, especially when you team up with the right partners.

London

HAVING DISCOVERED what I believed to be the richest source of philosophy of education in the English speaking world, I was delighted to move to London to pursue a PhD degree at the University of London's Institute of Education. In most universities at that time, philosophy of education was taught in the Faculties of Education, whereas at London University it was in the Faculty of

---

109 *From my book Philosophical Issues in Education*, p 142, 143.

Arts, indicating that it was beginning to be recognized as a specific branch of general philosophy rather than an offshoot of education. This is as it should be, employing as it does both the tools of modern philosophical analysis, yielding rigorous thought and clarity of meaning, as well as the more traditional concerns of examination of factual claims and the justification of values. Because my doctorate was technically achieved in the Faculty of Arts I was later able to obtain a cross faculty appointment between the Philosophy Department and the Faculty of Education at Simon Fraser University with interesting results, as we shall see.

En route to London in August, 1967, our family of four made two exciting stopovers, one in Montreal where we took in Expo 67, and one in Salzburg, Austria. My long-term friend, David, and his family, on holiday leave from Zambia, met us in Frankfurt, where we rented a vehicle and drove to Salzburg to take in the music festival there. Enjoyable as those both were, I was anxious to get to London and start studying with Professor Peters. I was fully aware that there at the Institute the coursework didn't count for much and one sank or swam entirely on the quality of a publishable dissertation. Seminars and lectures conducted by able faculty and visiting speakers were available, and while we were advised to attend some of them, they were essentially optional. In fact, there were no courses as such and no exams. The only examination was the 'oral' after the completion of the dissertation (PhD thesis). This method of study was very different from the American style which I was used to. It was much freer. Perhaps some would flounder without the structure and predictability of classes but I enjoyed it even though it did test one's discipline, focus, and perseverance.

Knowing all of this ahead of time, I had prepared an outline for my dissertation and was anxious to have this reviewed by Peters. My original title was 'An Analysis of the Cognitive Content of Morality with Implications for Moral Education'. Peters approved my submission and in the end eight out of the ten chapters appeared in my finished dissertation more or less as proposed. Because I came prepared, and because Professor Peters had me submit sections of my dissertation regularly (which he then criticized and we thoroughly discussed at regular meetings), I was able to complete my dissertation in only 22 months, perhaps a record time. Between lectures and seminars, often held after public school hours to accommodate working teachers, I spent many gruelling hours in my little study carrel high up in Senate House Library furiously reading books, taking notes, constructing arguments, and writing and rewriting passages for my dissertation. Often I would battle sleepiness late into the night, my head buzzing with ideas to weave into my dissertation after an evening seminar. Often, too, I was bored and homesick for Canada. When I saw or heard Air Canada planes heading out of Heathrow, I wished that I could be on one of them. If only I could save face, end this torture, and get back to teaching English in Vancouver! What is more, it was hard to know when it would end, to know how much more work my dissertation needed. Peters would often say it was "coming along nicely". But what did that mean? Perhaps he was restrained with his praise because there was nothing praiseworthy there? Later, when another faculty member asked me how my work was going, I mentioned that Peters had said that it was "coming along nicely", to which the faculty member responded "He said *that*? That's the highest praise you can get from him." Apparently I had misjudged the British talent for understatement.

While I learned much from the professoriate and faculty and from reading, I also learned much from fellow students (an oft overlooked part of the educational process for anyone). Frequently on weekends faculty and graduate students would stage a conference on some topic or other in one of the many colleges in London's green belt. There we would read papers or parts of our dissertations to each other, subjecting our work to rigorous criticism, including pointed off-the-cuff assessments from faculty members. The academic world can be harsh sometimes. We were usually pleased if from one of these papers we could salvage a paragraph or two. It was all more or less done in good humour and without rancour. We developed the attitude of criticizing the ideas, not the people involved, which isn't always the case, even among academics. This attitude was severely lacking elsewhere, such as at SFU years later.

There, one faculty member told me, as an examiner for his MA student, that if I attacked his student it was an attack on him too. I responded by explaining that I was not attacking him or his student but only unwarranted ideas. It is surprising how many people, even high level academics, don't get that.

Sometimes a group of us Canadian students would meet in our house in Wembley for discussion on matters of concern to us, like how the Toronto Maple Leafs were doing. One character, Keith, a stickler for exactness of meaning, interrupted an historian who was about to quote from his findings by saying "We aren't even nearly ready for the facts yet!" This was an astute and often overlooked observation about the importance of conceptual clarity logically preceding factual assertions.

C. Hamm family in Edinburgh, 1968

Family life, I believe, suffered somewhat because of my late evening and therefore late morning schedule. Frequently I had little time to spend with Mary and the boys on weekdays. On weekends I tried to make up for that. On Fridays and Saturdays, Mary and I would often take in operas, concerts, movies, and other cultural events in which London is famously rich, as was New York. I was extremely lucky to have experienced both. For example, I was exposed to and learned about opera in two of the world's finest opera houses, the Met and Covent Gardens. When weather permitted, all four of us, parents often more willing than the children, went on long walks exploring the beautiful countryside around London. Aside from these long walks (Hampstead Heath, Sherwood Forest, and Kew Gardens for example) I did little sightseeing during this time in London. That would come later on my many return trips over the following decades. At that time, I stuck to the books. I was anxious to finish my dissertation, end the expensive living in London, and return home to Canada as soon as possible.

Colin and Martin, 1968

By the spring of 1969, I was deemed ready to start searching for a job teaching philosophy of education with R.S. Peters' blessing and recommendation, even though I hadn't yet technically obtained my PhD. Two positions in Canada were being advertised at the Institute, one at Queens University in Kingston, Ontario and one at Simon Fraser University in Burnaby, BC (a suburb of Vancouver). I applied for both, was interviewed for both, and was offered a position by both. Because we already owned a nice home in North Vancouver (within reasonable commuting distance to SFU), enjoyed the climate of the west coast compared to Ontario, and because in my estimation the academic considerations were about equal, we decided to take the SFU offer. But I still had to finish my dissertation.

Having already secured a job at SFU and with only the final chapter of my dissertation, the summation, to write, we decided to return home in July of 1969 even though I still wasn't quite finished. I could complete my thesis later during my first research semester. Our London stint was coming to an end. We had planned all along to buy an export model Rover car in London to take home with us and so we did. We drove it (even though the steering was on the wrong side and *we* were on the 'wrong' side of the road) from London to Liverpool with the 'boot'[110] bulging and the roof rack packed with all our possessions. In Liverpool we boarded a ship, the Empress of Canada, (car on board in the hold) and sailed for Montreal.

Aboard Empress of Canada, returning from London, 1969

A few events come to mind from that first and only open ocean voyage that I have ever done. We prairie boys don't take to the water so readily. As soon as we exited the Irish Sea, gale force winds arose and sent most passengers to their cabins with sea sickness. I was somewhat affected but not nearly as badly as the rest of the family. Continuing to try to eat something and keep it down, I returned to the galley several times only to find no one there, even at meal times. It calmed down after a few days. Dur-

---

110   Trunk.

ing one of these calmer periods, while sitting on the deck reading Velikovsky's *Worlds in Collision*, taking a break from reading philosophy, I heard the captain's announcement that the Americans had just landed on the moon, clearly and finally giving them the advantage over the Soviets in the, at the time, all-important space race. At a fun show for children, Martin and Colin won first prize in a skit competition, putting on a farce called 'The Early Worm Catches the Bird'. I took a picture of Colin at the ship's wheel, steering for a bit as the captain looks on. All in all an eventful enjoyable experience. Still I was also very glad to be back on land, my homeland.

We then set about driving across much of our huge country from Montreal back to Vancouver. Somewhere in the vastness of northern Ontario, another car overtook us and flagged us down to a halt whereupon the driver handed us one of our suitcases that had fallen off the roof-rack of our car. Now we knew that we were really back in Canada. When we reached Winnipeg, we stopped for a few days to visit my parents. I tried to explain to Dad what I had been doing in London, researching the possibility of moral education based on rational humanistic ethics rather than religion. He kindly suggested that I was wasting my time, for without God there was no possibility of being good. Much later, after Dad's death, I discovered in his writings that at the time I was considered to be '*verirrt*' (lost, gone astray). It was not unexpected. In fact, despite how it must have pained my father, in a way, I took it as a badge of honor to be '*verirrt*', having finally and at long last achieved freedom from religion.

On returning to our home in North Vancouver, we found the house in terrible shape with much damage to the furniture and carpets. Apparently our reliable friend, despite exercising every precaution, had leased our house to someone who turned out to be from the criminal world, and allegedly used our house for dealing drugs and who knows what else. For months after our return we noticed police patrolling our little cul-de-sac and eyeing our house in particular. When the renter returned to get his damage deposit, I pointed out that the cost of repairs was many times higher than the deposit. I held my ground and after arguing over this for a while, he left in a peeve. A few weeks later we saw in the paper that he had been shot dead in a backstreet in East Vancouver.

That fall, 1969, while Mary busied herself refurbishing the house and getting the kids to school, I began my long career at SFU.

Early Years at SFU

IT WAS WITH some trepidation that I began my first semester at SFU in September of 1969. I had been hired by an Acting Department Head, an Acting Dean, and an Acting Academic Vice President. I was wondering what the real brass would be like. I knew too that there was not full harmony in our Department of Social and Philosophical Foundations in the Faculty of Education. It was 1969 after all and on University campuses everywhere there was social unrest and ours was no different. In fact SFU, though quite a new institution, founded in 1965, already had a reputation for attracting both student and faculty 'radicals'.

One member of our Department when interviewing me briefly in spring in a worker's waterfront pub, asked if I was a conservative or "one of us", meaning a radical socialist. I responded by asking him, "conservative or radical with respect to what?" He then said, "So, you're one of those wishy washy liberals. I'll tell you right now I will not vote for your appointment. Let's talk about something else." I would meet him again, this time as a colleague, supposedly working together and even teaching the same courses, at least by name and number. How would it all work out in this charged 'us versus them' environment? I didn't really know if I was an 'us' or a 'them'. I found out soon enough.

While registering students for courses on registration day, I was approached by a group of students, asking me whether I was the "dangerous Professor Hamm". I said "Yes, I carry guns and other weapons. Why do you ask?" They then explained that there were signs in the hallway reading "Don't take courses from Professors

X, Y, and Hamm. These people are dangerous." Once the Academic Vice President, the real one, found out, he had the signs removed. However, the 'damage' had been done as people flocked to my course to hear the 'dangerous' Dr. Hamm.

Many universities the world over were struggling with various social issues, student radicals, and even radical staff and faculty who weren't shy about questioning the status quo. At SFU one of the issues of contention was student representation on University committees such as faculty appointments, curriculum, or admissions. When students actually got many of their wishes, they found that it was difficult to fill those positions because it actually involved much time and work. Some departments wanted to reshape the whole institution into a 'people's University', whatever that is, and to remove the 'authoritarian' power structure altogether and replace it with a 'democratic' one. It was felt that one way to achieve that would be to eliminate the grading system. So some profs sent in no grades, some gave every student an 'A' so as to nullify the significance of grades, and others simply let their students choose their own grades.

The Faculty of Education at that time consisted of five departments, Social and Philosophical Foundations, Behavioural Science Foundations, Athletics, Professional Development, and Fine Arts and Music. The departments were constantly pulling in different directions and within each department there were warring factions. From its inception, SFU promulgated the view that the various disciplines should talk to and relate to each other. In particular the Faculty of Education should keep in close contact with parent disciplines. Education Faculty members teaching mathematics methodology, for example, should be in close communication with mathematicians and so on. We philosophers criticized our colleagues for sloppy thinking and they shot back with "you people are irrelevant". We philosophers, used to criticism, were ready to examine any sloppy or 'irrelevant' thinking that *we* might be engaged in but how does one respond professionally to "irrelevant people"? We argued for at least one mandatory Philosophy of Education course for all teachers, but we were told from other departments that "we do our own philosophy of education", revealing their total ignorance of the field.

Alone in my office, preparing courses and lectures and working on papers, I felt happy and successful but navigating the politics of the faculty and making an impact on the quality of public education in general was another story. To this day I regret that we philosophers of education were unable to have much impact on the school system itself. Who knows, perhaps we had some impact on the individual student teachers that took our courses, and perhaps that's the only way to effect real change, one student at a time. It was almost impossible to even engage a non-philosopher colleague in a philosophical discussion of any kind. The experiment to erase disciplinary boundaries by administrative arrangement was not working.

A couple of years into my career at SFU changes were afoot. A new Academic Vice-President rearranged the administration of our faculty, removing the departments of Athletics and Behavioural Sciences to other Faculties; in fact the whole departmental structure was changed. From now on there were to be only three 'programs' in the Faculty of Education: Graduate Programs, Undergraduate Programs, and Professional Development. At the same time several of us were made 'cross appointments' working half-time in the Faculty of Education and half-time in our parent discipline, attempting to keep the sought after linkages. For several years I taught half-time in the Philosophy Department in the Faculty of Arts but this didn't work out too smoothly either.

Meanwhile, I needed to complete my dissertation and return to London for my oral examination. Fortunately SFU operated on a trimester system with three sessions of equal length (any two of which would equal a year's worth of study) allowing me one full semester (four months) off each year for research and holiday time. On my first research semester, January to April, 1970, I diligently wrote the last remaining chapter of my dissertation at home and then hurried off to London to defend it. I hoped that I might even have a little time left over finally to do a little sight-seeing. Not so. On arrival in London, Peters quickly learned that I wasn't required back at SFU until May 1st. Well, he thought, Hamm ought to make good use of his time here, so he had me do some further research, rewrite my entire dissertation, and scheduled my oral for late April.

All semester I feverishly wrote and wrote, and then wrote some more. Finally in late April I was finished and sent the entire work off to be typed and bound. I got my holiday too – a whole day. In fact I spent a glorious triumphant day in Paris, marching up and down the Champs-Elysees, poking my head into shops and galleries, feeling free and light as a bird. It was a marvelous feeling finally to have that monkey off my back. However, the oral defence was still to come. Back in London, my examiners were Peters himself, Robert Dearden of the Institute, and John Wilson from Oxford University. I arrived at the Institute at 9:30 half an hour early and reported to Peters secretary. I hadn't even fixed my tea yet when the secretary beckoned me over and told me that my examiners had arrived and would I mind starting a bit early. Of course I wouldn't mind, wanting to get this final hurdle over with as soon as possible.

Professor Peters announced that Dearden had already 'signed off' on the dissertation and wouldn't be attending. Peters started by pointing out a few typos that had been missed and then asked me to explain a rather turgid bit of writing I had done. "No problem here," he said "but why didn't you write it the way you just explained it?" Wilson then asked me a few questions which I thought I fielded rather easily. Then Peters again, and then Wilson. Things were going pretty well so far, but were these just the warm-up questions? Wilson came in again with a challenge. Why hadn't I addressed the question of the uniqueness of moral language and did I agree with R.M. Hare's analysis of moral language in his book by that title? I responded that I had indeed addressed that question in a chapter near the end and, no, I didn't really agree with Hare. I didn't really have anything to add to what I had already argued in that chapter of my dissertation. To my surprise, Wilson revealed that he hadn't read that far. Then he asked if I would mind terribly if we just left off with the questions at that point as he wanted to get in some shopping before lunch. Each of us chuckled at this. We stood up, shook hands, and it was all over.

My tea wasn't even cold. Wilson was gone. It really was all over. Peters muttered something while lighting up his pipe about my not getting my money's worth. I retorted with, "If I succeeded in defending my dissertation, then I got my money's worth. By the way, you didn't say anything about my passing the oral." He looked at me with surprise and said, "Do you think I would have let you come this far in the proceedings if there was any doubt in my mind? Of course you passed." Before I left his office I handed him a set of Cornelia stone cuff links and a bottle of fine Scotch as a token of my great appreciation and esteem.

Just around the corner from Senate House was a small branch post office from where one could send telegrams. I hastened there to send Mary and department head Eastwood a telegram to say that all was well, signed off as *Dr. C.M. Hamm*. That done, I strutted off to a nearby pub where six or seven of us graduate students had arranged to meet to either celebrate or commiserate. Of course it was a celebration. Since I was the first of this group to undergo the dreaded oral, I was questioned in every detail. Lunch turned into dinner and dinner turned into a party. Unfortunately Mary's very proper Aunt Maisie was arriving at Heathrow early the next morning and I was expected to meet her so I had to spoil the party at about 2 a.m. and take a taxi home. The next morning was a bit difficult but I survived a day of sightseeing with Maisie and then flew home triumphantly the following day.

As a university professor, I was now responsible for writing publishable papers as well as creating and teaching courses in philosophy of education. One course that I thought should be available for students was 'Ethics and Education', using Peters' own book by that title as the main text. I prepared such a course, submitted it to Senate, and much to my delight it was approved. When I taught the course, both education and philosophy students took it and got credit upon completion. Yet when my colleagues in the Faculty of Education taught the same course, philosophy students were not eligible to receive credit for it. Why? Because the Philosophy Department deemed that professors whose doctorates were obtained from Faculties of Education were not qualified. So now we had a course on offer which did or did not grant credit based on who taught it, which was not supposed to happen. This and other issues arose from having a cross faculty appointment. In the end it was administratively too cumbersome for me to continue in both departments concurrently.

While I was in the Philosophy Department, I thoroughly enjoyed the cross-fire of ideas and I even got to teach a course that I had long been itching to teach, namely philosophy of religion. It had been many years since I had practiced or even thought about religion and it felt like a lifetime ago that I was studying to be a minister; but now I not only had the opportunity but the professional duty systematically to re-examine the issues of God and religion from a secular philosopher's point of view. I used John Hick's *Philosophy of Religion* as my main text and the course included topics such as the concept of God, grounds for belief, theodicy, revelation, and the nature of faith. In reassessing these issues from as open a mind as I could muster, and from my new more scholarly point of view, I came to the same conclusions I had arrived at earlier, namely that there was no evidence for belief in God. I confirmed my non-theist position and that the primary problem with religion is conceptual rather than epistemic; that is to say that the fundamental claims of religion lack meaning rather than merely lacking evidence for meaningful claims. Not only is there no evidence for God's existence but we don't even know what counts as evidence and wouldn't recognize it if we did.

However, soon I would leave the Philosophy Department and that would mean not teaching that course again. Once in a while I got a 'real' philosopher (from the Faculty of Arts) to give an address to my education students and sometimes we 'Education' philosophers might get asked to attend special Philosophy Department events, but for the most part departmental divisions remained. The Faculty of Education itself remained fractious and divisive and I was not particularly successful in the role of 'liaison' professor. There was not much solid ground upon which to build bridges. In-fighting continued within our faculty over issues such as promotion, tenure, course ownership, student allegiances to preferred professors, course prerequisites, and research versus teaching in the allocation of funds. Before I joined the SFU faculty I thought that universities were small havens of rationality in a fractious, irrational world. Now I wasn't so sure.

Certainly the faculty that I was in was not a very friendly and happy place to be working. After five years, I thought of moving elsewhere or even quitting and taking up farming, as I had long dreamed of doing, but had always concluded I couldn't afford to. However after much careful saving and calculation I was ready to explore some options. One day I conveyed my restless state of mind to the Dean, with whom I was quite friendly. He suggested not to quit but to request a half-time position until I was satisfied that I could both do and enjoy the farm work. That was sage advice. The problem was that there was no precedent for 'tenure track' professors to go half-time. I never cared much about tenure in any case. So if it were just a matter of dropping the tenure track part then I could do that. Figuring out how to run a farm half-time while teaching would be more problematic. I did have the Dean's support however and he told me to think it over and propose a plan to the Academic Vice President.

The plan I proposed was to take my position and basically chop it in half, half-time teaching, half-time research and holiday time, and half salary. I would 'work' from November 1st to the end of April, with November and December being my research and holiday time (two months instead of four) and my teaching semester (one instead of two) would be January to the end of April. This would leave me May 1st to the end of October to farm. Even though there was good fertile farm land in the Fraser Valley, just to the east of Vancouver, and that would seem the obvious choice, I didn't want to commute back and forth. The plan that I was dreaming up would allow me to go back to my beloved Peace Country up north, to do grain farming, with the short growing season for once working to my advantage. There were a few caveats however. I would have to keep current with my reading; I would lose tenure possibilities, but still be available for promotions; and I would have to provide for the other half of my medical and benefits package. To my surprise and delight my proposal was accepted almost in its entirety The very next chance I got, I flew to Dawson Creek in northern BC near the Alberta border to look for a farm to purchase.

Farming in Dawson Creek

THIRTY TWO MILES north and slightly east of Dawson Creek, on the Clayhurst Ferry (now bridge) Road, just before the rolling farmland of the Peace country dips down into the rugged valley of the mighty Peace River itself, lie the ruins of a barn and farmhouse that were once my beautiful and well cared-for farm buildings. A Quonset machine shed and metal granaries are still extant and useful. There I spent five half years (May through October) relearning how to be a farmer, this time a grain farmer with a few animals on the side. I purchased the farm from the local member of the BC legislature and owner of the local newspaper. It just so happened that the paved road ended literally at my front door. I bought the property in the fall of 1973, with the intent to start my farming operation in the spring of 1974. In the intervening time I bought and read books on farming, farm machinery, gardening, and how to care for farm animals. I also took a night school welding course at Van Tech (of all places) which turned out to be a good move, for Dawson Creek, the nearest service centre from my farm, was 32 miles away and going there for a small repair would prove time consuming and costly. I then set about acquiring the many expensive machines needed to run a modern grain farm.

The expenses started to mount. Mary had inherited quite a comfortable estate but I was uneasy about relying on her inheritance to start my farming operation. I wanted the farm to be a success in its own right, to fail or succeed under my own steam so that I could enjoy the success all the more if and when it came and be proud of my achievements. We not only owned our nice North Vancouver house together but we had purchased a property and built a cottage on West Pender Island[111] as well. When we sold that at a profit, we bought a small farm in the Kispiox Valley in north-

---

111 In the Gulf Islands roughly between Vancouver and Victoria in the Strait of Georgia.

western BC as an investment.[112] So for this new project in Dawson Creek, we sold the Kispiox property, split the proceeds and Mary bought from me my share of the house. Thus we split all our joint assets, which together with a short term farming bank loan and a loan from Mary's estate, was sufficient to get me started. I was financially set to run the farm and for better or worse Mary and I were now fully financially independent.

On the last weekend in April 1974, having pushed myself hard to finish a paper[113] so that I could pop it in the mail and be done with it, I prepared to leave for Dawson Creek. With pickup truck and trailer loaded with gear of all sorts, I took off for Williams Lake early on Saturday morning. Williams Lake, where my brother Martin, his wife Adeline and family live, is roughly half way to Dawson Creek, a good seven hour drive on its own. So it became routine over the next few years to stop, visit and spend the night there when coming and going. I can never thank them enough for the many enjoyable times I have had there and at their cottage on nearby Chimney Lake.

Just after sunset the next day I arrived at my very own farm. My heart was beating fast as I turned onto my paved driveway. As I stepped out of the pickup in front of the house, I was overwhelmed by the beauty of the place and a sense of peace immediately settled in. And then I heard it for the first time. The sound of absolute silence. Never before had I heard that in my entire life. I would never forget it. Without having done a thing, I already felt successful in my venture.

Then I frantically went to work. Not only did I have to make the house liveable but I had a lot to do to get started farming. I scrambled desperately to bring together all the things necessary so I could take to the fields as soon as the weather would allow: machinery, seed grain, fertilizer, tools, fuel, provender, and provisions for me. The spring thaw was late but that suited me just fine as I

---

112 We had tenants who ran the farm there.

113 I believe it was 'In Defence of the Bag of Virtues' where I take Kohlberg to task for demeaning the practice of establishing virtues in children.

needed a bit of time to get ready. I purchased most of my much needed machinery locally, but for the set of seeding drills I had to go to Fort St. John, a distance of over 40 miles. There I acquired a 24 foot International Harvester drill set in two 12 foot sections. It took me two long painstaking days to haul the drills, one set at a time, to my farm, dangerously towing them behind my pickup along the Alaska Highway. It was exciting when I finally had all of my gear assembled and started the cultivation on May 20th, using a rented FW IH4100 tractor pulling a 29 foot Co-op cultivator. The tractor I was buying, an articulated four wheel drive Steiger, under the Co-op name Wildcat, hadn't arrived yet.

When later in the summer my Wildcat did arrive, I found myself the proud owner of a fine set of new machines, save for the old combine. The following year, I brought that up to date by buying a new Massey-Ferguson MF510. With a grain auger, a 20 foot self-propelled swather, 50 feet of harrows and a 20 foot disk, eventually, I rounded out my equipment purchases. I now owned sufficient machinery to work my two sections (1280 acres) of land more or less single handedly. The only older machine I had was a 1957 two-ton GM truck which I used for seed grain in spring and for hauling the harvest from the combine to my granaries in fall. I hired professionals to truck my grain to town over the winter. I also had an old McCormick two wheel drive tractor for picking roots and rocks on the breaking quarter and for doing small jobs around the farm, like hauling manure from the barn to the expansive vegetable garden.

It was gratifying when, in the middle of January after my first crop was in the bins, the elevator agent phoned me in Vancouver to ask if I had more of that premium Olli barley. He wanted to sell it at a premium malting quality price. Ah, supply and demand. I had it and he wanted it. We both made money.

Anyone who is brought up on a farm knows that any kind of farming is a lot of work, even hobby farming. My farm of 1280 acres, about average size for the Peace country, was not a hobby farm by any means. Because I worked on in it for only six months of the year, I had to squeeze all the jobs that needed doing into that half year. During seeding and harvesting, I often worked very long hours, up to 16 hours a day not including house and barn chores, feeding myself, or servicing the equipment. The long days of summer sunlight in the Peace allows one to work late into the evening. However, even with all my efforts, I still could not do it all entirely by myself. In the busiest days of seeding and harvesting I almost always hired some help. Sometimes city friends would stop by the farm for a quick taste of country life, and sometimes they would even be a help. Otherwise I would just advertise locally for casual labour. Young women neighbours would often take an hour or two to shop for groceries and prepare meals, and I usually managed to find someone (often a student, a nephew, or a neighbour) to help with the heavy work of seeding and combining. Combining was definitely a two person job, with one person driving the combine and one driving the grain truck. Keeping that combine going during the short period of favourable harvesting weather was essential.

In addition to grain production, mostly wheat and barley, which were the main cash crops, I also grew alfalfa and clover in rotation. Not only did they replenish the soil with nitrogen, meaning less reliance on fertilizer, it was also excellent fodder for our animals. The alfalfa crop was sold standing to a local company, 'Dehy', which had an experimental process of drying and pelletizing the hay. It was a good idea but the company had difficulty fulfilling the contractual agreements they made with the farmers, often failing to pick up the hay and to pay up on time. Dehy provided me with considerable frustration in an otherwise smoothly running farm operation. Our animal numbers fluctuated a bit from year to year but we typically had a milk cow, a steer, fifty chickens, four to six swine, and a couple of sheep. Our milk cow was prodigious and could provide more than our family, including two now teenage boys, could consume and so in addition to grain and alfalfa our animals dined on milk and table scraps as well. This high quality diet produced very high quality meats and dairy products and would sustain us for the whole year. I always took a freezer full of meat and produce back to Vancouver with me in the fall.

Our small farm animal operation and our big vegetable garden provided ample opportunity for our boys to earn some pocket money and to learn the concept of work. One of my reasons for wanting a farm in the first place was to teach the boys how to handle animals, how to operate vehicles, and how to buckle down to do a job and finish it properly. And learn they did: not only the basics of farm work but also how to handle and shoot a gun, how to ride a motorcycle, and even how to milk a cow. One evening as we were sitting down to dinner at 6 p.m. as was typical, I asked Colin, whose turn it was to milk the cow, if he had done his chores. He replied that he had not and that he would do them after dinner. I reminded him that it didn't work like that; 5:30 a.m. and 5:30 p.m. was milking time and there were no exceptions or delays allowed. I explained that animal comfort takes precedence over human comfort, and insisted that he go immediately to look after the milking before he ate his dinner. He did, and never failed in that regard again.

The boys had their chores to do, but they also had lots of free time to build forts, go swimming and fishing, ride motorcycles, and entertain guests. Several of their cousins and city friends from Vancouver and beyond visited and stayed with us for varying periods of time in the summer. In the last year or two, Martin, our oldest, at age 15, learned to operate my big tractor, cultivating the summer fallow. Operating big machinery can be quite easy and enjoyable, like driving a car, but this is only after caution becomes second nature. The actual learning of how to operate machinery takes a great deal of caution, as one little mistake can have severe physical and financial consequences. I think my insistence on the practice of caution was what made our five years of farming accident free. For many rounds I sat with Martin in the tractor constantly reminding him to keep an eye on the furrow and an ear to the engine, until finally he got the feel of it so that we could have a conversation as he smoothly made the rounds. I tried to teach the boys proper safety in the driving of vehicles, motorbikes, and machinery, and caution in handling animals, tools, and firearms. I practiced caution myself. However, even with all that caution, there were still some close calls.

On one such occasion in the late fall when Mary and the boys had returned to Vancouver to start school there, I was checking the grain for heating (i.e. unwanted fermentation of moisture in the grain). I noticed that the wheat had been somewhat tough when combining. I set up my 24 foot aluminum ladder on the outside of one of the enormous round metal bins for storing grain, in order to climb to the hatch at the top. It was no problem climbing up the ladder, up the roof to the hatch, and dropping down a couple of feet into the loose grain to check for warm spots. The grain was fine and I was about to exit when I heard a loud clatter of aluminum on tin as the wind carried away my ladder which crashed to the ground below. Now what? With my hands, I piled up enough loose grain so that I could stand with my torso sticking out the top hatch and there I stood hoping to flag down a passing vehicle. Luckily I was in plain view of the one main road in the area; I could have easily been stranded a lot further away and out of sight.

Ours was the last farm on the paved highway before the rolling farmland precipitously dropped away into the deep and steep sided Peace River valley. From there, a gravel road wound its way down through the thick forest to the valley floor. I stood there in the harsh wind for about 10 minutes waiting for someone to come when I finally heard the sound of a truck slowly climbing up the steep embankment. I knew I had to catch the driver's eye immediately upon emerging from the bush, for then he would undoubtedly speed up and take off along the straight flat paved road once at the top of the hill. Then I saw him. It was a grain truck hauling grain to Dawson Creek. I waved frantically. He didn't stop. In fact, it seemed as if he deliberately looked the other way. I waved again as the truck inevitably sped up and sped off, my heart sinking as I realized that he hadn't seen me nor was he going to. After a short wait, I heard another truck coming up from the river valley. More frantic waving, and another truck speeds off without seeing me. After twenty more agonizingly slow minutes of nobody and nothing I was left figuring out how to tear up my clothes and imagining what the neighbors might say if they saw a half-naked professor clinging to the side of a granary with a makeshift strand of clothing.

I was looking for a place to tie off one end of the 'rope' when I heard another vehicle coming up the hill. I hurried to my perch and saw that the truck had already passed my drive way but the driver just happened to glance my way. I waved again vigorously. He must have been a bit surprised to see me there poking out of the top of a giant metal cone on top of a huge metal cylinder, a part of the landscape that was usually dormant. When he did see me, much to my relief, he stopped, backed up, and came around to rescue me. After a few laughs he was gone. Never again did I climb that ladder without a long strong rope in hand.

I believe the boys genuinely enjoyed their five summers on the farm, particularly early on; but then a time came when that started to change. They were teenagers and because they missed their friends back 'home' in North Vancouver, they would ask "Do we have to come to the farm even if we don't want to?" I didn't want to force them. Nor did I want to be without the family for the full six months of the farming season. Other developments also triggered the idea that perhaps it was time to consider selling the farm. Dehy had gone belly up and I could no longer count on them to harvest and buy my alfalfa crop. I didn't have the time or specialized equipment to do that on my own in addition to my grain farming. Land prices had also risen dramatically[114] and if I sold at that time, I could make a healthy profit on the land. I was also getting tired.

Typically when I returned to campus after six months of gruelling work on the farm, my colleagues at the University would take the view that I was through playing around in the countryside and it was now time to get back to work. When I left campus to go back to farming the next spring, invariably my neighbors would think that it was time to get back to work after playing around in the city all winter. Even though I did like both kinds of work, neither were the holiday that people were imagining. The final factor that drove me to sell the farm in the fall of 1978 was that I was actually enjoying the university work more and more, especially the lecturing and

---

114   They also fell just as dramatically a few years later, forcing many large prosperous family operations to close and move off the farm for good.

teaching part. In fact, often as I sat in my air conditioned tractor going around and around the fields in endless hours of tilling or combining I found that my thoughts would drift towards my lectures, rethinking and restructuring them, sometimes finding just the right wording for difficult to grasp philosophical points and stopping to write them down when I did so. I was also getting published. Not only was that a professional obligation but it was also a real joy to see one's work in print and to be taken seriously by other academics as evidenced by their responses and rejoinders. Not that I ever really find writing all that enjoyable in itself but I like to have written. I was getting comfortable with the idea of being a professor.

In any case, in the tug of war between farming and philosophy, philosophy won the day. After harvesting my last crop, storing my implements for the winter and planning for an old-fashioned farm sale by auction the next spring, I loaded up my pickup truck one more time with a freezer full of incomparable food and a few things I didn't want to sell and headed back to campus and the coast for good.

During the five years of farming in the Peace Country, there were periods of stress and frustration, disappointments and failures, and wearying long hours of work. But more often than not I think of those years as being filled with joy and excitement. Not only were there tangible rewards for my labour, along with some summer frolic and fun with the family, it gave me much confidence and hope for future endeavours. I particularly liked the immediacy of the reward in farming. When teaching students, one metaphorically plants seeds of thought but one doesn't know how well or badly one has done for a long time, if ever. In farming one plants the seeds and in a matter of days or weeks one can start to see a result. In no time, the grain stocks are swaying in the wind and by the end of the season the gold is in the bin. I calculated once that in one good season I actually harvested enough grain to keep 2000 people alive for one year. That is satisfying in and of itself. With the farm working out so well, with the situation at the University rapidly improving, with family life intact and the boys at their most delightful stage of maturing, I would venture to say that those five years were probably the best and happiest years of my working life.

Langley and SFU Middle Years

HAVING STOPPED farming in the Peace country, I was not automatically placed on full time again at SFU. There weren't any openings in my field at the time so I just continued on a half-time basis. Tenure was not an option and so the old maxim for academics of 'publish or perish' certainly applied. Not that I wasn't publishing a respectable amount already, I was; but now with more time on my hands, I could and did do more. I decided to put together a book of essays by various authors on issues in moral education. Even though it was getting some attention, the term 'moral education' was still "the name for nothing clear".[115]

As soon as I began the project, I realized that it was a task too big for me to undertake by myself, so I discussed the possibility of jointly editing the book with my colleague Tasos Kazepides and a visiting professor Don Cochrane. Our book was to be named *The Domain of Moral Education* with four sections: The Limits of Moral Education, The Nature of Moral Education, Form and Content in Moral Education, and The Developmental Hypothesis of Moral Education. We all took part in recruiting authors, in choosing papers, and in the editing. The delightful task of going to England to interview on their home turf, experts in the field including John Wilson, R.M. Hare, and G.J. Warnock from Oxford and Pat White and Richard Peters from London University, was mine. The book was published in 1979 by Paulist Press, New York.

Between 1979 and 1984, while on a half-time position at SFU, I actually did somewhat more than half-time work. In addition to the book, I also published papers on topics other than moral education. Two of the more successful ones were 'Constraints of Parents' Rights Concerning the Education of their Children'[116] and

---

115   John Wilson, N. Williams, and B. Sugarman, *Introduction to Moral Education*, Baltimore: Penguin Books, 1967, p.11.

116   'Constraints...' in M E Manley-Cassimir, *Family Choice in Schooling*, Lexington Books, Heath, Toronto, 1982.

'Critique of Self Education'.[117] Also, I attended more conferences and workshops than I had in previous years. I also spent three months at the Institute in London just reading and keeping abreast of my discipline. However, I didn't spend all of my time on University related matters.

Immediately after selling my Dawson Creek farm, I bought fifty acres of bush and pasture in Langley in the Fraser Valley of BC for a cattle 'backgrounding' operation. This simply meant grazing cattle to feed-lot readiness. I would buy a herd in early spring, fatten them up, and then sell them again in fall. Aside from keeping up the fences and ensuring a supply of water, salt, and at times extra feed, there was little work involved. I had time to clear some land for hay, to have a machine shop and hay-shed built and to design and build a cottage. I had the cottage framed up to lock-up stage. During the summer of 1982 Colin, our second son, helped me finish the interior. He earned some needed cash to go to University himself and I was overjoyed to have the small house of my own design finished. I remember the thrill that rose up in me one evening in late August to stay there overnight for the first time, the late evening sunbeams filtering through the trees and in through the many windows, the fresh air mixing with the delightful cedar aroma with just a hint of barnyard. Here I would spend many delightful hours

Cornel's Langley retreat

---

117 'Critique...' *Canadian Journal of Education* 7:4, 1982.

away from the din and commotion of the city, away from teenagers and urbanites and their annoying music. Here I could read, write, and contemplate to my heart's content and when I tired of the quiet, I could listen to good music in full volume without fear of interrupting or annoying anyone else.

That first evening alone in Langley was not the official ending of our marriage, though it serves as a reference point as good as any. At that point, the cottage was still a 'retreat' and a place to be when looking after the cattle. For many more years, Mary and I would live together periodically and then separately again. The truth is that long periods of separation every year during the Dawson Creek years had taken their toll on our marriage. We had not only become independent financially but also psychologically and emotionally. It seemed that we were simply more content living apart, each doing our own thing, though we got together for travel, to attend events, and for family occasions. In fact even up to the time of this writing, as much as possible, we still all get together for regular family dinners. For a while, the four of us core family members all took turns hosting Sunday meals, but I'm getting ahead of myself. We never really had a 'break up' nor a precipitating event for separation, nor even an ending date really, we just slowly drifted apart until one day I just filled in 'separated' on my income tax form.

My offer of a formal written separation agreement was rejected by Mary. Neither of us wanted to marry again so there wasn't really any need to do all the paperwork of a divorce and there were some financial advantages to staying married. However, the magical romance of our early marriage had ceased. Despite outward appearances, I hadn't really contrived the separation, or planned it, or even wished for it. It just happened. If one has to put a date to it, the last time we cohabitated was in mid-1985 and since then I haven't lived in our marital home in North Vancouver, where Mary still lives. We had our usual little frictions and differences of opinions, but like so many married couples we had learned to deal with those along the way. It may have been a strange marriage by some standards but then again I would imagine that every marriage is unique. We didn't end up with strong feelings of animosity or acrimony, in fact we are still good friends. Sadly, like it does so frequently, love just fled without stopping to tell us why. Only memories were now left to console us. Yeats says it so much better:

> When you are old and gray and full of sleep,
> And nodding by the fire, take down this book,
> And slowly read and dream of the soft look
> Your eyes had once, and of their shadows deep;
>
> How many loved your moments of glad grace,
> And loved your beauty with love false or true;
> But one man loved the pilgrim soul in you,
> And loved the sorrows of your changing face;
>
> And bending down beside the glowing bars
> Murmur, a little sadly, how Love fled
> And paced upon the mountains overhead
> And hid his face amid a crowd of stars.[118]

During the years at Langley, with more time to devote to my university affairs, I felt confident that my teaching and research were going well. So did others. In the fall of 1983 I received a letter from the Dean of the Faculty of Education from Melbourne University, asking me to apply for the 'Scholar of the Year' position. My old friend from the London University days, Keith, now a member of the Melbourne faculty, had nominated me. So, just for the fun of it, I sent my CV and personal details off to Melbourne University, thinking that I would never hear from them again.

Meanwhile, the Dean of Graduate Studies, back home at SFU, invited me to become the Assistant Dean. I guess he felt that if I could run a successful grain farm while holding down an academic position simultaneously I had to have at least some administra-

---

118   Yeats, 'When You Are Old', 1893.

tive abilities. In fact, we had even discussed farming, he being a scientist specializing in Pestology. I suppose that I could have been quite an able administrator but I wasn't really interested in that, at least at that time. As I was sizing up the offer, word came in from Melbourne that I had been selected 'Scholar of the Year' for the coming academic year, including a one term posting in Melbourne, Australia, and all agreed that that was sufficient reason not to take the administrative post of Assistant Dean.

Awaiting commencement ceremony at SFU, 1983

Melbourne

EARLY IN THE YEAR 1984 I flew to Los Angeles to catch my Qantas Air connection for the first leg of my round-the-world junket. This connection required me to lay over in LA for a day. Since I had often heard of Palm Springs and had yet to visit there, I took the opportunity to bus to Palm Springs on that extra day. I loved the city immediately – the air, the light, the palm trees – and decided then and there that I would come back as soon as opportunity allowed. From then until now, I have holidayed and/or resided there in winter every year except for one, and that was only for reasons of ill health.

North Vancouver (1963 – 1984)

From Los Angeles it was off to Tahiti and Bora Bora, where I holidayed for a week, and then on to Melbourne via Sydney. In Melbourne, Keith greeted me at the airport and showed me the beautiful campus of Melbourne University and then introduced me to the Dean of Education, who fixed me up with an office and accommodations. I was slated to stay at the International House, which I found a bit stuffy and too far from my office. Instead, for a little extra money, I was placed in the graduate student residences, which I enjoyed very much. In some ways it seemed like an 'International House' itself, accommodating not only Australians, but also students of many different nationalities, including Americans, Brits, Germans, Italians, Japanese, Indians, and also other Canadians. I made a number of good friends, some of whom I keep in touch with to this day.

My contract with the university included teaching and research in exchange for accommodations, a salary, and a few extra perks. The teaching part I fulfilled by conducting a graduate seminar in Moral Education, which lasted four months. My research period was ongoing over six months, two weeks of which was holiday time. It was expected that I would produce a publishable article. As it happened, because my marking chores were light (I only had 6 or 7 students in the seminar), and the preparation easy (I had given the seminar before and indeed edited the text), I was able to produce two publishable papers, 'Moral Education as the Achievement of Virtue'[119] which I read to a Faculty of Education forum and 'Moral Education and the Distinction Between Social and Personal Morality' which I read to a Philosophy Department forum, my work as always being a bridge between pure philosophy and the real life issues of education.

The first paper contained the main ideas which I later presented in my book *Philosophical Issues in Education: An Introduction*, published in 1985. There, in a chapter on moral education, I propose a model of moral education described as "the achievement of virtue", using a three-pronged methodology I call exemplification,

---

119 Published in *Melbourne Studies in Education*, Vol. 27, Melbourne University Press, 1985.

encouragement, and enlightenment. Under the rubric of 'enlightenment' I propose instruction in moral concepts, in moral rules and principles, in moral reasoning, and in moral philosophy.

In the second paper I argue that the perceived crisis in moral education is not nearly as severe as thought if one makes the distinction between social morality (those rules and principles which apply to inter-personal behaviour such as truthfulness, refraining from theft, or being fair in general) and personal morality (those ideals that I have that pertain to my own personal integrity). Readers who are interested in these things can of course read the papers or the book for further details.

On my two week vacation time, I did a quick circuit by air visiting Adelaide, Alice Springs (and Ayer's Rock), Darwin (and Kakadu National Park), Cairns (and Atherton Tablelands), Brisbane, Sydney, and Canberra. I also visited Hobart, Tasmania on a separate lecture stint. On my way home from Australia I was lucky enough to see Perth for a few days and found it to be a real jewel of a city. Altogether I got a lot out of my time in Australia, both professionally and as a tourist. I just loved Australia overall and swore to go back as soon as possible. I didn't, and haven't, and now probably won't. I'm very glad that I not only had the opportunity but took it when I had the chance.

As I continued on my open ticket round-the-world tour, continuing westward and stopping wherever I liked, I made my next stop at Singapore, where I was fitted out with a couple of summer suits. Next was Bangkok, Thailand and then off to Athens to see the Acropolis. After that I met up with Mary in Rome and we spent a week sightseeing there. Then it was on to London, where my brother Martin and I began a bus tour of the major capitals of Europe. When we got back to London, I noticed a sore on my lower lip that didn't want to heal. I had hoped to stay on in London for a while after Martin headed for home, but for the next few days I just couldn't stop my lip from bleeding. Despite wanting to stay a while longer in London, I was weary of travel and now in need of some medical attention, so I decided to hasten on home to see a doctor.

On the very day I arrived back in North Vancouver I went to see my family physician, who immediately sent me to a surgeon to have a biopsy excised. In a couple of days I was informed that I had "squamous cell carcinoma", in other words skin cancer on my lip, which would require surgery and radiation. While away in Australia, I had leased my farm in Langley hoping to return there when I got back, but now decided to stay with Mary in North Vancouver while I got my treatment and while I recovered.

Not too surprisingly, I was quite shocked and even significantly depressed about this development. Up to this point in my life, having enjoyed very good health for the most part, I felt invulnerable to disease, depression, and defeat. I had always thought that I could overcome any difficulty and conquer any enemy. Now, suddenly, my body had let me down. I had become my own enemy. Even though the surgeon told me that the cause of the cancer was UV light from too much exposure to direct sunlight, I was convinced that my years of smoking a pipe was a contributing factor. It was too much of a coincidence that the cancer just happened to be in the exact same corner of my mouth where I would always place my pipe. Then and there I gave up smoking the pipe for good.

My mid-life crisis came on with a bang. At age 53, I suddenly had to confront the fact that I was no longer a young man, no longer able to ignore caring for my body. The radiation treatment, though successful in treating the cancer, sucked the energy out of me that was once in abundance. I was not only fighting the cancer but the whole concept of ageing and weakening. I began reading voraciously on health, diet, and exercise. I was also particularly distraught over the slight disfigurement to my face (they had to cut away part of my lower lip). I no longer felt comfortable putting on my big broad expansive smile, pretending that I was handsome.

By late summer, 1985, I was well enough to return to my Langley farm and run some cattle. I continued for another two years doing that and commuting into the city to SFU, where I took on more and more teaching and research assignments. I was quite heavily involved with our off-campus teacher training program in far flung places such as Fort St. John, Dawson Creek, and Fort Nelson. This program, called the Alaska Highway Consortium on Teacher Education (ACHOTE) was specially funded by the Ministry of Education and involved the cooperation of the local Northern Lights College which has multiple campuses spread over several northern towns. I ended up being the Faculty sponsor of the program which meant that I was eventually working for SFU full time again.

An Inconvenient Love

COMING HOME from Melbourne to discover I had cancer was devastating and depressing, bringing on a mid-life crisis, but it wasn't nearly as painful or crisis-ridden as was falling in love and then dealing with it at the age of 58. And yes 'falling in love' is the right expression. Falling is not something that one plans or does deliberately unless one is acting or pretending. Suddenly I was head over heels in love. I didn't wish for it. There was no time for it. It interfered with my work and other commitments. It was totally inconvenient. But there I was, like an awkward teenager, finding it difficult to concentrate on anything except her, totally overwhelmed at the mere thought of seeing her again, flustered and intimidated by her presence. Nor was it simply mere sexual attraction; there was much more to it than that. In every thought expressed we were in total agreement, every nuance immediately understood. All the dreams of a perfect romance were becoming reality. All the old songs of love from our youth had meaning again: "All at once am I several stories high, knowing I'm on the street where you live"; "Love is a many splendored thing..."; "...And when I tell them how beautiful you are, they'll never believe me." An overpowering deep attraction gripped me beyond my power to control.

My own urge and desire to maintain control of my life vanished. I was drawn by some mysterious external force to go on this journey before any conscious decisions could be made. It wasn't 'yielding to temptation' so much as being captivated, a slave to a passion beyond my control. Within the mix of family obligations and social norms, falling in love could be considered a crisis, wishing at times that it didn't happen, but what a delicious crisis.

She had children that she couldn't leave, and so did I. She had interests that I couldn't meet and I had interests that she couldn't meet. What could we do? It was just as impossible to quit seeing each other as it was impossible to form a partnership. And then, in the midst of this lovely confusion, the guilt set in. Ah, precious guilt! Without the mechanism of confession and prayer to find expiation and comfort, guilt is the stand-in, helping to offset the unexpected and overwhelming joy. Come, blessed guilt and validate my love!

> This guilt cannot promote
> Some moral redirection
> It simply serves to validate
> The truth of my affection

Though one is hard pressed to admit it, one cannot survive long in the twin fires of guilt and overpowering love. I think that my love and I both knew that we could never form a partnership, but I was spellbound and couldn't take the necessary steps to break away. She could and did, breaking me up badly. Not certainly but perhaps probably it was for the best for both of us. Women sometimes have a better sense of those things. Life required that we both move on.

Painful as the experience was, it was also exhilarating and even as a mature man, I learned from it. I learned that it is definitely possible to love more than one person at one time, even if in very different ways. If that is so, why then is it so socially unacceptable and full of opprobrium? Shouldn't the practice of extramarital love be treated with more compassion and understanding?[120] Are social norms indeed more important than affairs of the heart? These are questions, enigmas that we humans are eternally wrapped up in. In any case, I learned never to take love lightly at any age.

---

120   As in the movie 'Silent Light', the only feature film I know of spoken in Plautdietsch, set in a Mennonite community in Mexico. Here a family man, and devout church member, has an affair with a married woman. The church community, who learn of the affair, treat the whole matter more like a social disease rather than a moral failing. Rather than shunning the two, the church members treat the pair with great sympathy and compassion and in the end coax them to return to their families.

The experience of my inconvenient love prompted me to express my sentiments in a number of poems, including the following two:

> My Mistress of Charlie Lake (1990)
> (The evanescence of love and religion)
>
> My spiritual mistress of Charlie Lake,
> In crystals of snow, when my soul needed you,
> You appeared on a cold winter's day.
> On a magical loom threading silvery dew,
> You carried my heart away.
>
> I adored you, mistress kind,
> My dream of Charlie Lake!
> With a love that would cure
> You made my heart pure
> And opened my eyes that were blind.
>
> I worshipped you, mistress true,
> My goddess of Charlie Lake,
> Your love changed my fate,
> Opened wide heaven's gate,
> You redeemed me, made me anew.
>
> I lauded you, mistress bold.
> Gen'rous sprite of Charlie Lake!
> In soul bearing missives, which set me on fire
> You charged my being with awesome desire
> And thoughts too rare to be told.
>
> My phantom mistress of Charlie Lake,
> While sun-dogs danced on a frosty morn
> You were fashioned one winter's day;
> But the crystals broke and my heart is torn,
> For in summer you melted away.

North Vancouver (1963 – 1984)

To My Lost Love (1991)

We cannot weep forever
For the love that went awry;
Life's urgency requires
That we kiss and say 'good-bye'.
There is nothing to be done
When as lovers we must part
Save store the precious mem'ries
In a corner of our heart.

We cannot grieve unending
For the happy days we had;
There are too many other loves
That soon will make us sad.
They too will swear upon the heart
To love us to the end;
But when sly cupid plucks the plume
New sorrows will descend.

We cannot hope for a reprieve
Of the magic that is past;
Love's wonder and entrancement
Never were in silver cast.
When again twixt toil and striving
We smile briefly as we fret,
We'll remember in our daydreams
The oases where we met.

CHAPTER 7

Burnaby and Yaletown (1989-2011)

Later Years at SFU

Now that I was back working full time for SFU (though still on a half-time appointment), and heavily involved with AH-COTE, which meant frequent trips to the airport, I found it too onerous to commute daily from rural Langley all the way to SFU. So in mid-December, 1987, I decided to lease my Langley property and reside closer to the University. I found a nice suite at the base of Burnaby Mountain, upon which SFU is located, and beside Burnaby Mountain Golf Course. I sold my remaining farm machinery, stored some tools and extra furniture, and wrapped up my farming life with mixed emotions. I was excited to dive back into full time academia but also regretting the end of the farming operation.

During that time I was asked to prepare materials for our introductory course in philosophy of education suitable for delivery in our Distance Education program. A colleague of mine, then a graduate student, came across these materials, liked them, and suggested I write a text for general distribution as well as for the distance education course. It proved to be a good idea and in the fall of 1989 *Philosophical Issues in Education: An Introduction* became a reality.

I actually did the final rewriting in a cottage beside a frozen lake in the far north of BC. I was still heavily involved with AHCOTE and was assigned to teach the introductory course to three separate groups, in Fort St. John, in Dawson Creek, and in Fort Nelson. Each of these three towns had local campuses of the Northern Lights College system. Since those places are a long way away from Burnaby and since I had to visit all three towns on a frequent basis the Dean and I decided that it would be more efficient for me to relocate there while I was teaching. So I installed a block heater and new snow tires on my car and drove north to a well appointed cabin at Charlie Lake, just outside of Fort St. John. It was a great arrangement and provided me with ample quiet uninterrupted time to finish work on the book. My text was to a considerable extent the reworking of the materials of other philosophers. Thus I needed permission from a number of them to replicate their work.

In a letter to R.S. Peters on February 9, 1989, I wrote, "The attempt in my text is not to write an original treatise, but rather to make more readily available to beginning students in philosophy of education the best work done in the field in simplified form." Peters responded by saying, "Using simple language [goes] a long way to help students' understanding and thinking. A simplified version of my writings ... I think would be of great value in keeping alive philosophy of education." Others from whom I sought permission were Paul Hirst and Robert Dearden from the London Institute, Israel Scheffler from Harvard, Keith Flemming from Melbourne University and Tasos Kazepides from SFU. All were most encouraging and helpful. When I sent the penultimate version of the text to M.W. Clarkson of Falmer Press, he sent me a contract to seal the deal. Apparently he agreed with Peters. The only work left was to hammer out the final draft, finish the exercises at the end of the chapters, and get it in print in time for the fall semester.

Although I was happy with the finished work and it fulfilled the needs of some of my academic partners, the book did not sell well in Canada and the US, where the 'British School' or 'Analytical Philosophy' is considered only one of several ways of doing philosophy of education. In England, Australia, South Africa, and elsewhere the book sold much better and over the years I enjoyed a few royalty cheques. The text was also translated into Korean, though I think I received nothing in royalties from that. No matter. It gives me satisfaction enough just to know that the ideas in the book are being promulgated in many far flung parts of the world, including Bulgaria, Turkey, Indonesia, and elsewhere. After 25 years, it is still selling and I'm still receiving royalty cheques here and there. It was a nice twist that the lad born in the Peace country could return there so many years later to complete his major publication. The peace and quiet of Charlie Lake was at least partly responsible for this success.

Charlie Lake in winter is a magical place. Thick ice topped with powdery snow makes the lake a natural playground for those interested in cross country skiing, dog sledding, or ice fishing. Several times a week I would ski across the lake to the few buildings that made up the hamlet of Charlie Lake to pick up supplies and mail, always hoping to receive a missive from a loved one. Sun dogs in the daytime and northern lights after dark often danced in the sky above me as I made the traverse.

As pleasant and peaceful as my Charlie Lake experience was, there were also some unsettling and hazardous experiences. I recall waiting many hours at cold airport terminals because of delayed flights. It was all small towns and small airports and small aircraft and there were many delays. This was, after all, northern Canada and in winter the weather is always a factor to contend with. Driving was difficult too.

Often I drove the 80 kilometers to Dawson Creek in complete darkness in order to make the round trip in a single day, the daylight hours being short-lived. On one occasion, I recall making my way down the winding, icy highway, my lights, windshield wipers, and heater all at full force, straining to compete with a full, fierce blizzard. Suddenly I was face to face with a huge semi roaring towards me, barely being able to make out his lights in the swirling snow. I dared not hit the brakes lest I skid off the road or worse, into the oncoming truck. I dared not steer away too sharply either lest I end up in the ditch. I could barely see the road itself, never mind any of the lines or markings. I only dared to release my foot on the accelerator a bit and held my breath as the truck and its blinding cloud of snow passed by.

Even having to drive slowly, I still arrived on time, in fact a bit early, having the habit of always allowing a little extra time for the unexpected. I realized how dirty my car had become from all the salt, sand, and gravel on the road, so I decided that a car wash was in order as befits a visiting professor. So I went for a coffee and prepared my notes while my car was being washed. When I was ready to go, I went to get in the car only to realize, much to my surprise, that all the doors were frozen shut. The only way in was through the window of the tailgate (it was a station wagon). So here I was, dressed in my professorial finery climbing through the back window of my car like a well-dressed thief. Had I been seen and photographed, it surely would have made the paper, perhaps with a caption "Visiting ethics professor breaks into vehicle." I told my story to my students who just laughed, all having had similar experiences.

Undergraduate Directorship

BACK AT SFU in Burnaby, one day in the late spring of 1989, the Dean asked me to join him for a business lunch at the University Club. We were joined by the Academic Vice President. It didn't take me long to figure out that I was being screened for an administrative post, the Director of Undergraduate Programs. At that time, the Faculty of Education didn't have a departmental structure, but consisted of three program areas, Undergraduate, Graduate, and Professional Development. The directors of these areas together with the Dean and Assistant Dean formed the Executive, which jointly made decisions on academic and budgetary issues. Individual directors, along with their own elected committees, made decisions on course approval, student counselling, off campus offerings, and the like. The Director was also responsible for the selection and appointment of short-term instructors and teaching assistants. So at the luncheon, I was being sized up for all of these tasks. I got the nod from the Dean and Vice President but I still had to gain the approval of the Faculty members themselves. After a bit of grilling on various issues, they too gave me their approval. I requested and was given tenure, a full time appointment, and commensurate salary. And so, by the fall semester, I was all set to start my four year stint as Director of Undergraduate Programs.

One of my first duties as Director was to hire Teaching Assistants (TAs) for the popular courses with large enrollments. To make my decisions, I had the prospective TA's application form, resumes, and evaluations from former students and course instructors. Since the TA job was a unionized position, I was required to accept the candidate with the most seniority if all other things were equal. In one instance I observed that the person with seniority had significantly lower evaluations both by course instructors and students. My approach was to select the best candidate for the given job – all things are not always equal – and so that is what I did. When the results of my hiring decision became known, I was immediately slapped with a 'grievance' by the person with more seniority. I was so naive in these matters at the time that I didn't even know what that meant. I found out in a pronounced manner very shortly.

The head of the TA union asked for an interview with me to ascertain why I had defied the union rules about seniority. If I had only said "In my judgement, the person I appointed was a superior candidate", which of course was true, it would have ended there. However, not knowing how to navigate these strange new legal and political waters, having some sympathy for the failed candidate and the union, and depending on compassion as a guide, I tried to give reasons why I had hired one over the other. The union leader found his opening and jumped on my explanations challenging the validity of my hiring process and the validity of the evaluations. After that lawyers got involved and it turned into a nasty litigious matter. Clearly, at least in my mind, I had done nothing wrong, but that doesn't necessarily matter. There are always ways to monkey with the evidence to construct a spurious legal defence. We ended up settling out of court with the University paying the failed candidate a semester's salary simply because it was cheaper than going to court. I was glad to put an end to this stressful episode but I would have preferred that the University fight it out in court. I'm sure I could have won.

That was only one such legal/political conflict, albeit a serious and disturbing one. For the first several months as director I kept wondering why *all* of the issues in my in-box were complicated and difficult to resolve. Then I began to realize that all the easy decisions were already made and taken care of by my capable staff. Everything that landed on my desk was both difficult and controversial. I suppose that's the life of any administrator. I had to make calls on grade disputes knowing full well that my decision could seriously affect the staff member or the student and I had sympathy for both. How does one decide between two equally qualified candidates knowing that both need the job? How does one decide between two qualified faculty members each having equally good grounds for arguing that it is their prerogative to teach X course at Y time? Grades are also highly political. The Senate was asking for lowering the 'out of control' high grades given out in the Faculty of Education. So do I side with them or with my own faculty? Do I sign the grade sheets to approve them or do I reject them? Are the grades really out of control or is it that we just have high quality students and excellent instruction? I came to realize and accept that making tough decisions was the name of the game.

Often I would mull over the pros and cons of an issue – not only in my office but also at home, on walks, in leisure time, and in the middle of the night – only to find that arguments and data on each side of an issue were equally compelling. One may as well have just flipped a coin. But decisions had to be made and once a decision is made, one is expected to be able to defend and justify it. So, to survive one has to focus on all the positives of one candidate and all the negatives of the other candidate when justification is inevitably called for in a meeting or by a colleague. Thus one can come off appearing quite wise and rational to the group or individual discussant; but deep down, despite carrying the day with aplomb, one knows that it could have gone the other way just as easily.

All people have pros and cons and by simply choosing one's focus one can paint the picture one wants to. It is a way of surviving in administration but one ends up feeling like a misfit, like Hamlet:

> *The time is out of joint: O cursed spite,*
> *That ever I was born to set it right.*[121]

Not surprisingly, I found my four years in administration quite exhausting, mostly because I cared enough to try to make the right decisions. I can truly say that those years were the most difficult and stressful in all my professional academic life. At times I felt that I wasn't going to get through another year of that. At such times I was content to just keep things rolling without too many bumps, or, to mix a metaphor, just to keep the lid on a boiling pot. At other times I felt quite successful in my role and thought that I was actually instrumental in innovating and consolidating improvements in Undergraduate Programs. I did the best I could.

Those were years when a month's holiday, usually in August, was most needed and relished. It was during these years that my good friend David and I made our road tours in Canada and beyond. We went on nice long trips to Alaska, across Canada to New Brunswick, to Lack La Range in Saskatchewan, and also one summer to revisit London and England.

Cornel and David as travellers, circa 1989

---

121 William Shakespeare, *Hamlet*, Act 1 Scene 5.

Despite the challenges of the job of Director, I am now very grateful for the experience. I now have much less animosity to administrators and politicians, having seen and experienced what they have to deal with. Before that time, I had always felt, and to some degree still do, that administrators and politicians make at best arbitrary and at worst entirely self-interested decisions. However, even when there are weighty arguments on both sides of an issue, *someone* has to make the call and then take responsibility for it. At times, even with the best intent, some decisions will turn out to be the wrong ones. So when I see administrative mistakes now, even knowing that some decision makers are less than fully honest, I tend to sympathize more than to blame.

In 1995, at Christmas, my administrative post and in fact my whole teaching career had more or less come to an end. I did conduct a few more graduate seminars off campus for SFU in the next few years on special assignment, but I was heading out to pasture. In Vernon, BC, and Prince George, I remember the sessions going very well indeed. I can honestly say that I went out on a career-ending high. Though my employment at SFU had come to an end, my salary continued for another year and a half, thanks to the times when I worked full time for half salary. Not losing my salary immediately was a great boost to my overall financial picture and set me up well for retirement.

Retirement

SO WHAT DOES one do in retirement? Working people are fond of asking this question. A glib answer, one my brother Martin sometimes used, is "Tell me what day you have in mind and I'll see if I can remember." The real answer is, of course, anything and everything. There seems to be so many things to do that I can honestly say, along with many other retirees, that I'm so busy now that I don't see how I ever had time for a job. The last thing I feel is boredom for lack of something to do.

As one gets older, one slows down considerably, both physically and mentally. Thus it takes more time to go shopping, preparing for a trip, seeing the physician, picking up prescription drugs, cooking meals, doing laundry, or doing just about anything. A good part of retirement is just doing these mundane but necessary chores. Beyond that, the bulk of my time in retirement has been taken up by the following: reading, listening to and seeing musical performances, participating in sports (tennis, while I still had the legs for it, golf, and daily brisk walks), writing, hobby farming, and other forms of entertainment.

Reading is not only pleasurable for me but I find it is the easiest and quickest way to fill in the gaps in my general education – and yes, I'm still working on my general education. Not only was my overall education skewed by religion, but also in our childhood and youth there was little leisure time to read. And when we did have leisure time the great works of literature and non-fiction were not available to us. So huge gaps remained, and still remain, in my general knowledge; not only in fiction, but also in history, mathematics, and physics. So in my retirement years I have begun to fill in some of those gaps; and I'm enjoying it immensely.

For example, in a three month period, wintering in Palm Springs, I spent all of my spare time reading up on Russian history and even learning a bit of the language in preparation for an upcoming trip to Russia. For a period of two years I focused almost exclusively on science, particularly physics, in my reading program, in the effort to understand at least something of the strange concepts physicists use and mind-boggling claims they make. Among theoretical and experimental physicists I have read and at least partly understood are: Stephen Hawking, Brian Greene, Steven Weinberg, Peter Voigt, and Leon Ledermen. Nobel physicist, Steven Weinberg once remarked:

> *As human beings we are perennially in the tragic position of not ever being able to understand completely why things are the way they are. For even if we find the grand unifying theory (GUT) we will still ask 'Why is it that way and not some other way?'*[122]

---

122 – Johnathon Miller (presenter), *The Atheism Tapes*, 2004, BBC TV Program.

That remark prompted me to write the following poem:

The Mystery (2012)

Democritus the *a-tom* sought,
But find the damned thing he could not.
Then other Greeks would take a look,
On *telos* though they closed the book.

Christians too laid down a plan
For the significance of man
Which they spread in word and song.
Did they ever get it wrong!

Newton in a word or two
Started wisdom all anew.
A smarter man you could not find
Then Einstein left *him* far behind.

Now we're closing in on GUTS;
That I'm not denying.
But whichever way it cuts,
Life *still* is mystifying.

Soon I will be going.
Time's up; and I lament
That I'll go not knowing
What life really meant.

In more recent years I've also returned to reading philosophy to try to finally grasp the full impact of some of the more difficult works of thinkers like Kant and Hume. If there were not so many other worthwhile and interesting endeavors to pursue, apart from keeping myself alive and healthy, I could easily spend the rest of my life just reading non-fiction.

Modern technology has made it possible to access a vast treasure of film and music for those so interested. And I'm so interested. In fact, to me, listening to great music before the ears go deaf is a must. Old movies and music that I have seen and heard need repetition. Watching 'live' opera simulcasts from the Met and other great opera houses, complete with sub-titles and close-ups, allows me to enjoy the highest quality operas without leaving town. In this way I have just begun to understand and appreciate Wagner (his music really is better than it sounds). That by itself is a whole new field of interest that could keep me busy for years. In addition to music and film, I also spend many enjoyable hours listening to talks, lectures, interviews, nature studies and more.

Retirement has also allowed me to travel more extensively. When working for SFU I had to travel a fair bit for professional reasons, as I was expected to attend conferences, to give and receive academic papers, and keep abreast of developments in my discipline. Thus I travelled to many places on business, all over Canada and the US, England, Australia, South Africa, and even Bulgaria. However, upon retirement I could travel more for enjoyment and choose locations that I had always wanted to see: Eastern Europe, Turkey, Egypt, Russia, China and elsewhere. I also took cruises through the Panama Canal and around the Baltic. For each of these trips I prepared vigorously, reading up on history, geography, and culture and even trying to learn a bit of the local languages.

This was particularly true for my trip to the Ukraine, in the fall of 2001 just after 9/11. This tour for me was the most memorable of all the tours and cruises I went on because it was a 'heritage cruise' and designed as an opportunity to discover and explore my Mennonite roots. Beginning at Odessa and anchoring at various ports around the Crimea and points along the Dnieper River and ending at Kiev, the cruise made a significant stop at Zaporozhe. Here we disembarked our cruise ship and travelled by bus to various locations where my forbears had lived and died. I even entered the house in Borozenko that my great grandfather Kornelius Penner had built in 1873 and had tea there. I also got to visit the house my grandfather lived in and where my father was brought up. I saw, too, where Mother's family had lived and farmed.

Burnaby and Yaletown (1989-2011)

Former great grandparents home of K. Penner, in Schöndorf, Borozenko, photo by Cornel, 2001

Former M.Hamm home in Schönau, Zagradovka

Former J. Warkentin home in Schönau, Zagradovka

It was also pointed out to me that half a mile away or so where the forest began was an unmarked mass grave, where my grandfather was hastily buried after his murder at the hands of the marauding bands of Makhnoists[123]. To see and enter the buildings my forebears made, to walk the land they walked on, to see the forest that was my grandfather's place of burial left me with a deep sense of belonging, completeness, and connectedness that is virtually indescribable. It was as though I had come full circle and could now happily die without missing anything.

At that point in my life, I was in the habit of wintering in Palm Springs, California and I do not really consider going there vacationing as such. Since I fell in love with Palm Springs on my first visit there in 1984, I have returned every year save one. At first it was just for a brief stay around Christmas and then that expanded to a few weeks and then upon retirement about three months a year. For a period of about six years I owned a suite at the Palm Springs Golf and Tennis Club, which I sold again at a fair profit. Now I find it cheaper and easier just to lease a place when I go there. Often when I leave my Vancouver residence to fly south as a 'snowbird' I wonder why I am doing this. After all, Vancouver is a world class city and frequently in the top echelons of the most desirable places to live. However, as soon as I arrive at Palm Springs and step out of the plane greeted by the warm desert air, I remember why I like to go there. The air is so pure, the light so penetrating, the warmth so pleasant. The aches and pains in my bones seem to disappear and I am again walking, hiking, playing golf and tennis, keeping active and exercised. How long I'll be able to continue with this I don't know, but for as long as I can, and health allows, I will.

Part of my reasonably good health for my age I attribute to sensible eating and regular exercise. My snowbirding venture is part of that. In Palm Springs, the fruits and vegetables are fresher,

---

123 The Makhnoists were a band of anarchist guerilla fighters who violently opposed any order in southwest Ukraine and basically fought anybody they came across who wished to impose order. They fought both with and against the Red Army during the Russian civil wars following the Russian Revolution.

Balcony view from Cornel's place, Palm Springs, CA

Ready for golf (l. to r.): Wayne, Cornel, Norm, David

tastier and cheaper, the outdoor activities, at least to me, more luring and attractive. Here at home in Vancouver, I also exercise regularly but one has to survive torrents of cold rain all winter. Regardless of where I am, my first activity each day is to go for a brisk 20 to 30 minute walk. Earlier, before I hit 60, I used to run. After the warm-up walk, I do a series of stretching and strengthening exercises for about 15 minutes more. If I am not golfing or shopping or being active in another way, I also go for a walk in the afternoon. I've been doing this for years and it takes no force of will whatsoever to make myself do it; it is second nature to me now. My eating is also well regulated: I eat home cooked meals as much as possible. low in fats and meats, high in fresh fruits and vegetables, and low in sugar and salt.

Over the years, particularly while living by myself, I managed slowly to learn how to cook for myself, even learning to enjoy cooking and serving respectable meals to guests. Usually about once a week I entertain a friend or two around wine and dinner. Most evenings are conversational but occasionally music or film take centre stage. I also get asked out for reciprocal dinners and drinks. In the late 1990's and early 2000's, I particularly enjoyed soirees and an annual big party at David's place in West Vancouver. There he would, after a delicious dinner, have instrumentalists (from the Vancouver Symphony Orchestra) and singers perform and readers present poetry and drama. For at least five years in succession I recited and read poetry at these galas. So there I was, in my advancing years, going back to my childhood love of reciting poetry. In fact, before I retired, I used the SFU recording studio to record a CD of poetry with my grandchildren in mind. I think I enjoyed it more than the grandchildren did or ever will. We'll see.

Despite all the attention to and time given to reading, listening, travelling, and writing, I still had a yen to do some farming and stay connected to the land. I just could not live in peace for very long without owning and improving a piece of land. For a year or two after retiring I just sat on my laurels and rested. When I finally quit teaching I really felt exhausted and relished the opportunity to recharge my old batteries. However, as much as I needed the rest, I just couldn't sit around for long. So in 1998 I started looking for a new property to work on. This time I wanted a mountain property a little inland away from the coastal rain belt, yet a driveable distance from Vancouver. The location and drier micro-climate of Princeton, BC appealed to me, the driving time being just 3 ½ hours. I had my eye on an 80 acre tract in the hills just a few miles southwest of Princeton but it was bought up by somebody else. So I kept looking.

That fall, while down in Palm Springs, a single joined our golf threesome. He looked a little familiar and amazingly turned out to be the very same realtor from small town Princeton, BC who sold the aforementioned property that I was interested in. I asked him if he thought that the property might go back on the market. He said that he would give the new owners a call. As it turned out, the owners

Nigel Shiraya, and Devin, our grandchildren

did have second thoughts and decided to sell. When I flew home for a couple of weeks for Christmas that year, I took the opportunity to bus out to Princeton to have a closer look at the property, now under a blanket of snow. The ponderosa pines and large Douglas fir trees poking their head out over the tops of the lodgepole pines made a stunningly beautiful scene. I knew right then and there that I wanted to go ahead with it but I also noticed some downed fences and asked for a discount. I got it. 'Hammstead' was now mine.

That spring I bought a 15 foot house trailer and towed it into place which was to be my home at Hammstead for the duration of my time there. Later that year I also cleared and fenced a home site near the centre of the property with the intention of planting a garden and fruit trees. The site afforded a sweeping 300 degree view of trees and mountains. The following year, I brought in a water line from the edge of the property and put in the garden and orchard. I was considering hooking up to the BC Hydro electrical grid as well but instead opted for solar energy. I had never fully understood electricity and even feared it a bit, but I set to work studying up on the matter in all its multifarious dimensions. I calculated the amount of power I would need, bought sufficient solar panels and installed and wired all of the various devices and contraptions in the combination pump-house electrical shed that I had built. In the end, I had a working solar system sufficient for my needs, even passing the required inspection by the authorities. I was both proud and content.

The Princeton property was to be the place where my son, Colin, could establish himself in a semi-wilderness setting and I could visit him there and he look after me in my dotage. I had hoped to establish a small ranch with cattle and sheep and at the same time sustain a small woodlot operation. In the end, Colin wasn't interested in that arrangement so I used the lot as a recreation property for a period of eight years. It was certainly suitable

Vista at Cornel's Princeton property

for that. By 2006, I was getting weary of commuting back and forth for short trips and felt too isolated while I was there for longer ones. It was time once again to sell. I made somewhat of a profit and now wanted to use the funds to buy a more permanent residence in Vancouver.

In the meantime, several friends of mine, including my dear old friend, David, had moved to Yaletown, a revitalized area on the edge of downtown Vancouver. That area appealed to me too. However I first needed to sell my apartment in Burnaby, near the main campus of SFU. When I first moved to the Burnaby Mountain area, I was renting but then I decided to buy a suite there to take advantage of the steeply rising real estate market. That I did in 1994, but soon realized to my dismay that I had bought a 'leaky condo'. So instead of profiting from my investment, I had to shell out a large amount of cash to fix the exterior walls which were mouldy and moist and had to be replaced at great expense.

With repairs to the outer building and the replacement of windows and walls, with the lost interest revenue and lost appreciation in value, I figure that I lost about $75,000 on that deal. And I wasn't alone. This was a widespread phenomenon. The 'leaky condos' saga of the 90's in greater Vancouver was, and perhaps still is, a massive scam and injustice, deserving of shame and guilt on the part of questionable builders and the failure of local and provincial authorities to regulate them. There is no excuse for such shoddy business and poor government supervision. I am still waiting for someone to write a definitive exposé on the whole 'leaky condo' phenomenon. Luckily, I was in a financial position such that I could weather the storm, but it was not so for everyone. After waiting for the interminable repairs to finish in my leaky condo and waiting for the market to recover, I put my place up for sale. I was relieved when it finally sold in 2006, the same year I sold the Princeton property, and was now in a position to look into moving to the desirable Yaletown area of downtown Vancouver.

Yaletown

YEARS BEFORE moving to Yaletown I had visited with friends who lived in the area. They all seemed to enjoy the lifestyle and amenities of the newly renovated False Creek / Yaletown area of downtown Vancouver. Before committing to buying, I wanted to test it out a bit so I started by renting a place on the tenth floor of a high-rise with nice views of Yaletown marina, False Creek, and the Cambie bridge. Not only did I have a great view and many conveniences at hand, I also enjoyed the general ambience of the area. One of the attractions was the diversity in race, colour, culture, age, social status, and educational level of the inhabitants. The proximity to shops and services was particularly nice. Almost everything I wanted, and a lot more, was within easy walking distance.

I didn't even really need a car anymore for I could walk to the dentist, the doctor's office, the hospital, to movie theatres, friends' places, concert halls, banks, shops, grocery stores (including a farmer's market), the library, and the liquor store. And if my shopping bags got too heavy to walk with I could always take the bus or the nearby skytrain. So I sold my car and I don't miss it.

Being free of the car habit is actually a wonderful release; and it saves one a lot of money. On occasions when I do need a car – to go golfing, to carry heavy shopping items, to visit out of town – I use

Balcony view in Yaletown

co-op cars several of which are within a few blocks of my home, the closest being just outside the front door of my apartment building. These cars, and the occasional use of a taxi, aren't free but compared to the costs of owning and operating a car full time (depreciation, gas, insurance, and so on), it's far cheaper and I can almost cover my entire transportation costs by simply renting out my coveted downtown parking space. Not only does not owning a car make sense financially for me, I benefit greatly by keeping fit from all the walking I do.

Convenient though the location and pleasant though the available amenities, Yaletown has some disadvantages as well. A big problem is noise. Local parks and beaches offer many enjoyable festivals and events, which is great when you want them; but less so when you don't. Many jazz concerts and fireworks displays have intruded on my peace and quiet. The constant thrum of regular traffic noise, punctuated by sirens and excessively loud motorcycles at any time of day or night, can, at times, be downright annoying. Noise from my immediate neighbors also seeps in through the surprisingly thin wall of my not so inexpensive apartment. Would a little soundproofing from the builders be too much to ask for?

Vancouver is often listed as one of the most desirable places in the world to live and Yaletown is one of the more desirable neighborhoods there. Furthermore the city prides itself as a model for green, high density living; so it is to me astounding that there are still so many problems to solve before it is truly cultured and comfortable. The high-rise buildings, though sensibly spaced, structurally sound, and even aesthetically pleasing, are, in my view, shoddily finished, at least most of the ones that I have been in. And I have been in many. Not only is the sound of partying and children playing clearly audible and somewhat annoying, but even the smells of tobacco smoke and perfume come right through the walls! The hollow metal doors banging on hollow metal frames frequently echo through the hallways. The required mechanical door closers make this even worse. We're good at making buildings safe such that they don't fall over or burn down all that often and we're good at making them look nice but we're less good at making them comfortable, low stress places for human beings to relax in.

It's not just the design and construction of the buildings themselves that is the main problem; it is people's lack of regard for others. It may well turn out that in the long run the greatest challenges to having comfortable high-density living are not really design or engineering issues but rather people's attitudes and behaviour. Ethics and etiquette are ever important. Nevertheless getting the building design and construction right would be a good first step in helping neighbors not to annoy each other. We as a culture are just starting to figure out how many ways stress is unhealthy to us but I think that a lot of people don't realize how much unwanted sounds add to this ever mounting stress of modern urban living. Despite the annoyances of noise, smells, improper management of pets, and, at times, overcrowding, there are still many periods of time when I am ever so delighted to be living here in Yaletown.

How many more years (or months for that matter) do I have until the end of my journey? Who can say? What I do know, is that however long life lasts, it will be too short. Given reasonable health, I would like to spend my next decade or so much the same as the last: reading, listening, golfing, travelling (though perhaps a bit less), writing, and participating in politics. If I do live long enough, I also hope to get involved in volunteering for social causes. In the next year or so, after I get through reworking the first draft of this memoir, I would very much like to do a thorough study of the myths alluded to in Wagner's operas. I also want to write more poetry.

Even if I can't expect to achieve much, I can, and do, enjoy just being alive, watching the world and time slip by in endless magnificence. I try to look on "all things lovely every hour".[124] I feel so fortunate to have found my intellectual freedom, my way out of the metaphorical Damascus, and to have landed in Yaletown. What a journey it was! It was indeed a long and winding road, complete with pitfalls and confusion, always difficult to find my way. But find my way I did. To freedom. To happiness. To a vision of the New Jerusalem.

---

124   From 'Farewell' by Walter De La Mare.

CHAPTER 8

The Road Back

Losing the Faith and Growing Up

SOME YEARS AGO, while standing on the street corner waiting for the light to change at a busy Burnaby thoroughfare, I was approached by a smartly dressed handsome young man holding some papers in his hands. He obviously wanted to talk to me and when I turned to look at him, he said "Excuse me, do you live in Burnaby?"

"Yes", I replied.

"And have you always lived there?"

"Oh no, I was born in Alberta and have lived in many parts of the world."

With that, having found his opening, the young man then said, "If you were born in Alberta you will have heard of the Lord Jesus and the Gospel."

"I most certainly have."

"And were you saved?"

"Yes."

"And were you baptised?"

"Yes. Saved, baptised, choired, churched, Sunday Schooled, Bible schooled, and more – the full catastrophe."

"You're still a believer then?" he urgently inquired.

"Oh no! Not at all."

"What happened?" he asked, anxiously this time.

"I grew up."

With that his chin dropped and a puzzled look came over his face as he put away his gospel tracts and turned away. The lights changed and as I made my way across the intersection I thought to myself, "There, but for good luck go I." How could I have been so fortunate as to achieve freedom from all that this young man represented – all those zealots, wasting their time proselytizing to pacify their conscience because others do not share their mythology? It could have been me. In fact for a short while it *was* me.

Perhaps it is an oversimplification to suggest that acquiring freedom from religion and the effects of indoctrination is simply a matter of growing up. Though perhaps also I had been more right in my quick retort than I had wanted to be. Perhaps I hit the nail right on the head, for there is, in the end, no excuse for not leaving behind childish myths and beliefs if they are not supportable, especially if they cause harm and distress to others. Nor do I apologize to this young man for suggesting he was not grown up. Sometimes it is impossible not to offend if one wants to awaken someone from their dogmatic slumber.

This incident reminds me of how frighteningly close I came to being professionally caught up in very similar religious activities. I was very nearly trapped for good by all of that religious indoctrination that I grew up with. How happy I am that I took those difficult and tentative first few steps toward intellectual freedom, and then a few more, which in turn became leaping strides along the long road back from Damascus. This was made possible because early on in my struggle with doubt I allowed myself to retain within me settled pockets of disbelief.

Pockets of Disbelief

THE PHENOMENON which I have called 'pockets of disbelief' is, I think, quite widespread amongst any community of believers. For example, when internal conflict, the battle between faith and reason, became too severe for me, I just declared to myself that I just didn't believe that particular item. I was a small-time heretic, but if I kept it to myself I could still keep the bulk of my faith and not harm the fellowship of family and church. My own father, a devout church member and community leader, had let slip at least one such pocket, and that gave me tacit permission to do the same.

Once, after discussing evolution at school, I approached my father to ask whether he believed in evolution. To my great surprise he said that he did, though of course he fit it within the Christian context: "to God, a day is like a thousand years". And so the door was open to non-literal interpretation of the Bible and thus I thought, if a thousand, why not a million or a billion? It was quite liberating, but Dad suggested rather strongly that I shouldn't mention this to Mother. So here too was Dad, a lay preacher in our church, holding on to this little secret pocket of disbelief. In this instance he deliberately and consciously chose a non-literal interpretation of the Genesis creation story. I started thinking that perhaps all believers are forced by blatant contradictions in the Bible to interpret at least some passages symbolically, even if that is against their inclination or teachings. After all didn't Jesus himself scold Nicodemus for trying to take the notion of being 'born again' literally?[125]

For me, another pocket of disbelief concerned the reality of hell for non-believers, who, through no fault of their own are condemned to eternal suffering (supposedly by a beneficent God) simply because they haven't heard about Christ or the Gospel. I reasoned it this way: if God is just and fair and loving and all

---

125   John 3:1-21.

good and all powerful, as we had been taught, then He could not cause millions or perhaps billions of human beings to burn in hell forever simply because of ignorance. And there are other attendant problems as well. What about those who lived before Christ arrived? How far back does one go? If evolution is correct, and the evidence for it is overwhelming, then how far back into pre-history does God go to gather fuel for his hellfire? What about intelligent non-human species? Will dolphins burn in the big barbecue? I had to, out of compassion, conclude that hell didn't really exist for these innocents. So there I was, entering my second year at PBI with the expectation of preparing for the ministry, not believing in hell for heathens. This took some of the urgency out of missionary work and so I focused on home ministry work or teaching instead. The rest of my religious beliefs held firm more or less, at least at that time. Eventually however, I acquired more and more pockets of disbelief until my religious edifice grew hollower and hollower.

I noted earlier that it is not uncommon for religious believers to have such pockets of disbelief, who nevertheless stay in the fold their entire lives. A number of those who have left the Church have related to me how uncomfortable it was to maintain religious practices and observances while their pockets of disbelief mounted, particularly those who had been professionally involved. In some cases preachers have continued preaching long after their faith has collapsed, simply to put food on the table and protect family and community cohesion and appearances. I feel very fortunate to have escaped all of that. What helped me to get there were some fundamental shifts in my attitude towards reason and rationality.

At least three important ground breaking insights and changes in attitude enabled me to break away from religion. First, I became entirely convinced by the embededness of reason in human affairs and a growing trust in my own use of reason. Second, I experienced a growing awareness of human beings' capacity for grand delusions, including self-delusion. Third, I embraced the philosophical notion of the absolute necessity of conceptual clarity for knowledge claims.

The Embeddedness of Reason

IN THE ABILITY to use reason lies human beings' uniqueness as a species. The power of reason has enabled us to become creatures of rational thought and to create at least the beginnings of a civilized existence. Not only do we have a right to use and refine our reason, which is tantamount to our right to be human, we also have the responsibility to use reason in the quest for human betterment and perfection. It would therefore seem silly, even perverse, for people to try to make a considered case against the use of reason, not least because it takes reason to make the case. Yet that is exactly what happens in the minds of many when it comes to religion. That is what I did in my youth when I had doubts about some religious tenet or dogma. I just deliberately stopped applying reason and continued to believe as I was supposed to. I am convinced that that is what the vast majority of religious people do. They apply and follow reason up to a certain point in a debate (be it public or internal) and then suddenly abandon reason at some arbitrary point when faith becomes threatened. That point differs from person to person depending on their ability to think, their level of comfort with ambiguity, and their ability to admit failure or ignorance.

Let's again take the creation story in Genesis as an example. Some people who take the Bible as the literal word of God in every detail will take the story at face value and simply dismiss the overwhelming evidence against it being literally true. My mother would have been of that persuasion. My father, however, was able to take the Bible more metaphorically, though he still insisted that there had to be a God who used evolution as a mode of creating mankind. He had to fit his reasonable doubts within the context of his strong personal faith and social expectations. He believed in the God-as-designer idea, assuming as many religious people do, that any complex thing has to be created by a more complex being. That is easily negated by "Who created God?", "Who designed the designer?", and pointing out the infinite regress in that line of argument. However, the religionist at this point, falls back on the notion that God has always existed. As my Dad would say, "From everlasting to everlasting He is God" (meaning that God needed no creator). At this point reason is abandoned, just like the literalists, such as my mother, only at a slightly different level.

Reason does not allow infinite regress as an explanation for the existence of an object or being. My father probably sensed that and so arrested the regress using the 'First Cause' argument and referred back to an 'everlasting' notion of God. Others, who might not think as deeply, just don't engage or even think about the infinite regress, they just accept God as always having been.

Knowing and believing are very different states of mind, as Plato, perhaps first, pointed out. He and other great minds insist that to *know* something you must have some kind of evidence for what you believe to be true. Religion, however, has no 'truth test'. Since there is no evidence for religious claims, religious *knowledge* cannot exist. One cannot *know*, based on faith, as if faith is some kind of special emergency tool to escape the demands of reason. There are no special exceptions, no protected zones, where reason and rational demonstration cannot go to validate knowledge claims. There is no special case of access to truth called "revelation", "faith", "divine illumination", or any other form of insight peculiar to religion. There is only reason; that is the entire mode of access to truth. There is no special tool in the tool box, as George Smith would say[126], to be pulled out and used only when it comes to religion. Reason is the entire tool box. That is why reason and faith clash, why ultimately faith and reason are incompatible.

This was already widely discussed in the middle ages. St Thomas Aquinas, probably the world's foremost Christian philosopher, argued that demons have so much evidence for the teachings of the church that they have no choice but to believe in God and his teachings. Hence their faith is forced by the weight of the evi-

---

126   George H Smith, *Atheism: The Case Against God*, Prometheus Books, NY 1989, p 110.

dence. They have no choice but to believe. Therefore their faith has no virtue and they are not eligible for salvation. Christians, by contrast, believe in God not on the basis of evidence, but through faith alone and therefore their faith has merit and they become eligible for salvation:

> *As incredible as it may seem, Aquinas is arguing that the faith of demons, because it is based on the evidence of 'signs', is more rational than the faith of Christians. Thus the evidence available to demons is so strong as to leave them no choice but to believe, and it [is] precisely because of their rationality that demons should not be praised as virtuous. The belief of Christians, in contrast, is morally superior because their faith is not based on evidence that is sufficient to compel their assent. Christians, motivated by their love of God, choose to believe without sufficient evidence, and it is the voluntary assent that renders them praiseworthy.*"[127]

Within the framework of rational discourse, it is fairly easy to demonstrate that religions of all forms, particularly the big three monotheistic religions (Judaism, Christianity and Islam), are irrational and unreasonable. Rational arguments for the existence of God simply do not work, and using the Bible or other religious documents as 'proof' is faulty because these documents are not only unreliable as historical documents, they are full of contradictions and discrepancies. Over hundreds of years of examining these documents and discussing them, no one has ever even come close to a coherent explanation of the contents. There is not only a lack of evidence for certain claims, it is not even clear what the claims are or what counts as evidence. Thus the believer has a problem of having to justify believing in something that is incomprehensible and lacks all evidence, a truly horrendous state to be in for those inclined to rationality and intellectual pursuits.

---

127 George H Smith, *Why Atheism?*, Prometheus Books, 2000, p 89.

What's even worse is that believers apparently don't care about reason and rationality. The lack of evidence doesn't bother them; they just assert the impoverishment of human reason and cling to the notion that it is impossible for us mere human beings to understand. They are even perhaps smug in their imperviousness to reason and this often creates an unyielding roadblock to even enter into real discussion or debate about religion.

What brought about my abandonment of faith and acceptance of reason was a process of gradually trusting reason more and more as I progressed through school and as I interacted with educated people. Trusting one's own reason comes slowly, if at all, if one's youth is dominated by religion. At first, on the road back from Damascus, I was quite excited to follow writers and speakers and to try to understand their arguments and insights. Then I became aware that it was possible to discover flaws in their thinking and it even became quite a joy to find these and expose them and discuss them. More pleasurable still was to have those criticisms accepted. It took courage to stand up and object. However, the more I spoke my mind, the easier and more enjoyable it became.

To think new thoughts was riskier still and took still more courage. Many of my thoughts about religion that differed from orthodoxy, I kept to myself, thinking that my own ideas were crazy, and no doubt some of them were and are. In my thinking I had almost come to the same conclusion reached by Plato. In Euthyphro, he argued that even God could not make a thing good merely by commanding it. If 'God is good' is literally true by definition then one can dispense with one of the terms. If they are equivalent then only one word is needed, leaving us to judge what is moral based on our own moral insight. If 'God is good' is not true by definition but a description of an attribute of God, one still has to rely on one's own moral insight to make that ascription. Hence morality is autonomous. In other words, if God is to be described as being good, He has to recognize and obey the same moral principles we human beings recognize and obey. Even He cannot make something 'good' simply by wishing and commanding it. When I suspected that one could be good independent of God, against the teachings of the church, I was on the verge of my big breakthrough. I had almost come to that conclusion entirely by myself and it was a great comfort to me when I discovered that respected scholars thought the same. Not only was this an invaluable insight but it also meant that I could trust my own reason, my own independent thought. The door out of Damascus was now open and I was on my way.

The Human Capacity for Delusion

ANOTHER GROUND shifting experience I had on my road to freedom from religion was my coming to understand the capacity and propensity of human beings to become deluded. I came to this realization not only by observing the delusional phenomena in myself and those around me but also by reading history. While the causes and processes of delusion are quite complex, the meaning of delusion is relatively straightforward: "a false persistent belief not substantiated by sensory evidence. Syn. illusion, fallacy, deception, error, hallucination."[128]

Individual beings, large groups and even whole populations often delude themselves in order to escape an uncomfortable reality. We, for example, may delude ourselves into thinking that a prospective lover's rejection is just a momentary misunderstanding, because we don't want to face the reality of rejection. We can become deluded about many things in ordinary life from thinking that buying that lottery ticket every week, week in week out, year after year, will eventually make us rich when the statistics say otherwise; or be deceived into believing false claims about consumer products, such as there is no danger in smoking. There are still many people who deny that human activities are speeding up global warming, despite the evidence that we are. Or as a society we invent and perpetuate stories about an afterlife because we cannot face the reality of a permanent death. The most frequent and most serious delusions tend to be of the religious kind.

---

128   *Webster's New Twentieth Century Dictionary*, Unabridged (2nd edition), 1975.

My own religious delusions began early in childhood. I was engaged in a long-standing human practice which Richard Dawkins thinks of as the 'Binker phenomenon'[129]. This refers to human beings' ability, particularly in children, to delude themselves into thinking that they have a ghost-like companion who communicates with them, befriends them, and watches over them much like the character 'Binker' did in A.A. Milne's *Now we are Six*. It was not until my late teens that I started to suspect that when I was talking to Jesus, and He to me, I was just talking to myself.

Another self-delusion that I struggled with was the attempt, strong in my Bible school years at PBI, to try to surrender all to Jesus. Time and again there were altar calls for us to come forward and surrender all to God, even though we had all done so before. In sacrificing ourselves and surrendering to God, we were letting God take charge of our lives and letting Him lead the way and make decisions for us. Then I started to realize that if I was consciously deciding to allow God to make all my decisions for me then I was still in charge after all. I decided that I just needed to try harder to actually surrender. But I realized that if I succeeded then it was still me who was succeeding and I could not remove myself from the equation no matter how hard I tried.

If and when I let God have his way with me, I would want to know what He had in mind for me. How was I to know? Through some kind of sign or test? But I would have to set up the test, read the results, and interpret them. It was still all up to me. I had already done my 'fleece test' and found that process to be quite flawed. So what to do? I finally decided that surrendering oneself to God or anyone else is, in the end, illusory, comfortable perhaps, but not a genuine acceptance of what we essentially are: independent beings. Giving your life to Jesus, or to anyone or anything else, denying your free will, pretending not to be making decisions, letting others use you and manipulate you is not facing up to reality; it is defaulting on one's potential as a human being and perhaps even harmful to one's sanity.

---

129 For a fuller discussion of this see Richard Dawkins', *The God Delusion*, 2006, ch. 10, p. 389-394.

Surrendering to Jesus is denying ownership of one's choices and actions; it is trying to shove onto someone else the responsibility for those choices and actions; it is a contradictory affirmation by making a choice not to choose. You are still choosing your own role, your own fate, your own destiny. Letting God make the choices for you, as if you were following along like a sheep, is disingenuous because you are not a sheep and it is *you* who is making the *decision* to be one. Self-abdication and self-disaffirmation are not the hallmarks of a rational person. Attempting to surrender to Jesus is like a failed suicide, trying to sacrifice yourself without success, leaving you in the cyclical trap of choosing not to choose. It is little wonder then that believers are permanently in need of prayer, confession, rededication, and the comfort of the flock to ease their troubled minds. Once you see the illusory nature of surrender, one takes charge of one's own life and accepts one's humanity.

Delusions can become so strong that they in fact may never be recognized as such in an entire lifetime, or even over many generations. Perhaps the majority of us live our whole lives under some delusion or other, as reality can be confusing and harsh at times. The human brain so desperately wants the comfort of clarity and answers. It may even be the case that not all of these delusions are such a bad thing. Most of us, I would think, overestimate our own importance in society. Is that a good thing, perhaps strengthening our ego and resolve to contribute more to society, or is it a bad thing? Is it better to acknowledge the fact, if indeed true, that I am of only average ability and intelligence, and am only a tiny part of a vast humanity, and am nothing special:

> *I am a walking shadow, a poor player, that struts and frets his hour upon the stage, and then is heard no more. [Mine] is a tale told by an idiot full of sound and fury, signifying nothing.*[130]

---

130 Shakespeare, *Macbeth*, Act 5, Scene 5, lines 22-28.

If this is what life is actually like, and it probably is for most of us, can our egos handle the harsh reality of being only such a tiny part of the overall play? Or are we better off giving in to our ego and deluding ourselves that we are more important than we actually are? Here, I can only speak for myself. I don't want or need the delusion. I can handle the truth (at least what I know of it). The truth matters. It matters supremely. Once we allow and cultivate little delusions, we become more susceptible and acquiescent to larger delusions, like the delusions of the great religions of the world, which indeed do untold harm. We must guard against that if we are to stop the endless cycle of hatred, war, and needless suffering. History doesn't have to keep on repeating itself.

In fact, we need to take steps to clear the world of delusions in religion and elsewhere. A good first step would be to introduce our youth, by making it compulsory reading in schools, to a great book on this subject, *Extraordinary Popular Delusions and the Madness of Crowds,* by Charles Mackay, first published in 1841, revised in 1932 and in the twelfth printing in 1962. Mackay's book is a detailed, lucid account of such horrible events as the Crusades, the Inquisitions, witch hunts and many more historical human tragedies. It sheds a great deal of light on the human capacity for delusion, from self-delusion to the delusion of the masses.

A good second step would be to make it a matter of habit constantly to examine one's own thinking, to examine one's own assumptions for error or contradiction, and constantly to entertain the possibility that we ourselves have been deluded. Part of this is to examine the consistency of our belief systems and the dissonance between those belief systems and actions, both for oneself and for others. It is easy to live with the intellectual pathology of accepting contradiction if one doesn't see the contradiction, if it is part of a long standing deeply held package of beliefs that one can't imagine living without. However, if you can listen carefully to the dissonance and allow yourself to feel the discomfort of the pathology, you also allow yourself to envisage an escape from it, and that escape is to let one of the contrary beliefs go. Personally, I found that I just could not live with the dissonance of the two Christian ideas of 'God is just' and 'God punishes innocent unbelievers with hell'. I could not believe that a loving God would be so unjust, so the latter belief had to go (and then eventually the former too). I was able to make this large stride towards my freedom and happiness because I allowed myself to listen to the internal conflict of my belief system.

The world did not come crashing down around me just because I had let go of a deeply held belief, even though at the time it felt like it would. I just lived on as before with one more pocket of disbelief. Nevertheless, after achieving that insight, it became easier and easier to add new pockets of disbelief, each one another step on the road out of Damascus. Eventually I did make it all the way, realizing that the entire package of religious beliefs that I had been taught was indeed a grand illusion.

I can imagine some friends and relatives asking "Do you mean to say that all of us in the family, in the church community, are all deluded?" The answer, I'm afraid, is: "Yes." And I would hasten to add that you have been living under that delusion for your entire life. In fact not only an entire generation of people but many generations over many centuries have been holding fast to the same delusion. Many other civilizations have deluded themselves into thinking their gods would protect them, give their life meaning, and then grant them life after death. The ruins of temples and religious shrines in every place across the Earth and in every time period tell a tale of our capacity, desire, and perhaps even need to become deluded.

Need for Conceptual Clarity

ANOTHER MAJOR SHIFT in my thinking during the years when I shed most of my religious doctrines was my growing reluctance to accept as true anything I couldn't understand. Even as a child I had some of this reluctance, which only grew stronger as I got older. When I studied the Bible, I actually tried to make sense of it, and frequently found myself saying out loud "I don't understand this";

but then another voice would quickly take over and say, "You don't need to *understand* this, just believe. Your doubts are from the Devil." This voice however, was not my own; it was planted in me by others, perhaps well-meaning others. Nonetheless those words and thoughts held me back for a long time. And so I would repeatedly miss my opening to start my journey back from Damascus.

My need to understand grew so strong that eventually I declared to myself that I would refuse to accept as true something for which I had no evidence and which I could not grasp the meaning of. Indeed, how could I even know what counted as evidence for a knowledge claim unless I knew what was meant by the claim. In other words, I decided not to entertain any statement as either false or true unless I understood what the statement meant. Meaning is always logically prior to the assertion of truth. For example, how could I search for evidence that the Trinity was true, without even knowing what that really meant? I grappled with that for many years, with reason battling against the idea that it was not meant to be understood. That conflict became increasingly uncomfortable. I tried my best to resolve this issue regarding one of the central doctrines of Christianity for both Catholics and Protestants alike. I could repeat the words, "Father, Son, and Holy Ghost" as I was compelled to ad nauseum, but I felt really uncomfortable saying the words without knowing what they meant. In the end I decided that if I could not come to terms with this seeming absurdity, then I would just have to add it to the growing list of disbeliefs.

Generally, in ordinary language, a 'person' is an individual human being, a centre of consciousness, capable of free will and premeditated intentional action. As an individual a 'person' is not more than one entity and cannot be by definition. If someone approached me and said he was Smith, Jones and Taylor (all three), I would consider him to be a candidate for the loony bin or at least in need of some psychiatric help. Surely there is no ordinary sense in which three people can be considered one or one person considered three. The Trinity just doesn't make sense in any ordinary way. However, clerics and theologians, at least externally, seem to be quite content and confident with the concept of the Trinity and continually try to explain it to those of us who just don't get it. However that is almost always without much success, likely because those who want a logical explanation aren't going to get one and those who have abdicated reason to take it on faith don't need one.

One such explanation of the Trinity even has a name and it is called, 'perichoresis', which in Greek means 'going around; to envelop'. Hilary of Poitiers (c300-c370) in 'Concerning the Trinity' says the three persons "reciprocally contain one another, so the one permanently envelops and is permanently enveloped by the other whom he yet envelopes". Does that make it clear? I don't think so. One could go on citing many such attempts at clarification of the trinity concept, but none really help. Many writers on the subject just give up. Thus, George Joyce said in 1912:

> Moreover, our Lord's word, Matthew 11:27 'No one knoweth the Son, but the Father', seems to declare expressly that the plurality of Persons in the Godhead is a truth entirely beyond the scope of any created [human] intellect.[131]

I would agree that the trinity idea is beyond the grasp of our intellect, not because it is a revealed truth too profound for ordinary human beings to understand, but because it simply makes no sense. Three persons are not one person; one person is not three. It's a matter of simple logic and cannot be abrogated without dispensing with reason and rationality. So why did I not, as most Christians do, simply abandon reason at this point and *believe* anyway as our parents and clergy had taught us? Could I not just go along with the notion of the Trinity and get a warm fuzzy feeling from it and put my heart into singing about it like everyone else in the choir? No, I could not. Truth matters. It matters a lot, not just to me but truth is one of the pillars of human civilization and human continuity and cannot be simply dispensed with without serious repercussions.

---

131   George Joyce, 'The Blessed Trinity' in the *Catholic Encyclopedia*, NY Robert Appleton.

My rejection of the doctrine of the Trinity is based on a very simple claim, one that I think every rational person would subscribe to, if they are true to themselves and haven't actively shunned reason. If one does not know what something is or means (let's call it X) one cannot make true statements about X. In fact, it borders on insanity for one to say that they don't know what X means, but not only insist that it's true but also to describe it in detail. In the case of the Trinity we have an X which we do not and cannot understand. Yet most Christians believe in the Trinity and make specific statements about it they claim are true. Actually, this *is* a kind of madness. If only one or two people made similar nonsensical claims, they would be considered mad and either quickly dismissed or placed under care. But if millions subscribe to the same nonsense, pretty much anything goes. As long as they register as a 'Church', they achieve a privileged position in society, including tax breaks, with the blessings of government and society at large. My trust in reason, my awareness of mankind's capacity for delusion, and my demand for conceptual clarity just would not let me go along for that ride, even though I was well strapped in.

The Accretion of Disbeliefs

AS I GREW OLDER, gained confidence, and learned more, particularly between 1951 and 1960, the decade of my twenties, I wrestled with many religious doctrines. Sometimes I would doubt a particular tenet of the faith for quite a while and with varying degrees of intensity before I finally acknowledged to myself that I definitely did not believe that doctrine. When the rejection of an item of faith came, it was firm and final and constituted a 'pocket of disbelief'. As these disbeliefs mounted up they became more frequent and easier to accept until eventually an avalanche brought down the whole structure of my faith.

While it is impossible in a short space to list all of the doctrines I rejected, I can share some of the key ones to illustrate what kind of issues I wrestled with and to hint at the reasons for rejecting them. They are listed here in rough historical sequence:

1. The Genesis account of creation is literally true. (Both modern cosmology and the overwhelming evidence for evolution argue convincingly against that.)
2. Immersion is the only acceptable mode of baptism. (All modes of baptism are symbolic. Any type is as good as any other.)
3. Hell (everlasting torment) is a suitable punishment for all non-believers in Christ regardless of their innocence or lack of knowledge of the Christian story. (A just God could not be so cruel as to punish innocent victims with eternal torture.)
4. The Bible is the perfect word of God, literally true and infallible. (It is neither of these. It is full of human error and contradictions literally too numerous to mention. At best the Bible *contains* the word of God, which has to be assiduously sought for with careful scrutiny.)
5. The Bible is flawed but still contains the word of God. (It only contains the words of human beings and even if taken metaphorically it is still full of contradiction, errors, and even vulgarities. It is simply not a very nice book.)
6. God answers prayer. (The best evidence from modern research shows that God does not answer prayer and that prayer makes no difference in human affairs except in the minds of those who pray.)
7. The central message of Jesus Christ is eternal salvation, a pleasant life after death, in return for suffering and self-sacrifice here on Earth. (Self-sacrifice now for heaven hereafter was Paul's message. Christ, saying that the kingdom of God was at hand, favoured amelioration of the human condition through human love here and now.)[132]

---

132 Mark 1:15.

8. After life on this planet, there is everlasting life in heaven for some and hell for many. (This is almost certainly not true, for there is not a shred of evidence for these claims. In fact, it is doubtful the term "life after death" makes any sense.)
9. God is all knowing, all powerful, and all good. (Not as long as there is evil in the world. The problem of theodicy looms large here; but I was struggling with the more basic problem of what the *meaning* of an 'all-powerful' or 'all-good' being might be).
10. Deism is a good way to get around the fallacies of the Bible and still believe in a Christian God. (It worked for me for a few years in my early twenties, until I figured out, that that too, couldn't stand up to scrutiny.)
11. God created man in His image. (Clearly, it must be the other way around. God is an anthropomorphic projection.)
12. God is a non-anthropomorphic being; or in P. Tillich's words, He is "the ground of being"[133] (This is perhaps even more meaningless than the traditional definition of God as a supreme being. It just takes us further into the conceptual mire.)
13. God created and sustains the universe and everything in it. (There is no evidence for that. We don't even understand the meaning of the attributes ascribed to Him. For example, we don't even know what it means for God to be omnipotent.)
14. Overall, despite its flaws, religion in general, and the Christian religion in particular, is a positive force in the world. (All religion is at best nonsense and at worst a deep human tragedy.)

---

133 Paul Tillich, *Systematic Theology, Vol. 2: Existence and the Christ*, p 10/11, University of Chicago Press, 1957.

While I had many such doubts and internal conflicts prior to 1951, as already noted, I did not, could not, admit to myself (let alone anyone else) that I, in fact, was actually doubting my religion. I was becoming a heretic. In the summer of 1951 I finally admitted to myself that I could not accept the concept of hell for the innocent while believing in an all-powerful all-loving God. By 1960, I had admitted to myself that there was not sufficient evidence to believe any of the Judeo-Christian Bible story, nor any reason to believe in the Christian God or any god.

Even as a child I wondered why sometimes God answers prayers and sometimes not. Even at an early age I was starting to wonder how one could tell the difference between a definite 'no' response and no response at all. If one prays for rain tomorrow, and it does rain, how can one know if it would have rained anyway or if it was God's hand? During my agonizing 'fleece test', how could I be sure God was denying my request as opposed to not hearing my request? In my youth I often prayed for good marks and got them but then again I got good marks even when I didn't pray. And it just so happened that if I didn't study and prayed for high marks, God would always refuse to oblige. Suffice it to say that I found the idea of prayer and God responding to it as problematic.

An opportunity to examine the efficacy of prayer presented itself while I was taking a Philosophy of Religion course at summer school at UBC. The professor was Dr. R. Fitch from the Pacific School of Religion, in Berkley, California. For an essay assignment I chose to write on the question "Does God Answer Prayer?" I read everything I could lay my hands on about that question in the available time but couldn't come up with a satisfactory answer. Some writers asserted that God did indeed answer prayer and some concluded that He didn't. Research just wasn't helping to come up with a definitive answer. I therefore proposed setting up a 'scientific' experiment to test the power of prayer.

The experiment design provided for true believers praying for success in finding needles in a haystack, with a control group and other features necessary for scientific research, though I didn't actually do the experiment. The professor remarked that God couldn't be pinned down that easily (a classic response) nor would the praying believers be bothered to pray for such trivial matters. Subsequent research (some of it very recent and extensive) bears out that there is no evidence that prayer makes any difference in the real physical world.

It is worth noting that I am not making the assertion that I believe that God does not answer prayer, I am only saying that I do not believe that He does. He might answer prayer, I just have no reason whatsoever to believe it to be true and I'm not (or should I say not any more) prepared to abdicate my reason in order to believe that He does just because others do and want me to as well. Some people of course will say, "I know God answers prayers because I talk to Him every day and He answers me". That, however, does not count as empirical evidence. For it to be so there has to be some observable and repeatable phenomena in the real world and it has to be shown to be linked to God and not just perceived in the head of the believer.

The trustworthiness of the Bible as God's word, literal or not, was another important issue. It's ironic that it was Bible study that was largely responsible for my low opinion of the Bible and therefore part of the dissolution of my faith. As already mentioned, there are so many contradictions and inconsistencies in the Bible that a thinking person simply cannot help but have at least some doubt after studying it carefully. The only astounding part is that believers somehow manage *not* to notice, *not* acknowledge, or to trivialize these obvious and serious discrepancies and contradictions. Or worse yet, believers just say that there are mysteries too deep for the human mind to grasp and assert that God's revelation is perfect and it is human error and imperfection that causes the confusion. That is supposed to be the end to criticism and the cue to turn off one's rationality. Often it works.

Not only is the Bible plagued with inconsistencies with regard to the word of God and His instructions to humans, it is flawed in its historical accuracy, coherence, style, flow and originality. Secular

Biblical scholars point to many Bible stories that have their origin in other ancient religions, particularly Egyptian ones.[134] Actually studying the Bible reveals much confusion and contradiction and can only serve to undermine rather than enhances one's faith. No wonder that in the world of Catholicism, lay people are discouraged from reading the Bible, if not forbidden. One would think that if God, omnipotent and omniscient as He supposedly is, wanted to reveal Himself in a written work, He could have done a lot better than the Bible.

Even if one were somehow able to come to terms with and resolve the inconsistencies, discrepancies, and contradictions in the Bible (impossible in my view), the problems with the book continue, one of which is the unsavory depiction of the character of God in the Old Testament. Dawkins has described him as follows:

> *The God of the Old Testament is arguably the most unpleasant character in all fiction: jealous and proud of it; a petty, unjust, unforgiving control-freak; a vindictive, bloodthirsty ethnic cleanser; a misogynistic, homophobic, racist, infanticidal, genocidal, filicidal, pestilential, megalomaniacal, sadomasochistic, capriciously malevolent bully.*[135]

Others have argued that, because of the gruesomeness of some of the stories in it, the endless graphic violence, pornography, and human abuse, the Bible should be restricted reading for children. If one were to reproduce accurately those descriptions in a modern movie, let's say, it would surely get an 'R' rating or worse from regulatory bodies. If one takes the Bible at face value, without a fancy leather cover and gold dressing, without the word 'holy' in its title, without the 'magic glasses' of group delusion and reads it with an

---

134 For example Tom Harpur's *The Pagan Christ: Recovering the Lost Light*, Thomas Allen Publishers, Toronto, 2004 or Bart D. Ehrman's, *Misquoting Jesus: the Story Behind Who Changed the Bible and Why*, HarperCollins, San Francisco, 2005.
135 Richard Dawkins, *The God Delusion*, Houghton Miflin Co., New York, 2006, p. 31.

open critical mind, the Bible comes through as something entirely different from what it is purported to be. Isaac Asimov once said, "Properly read, the Bible is the most potent force for atheism ever conceived."[136] In any case, it is simply a not very nice book about a not very nice God.

Even if one is forced to accept that the Bible is flawed and that it does not provide sufficient reason to believe in God, then perhaps it is possible to prove the existence of God by other means, perhaps through pure reason. Indeed many philosophers over the centuries have tried to do this, to come up with some standard classical proofs. They always fail. Not only do the many attempts to prove the existence of God not work but many arguments against the existence of God do. Theodicy, the attempt to reconcile the three propositions 'God is good', 'God is omnipotent' and 'There is evil in the world', has not succeeded despite an army of people through the years who have tried and are trying. I have read as many as twenty or more versions of theodicy written by religious apologists and they all fail to convince and they all fall back on a leap of faith, i.e. that God's ways are beyond our understanding. A recent attempt by Francis Collins, ends the same old way, "Belief in God will always require a leap of faith."[137] How perverse it is to apply logic up to a point and then arbitrarily abandon it when the going gets tough.

Post-war liberal Christian theologians such as Paul Tillich, R. Niebuhr, R. Bultmann and others[138], sink deeper into the morass when they proclaim that God is not a being at all but rather the 'ground of being'. Now what does *that* mean? Does one pray to a 'ground of being'? Does the 'ground of being' care at all about human affairs? The point I'm trying to make here is a relatively

---

136   From a letter February 22 1966 as cited in, Stanley Asimov (editor), *Yours, Isaac Asimov: A Lifetime of Letters* (1995).

137   Francis Collins, *The Language of God*, Free Press, New York, 2006, p. 201.

138   I like to think of these thinkers and their like as apostate atheists. Dan Barker says of them: "Attempting to learn what a liberal Christian believes is like trying to nail jello to a tree" in his *Losing Faith in Faith*, Freedom from Religion Foundation, Madison, Wisconsin, 1992, p.30.

simple one really. If one doesn't know exactly what one is talking about how can one make any knowledge claims at all about that thing. Without an understanding of what God is, there can be no proof of His existence. Am I implying that most of theology is just sophisticated justification of nonsense? Yes. In fact, I'm not just implying that, it is my considered professional opinion.

By 1960, I was a full-blown, self-acknowledged non-theist and confident in that position. Not only did I reject my Christian beliefs but I did not believe in any religion whatsoever, nor in life after death. All of my religious beliefs were crushed in the crucible of conceptual confusion and despite some initial shock I learned to accept that with equanimity and even joy. My path in life was now unambiguous – to enjoy and to treasure this life to the full, to do as much good here and now as possible, to carve out a little bit of 'heaven' here on Earth. Did I regret that I would now not look forward to a life after death? No. No more than I didn't regret that I didn't have life before I was born. On the contrary, I felt as though a burden had been lifted. I felt overjoyed just to be alive. I felt like Emily Dickenson when she wrote:

> *That it will never come again*
> *Is what makes life so sweet.*

I'm not even sure that the term 'life after death' makes any sense. If we are somehow able to retain our self-awareness, identity, and memory; and have some kind of consciousness in some kind of 'soul' after our current physical body perishes, did we even die? Can there be disembodied souls? Where is the evidence for that? There is none. I am not saying with absolute certainty that there is no life after death; I am saying that I don't believe there is because there is no evidence for it. If there is a grand reunion in the sky, I'll happily join the festivities but I caution against betting too much of our current life on that happening.

Apart from a few early discomforts, the road back from Damascus was not all that rough. Obviously I did have a rough spell or two of emotional upheaval but they weren't all that frequent and didn't last long. My poem, 'Losing the Faith', below, alludes to such a spell. Most of my adjustments were intellectual and social rather than profoundly psychological. On the whole, my journey was smooth and safe, the main problem being that it took altogether too long.

Losing the Faith (1958)

Like dizzy dripping rain
On a November day in Vancouver
The acid of doubt leaked
Incessantly onto my heart
Souring the milk of hope,
Eroding the fabric of my faith.

Questions upon questions
Irreconcilable questions
Fired up my burning brain
While the leaves of faith
Fluttered down to die.
And the garden of my heart
Turned to desert; and like the desert
It wanted rain.
But the rains never came.

Being a Non-Theist

HAVING REJECTED the Bible as trustworthy and having no grounds for believing in the Christian God, or any god, I had become a non-theist. I prefer not to refer to myself as an 'atheist' not only because of all the negative baggage attached to that word but also because there is a subtle but important difference. A non-theist is a kind of atheist but one who does not make the positive claim that God certainly does not exist. I claim only that I do not believe

He *does* exist. There is an important difference between these two claims. I have not scoured the ends of the universe and I cannot claim on solid grounds that God absolutely does not exist. Nor has anyone else; nor is it even possible for the same reason I can't say with certainty that Unicorns or Bigfoot don't exist, or miniature tea-pots orbiting distant planets.[139] All I can say is that there is no evidence for believing in these things. Perpetuating these myths is fraught with peril.

Nobody can, with absolute certainty, prove that something does *not* exist. One can only say that there is no reason to believe that something does exist. Often people say "Unicorns don't exist" and while they are not really wrong, they are just using a shorter and easier way of saying "there is no evidence that unicorns exist and I, nor anyone else, has ever seen one". As a convention of language, it's easier to just say that they don't exist but there always remains a minute possibility that they do. The same can be said of God. The burden of proof always rests with those who make the positive claim that something or other *is* true or *does* exist.

If those making a claim are asked to show some proof or evidence, and they just say "Oh, I don't have any; I just believe it to be so, and so should you", that is not very convincing. In fact, it is a kind of intellectual cheating. Public discourse demands that the claimant provide some kind of grounds for positive pronouncements. So when one person says "I believe God exists" and another person says "I do not believe that God exists" they are *not* on equally rational footing. The onus is on the positive claimant to come up with evidence. The negative claimant may not be able to certify 100% that X does not exist but need not provide evidence because he is reporting on his state of mind (on which he is the authority) regarding a conjecture about the state of the world. He can also say, with reason, that the possibility of X existing is extremely low if there is a lack of evidence. The positive claimant, however, has a rational duty to provide evidence for his assertion about the world.

---

139   A famous example from B. Russell.

The improbability of the existence of both God and unicorns is extremely high. So why do people, including me, get excited and engage in endless debate about the existence of God and not unicorns? Why don't people such as me just shut up about something that we don't believe in? The answer is that there are far too many people who don't shut up about what they do believe in, without providing evidence. And it causes a lot of conflict and damage. I wish that we could *all* just shut up about God and other deities and all religion. Or at the very least if we do talk about these beliefs, we need to entertain the idea of doubt. Why can't people just say "I don't know for sure"? Is that so hard? It is my wish that we could advance our civilization to the level where we could leave the scourge of religious intolerance and religious conflict behind us. However we still live in a world full of religious zealots. If not directly involved in bombing buildings and sabotaging public education, many at least wish they could.

When the believers stop pushing their agenda on others that is when I will stop attacking the validity of their beliefs. I would love to live in peace in a post-theist society, but I fear that that is still a long way off. Until then, there is altogether too much damage being done by religion and in the name of religion for us non-believers who care about humanity to stand by and silently observe the decline of education and enlightenment, the deterioration of hard won freedoms and rights, the erosion of civility and social justice, the regression back to the dark ages, all in the name of some flimsy belief system or other. Religion may bring comfort to some; but despite some good intentions, it often spreads misery to the masses.

Myths About Non-Theists

BEING A NON-THEIST does not impoverish one's life as some religious leaders would insist. On the contrary, non-theism enriches life and is a desirable first step towards fuller human thought and action, social and moral behaviour, and in general a positive direction for the advancement of civilization. Indeed there are numerous misconceptions about non-theism, not surprisingly often promulgated by theists, that need to be exposed and debunked.

One such myth, that non-theists are somehow fundamentally evil because they reject theism, is false. There is no doubt that some non-theists are evil. Stalin was one; but even Stalin didn't fight wars and kill his own people in the name of 'not believing'. He was evil alright, but not *because* he was a non-theist. From my own experience I can honestly say that none of the non-theists I know could be described as evil. In fact it's the opposite. I find that they are *more* compassionate and *more* morally principled than the average believer. Among non-theists prominent in philosophical literature, I would cite Hume, Kant, and Russell as model moral figures.

As a matter of fact, the idea that one should be good because God is watching and recording our deeds for judgement day and because God wants us and tells us to be good, makes the believers morally suspect, not having reached what Kant would call the benchmark of 'good will'. One can make a good case that religion in fact *detracts* from morality by failing to encourage being good simply for the sake of being good.[140] If we do good, give to charity for example, just because God commands it, then that is not as pure morally speaking. We should want to do it simply because it is a good thing to do. As Kant and other eminent ethicists would argue, being good for its own sake is a higher order of good than doing good for some external reward or escape from punishment.

If one subscribes to the idea that "if God is dead, then all things are possible"[141] then one has not really understood what morality fundamentally means. For someone to be truly morally educated, the shedding of their belief in God should have no negative effect whatsoever on their moral awareness and actions. If anything, as described above, it should strengthen it. The myth about non-theists being evil is simply false, perhaps innocently arrived at, perhaps coming from malicious and selfish intent.

---

140   See my article 'Moral Education Without Religion' in D. Cochrane, C. Hamm, and A.C. Kazipedes (Eds.) *The Domain of Moral Education*, Paulist Press, NY, 1979.
141   As one of the brothers in Dostoyevsky's *Brothers Karamazov* says.

Another myth about non-theists is that without belief in life after death, life here on Earth is meaningless and without direction. That is also false. In fact the idea that life has 'meaning' is in itself wrong. Life can't have 'meaning'; it just is. It is people, with minds and intentions, that can have meaning. There is no reason at all why non-theists can't and don't have meaning in their lives. Their meaning is of their own making. It is not inferred from the outside, from God, or from any other source. "If we crave some cosmic purpose, then let us find ourselves a worthy goal."[142] It is often the non-theists and humanists among us who are the front runners in the meaningful and worthy goals of eliminating poverty, disease, conflict, war, creating art and promulgating real education and morality while we live here on Earth. There is indeed poignant meaning and direction in life for the non-theist. The non-theist is also *not* a miserable, unhappy, fearful being in the absence of religion as some theists might suggest. In fact, letting go of belief in God and life after death tends to have the opposite effect, at least it certainly did for me. If life here on Earth is just a temporary stop on the journey towards the eternal life to come, would that not significantly cheapen our existence here on Earth? Or at least give us a reason not to take good care of what we have here and now? Believing in an afterlife can be and indeed is dangerous to the health of beings on our current planet. If this life is all we have, as I strongly suspect is the case, then does that not make it all the more special?

Not being concerned with pleasing a vengeful God, not worrying about hell or judgement day, not trying to keep up a false reputation, not feeling constantly watched by a great Supervisor in the sky, is a joy and makes life much more pleasant. I was positively enthralled to be free of all of that and I wish others could be too. I was free to pursue the goals that I set for myself with confidence, commitment, and focus. It gave me a deep satisfaction and a sense of dignity that I didn't have before to realize that I was an individual contributing member of the human race, as far as we know, a race alone in the universe, in control of our own lives.

---

142   Carl Sagan, *Pale Blue Dot: A Vision of the Human Future in Space*, Random House, NY 1994, p 57.

Contrary to even more myths commonly propagated about non-theists, my sense of awe and wonder at the intricacies of the world around me, at the splendor of the starry heavens, only increased after my religious beliefs vanished. As I grow older and understand more and more about the universe and mankind I acquire in proportion more and more gratitude and respect for the courageous and dedicated scholars who awakened the human mind from the dark ages of ignorance and controlled thought. Just to understand a little bit more about how the world works and just to observe again and again the beauty of nature and human art, provides me with great delight, marred only by the thought that our collective wisdom and moral education has not kept pace with our knowledge and technology. We as a race, still mired in religious fanaticism and bigotry, could still blow ourselves off the face of the planet at any minute, but hope and optimism must keep the upper hand. I try to abide by de la Mare's advice:

> *Look thy last on all things lovely,*
> *Every hour – let no night*
> *Seal thy sense in deathly slumber*
> *Till to delight*
> *Thou hast paid thy utmost blessing.*[143]

On Being Non-Religious

MAKING A CASE for non-theism is not tantamount to making the stronger case of non-religiousness altogether, for there are some religions (or near religions) that do not subscribe to or posit a god, religions such as Buddhism, Taoism, and some forms of Animism. These religions lack a deity but retain most or all of the other attributes of standard theistic religions. I am a non-theist because I think it irrational to believe in any god; but I am also non-religious

---

143 From Walter de la Mare's poem 'Fare Well' st.3, 1918.

because I also think it is irrational to practice and engage in any form of religion. I do not subscribe to any of the central features and attributes of religions of any kind. The irrationality of religiousness extends beyond the irrationality of theistic religions. Irrationality is a characteristic of all forms of religion; and I attempt not to do irrational things and not to believe in irrational claims to truth. There are also other reasons why I oppose non-theistic religions, which I will get to shortly.

First, I need to make it abundantly clear what I take the concept of religion to be. 'Religion' is a concept notoriously difficult to define. The term is used very loosely these days. Thus some writers claim that secularism, agnosticism, science, humanism and even 'sportism' all qualify as some type of religion. In Sweden there is an officially recognized 'religion' called Kopimism, which is a new original 'religion' based on computer file-sharing. While Kopimism may be on the edge of what people honestly consider to be a real religion, some people take it even further and intentionally muddy the waters and add humour and sarcasm into it, like the 'pastafarians' for example who 'believe' in the Flying Spaghetti Monster, and even have a whole tongue-in-cheek liturgy designed around that. For whatever reason, likely because some people of only marginal religious persuasion wish to cash in on the favorable conditions and connotations associated with the idea, I would like to assert that the word 'religion' in its established sense is misused in these cases.

When I say that I am free of religion, I mean that I am free of what has traditionally been meant by the term, as in the examples of the three main monotheistic religions, namely Judaism, Christianity, and Islam. A very good article explaining what is meant by 'religion' in its ordinary sense is William Alston's in *The Encyclopedia of Philosophy*.[144] Here, he talks about what he calls "religious-making characteristics": belief in a supernatural being or beings; a moral code sanctioned by that being(s); the designa-

---

144 Vol. 7, pages 140-145, Macmillan Publishing Co & The Free Press, New York, 1967.

tion of some objects as sacred; rituals connected with the sacred objects; feelings such as awe, wonder, and adoration during worship of said God or Gods or in the presence of the sacred objects; communication with the God(s) (i.e. prayer); a world view specifying how the individual fits in; and a social group (i.e. Church congregation) dedicated to the advancement of all of the above. One doesn't necessarily need to meet all of the criteria but the more of them that one does meet, the closer one gets to meeting the definition of a religion.

Thus, when I say that I am not religious I mean that I do not believe in a supernatural being; that morality is not dependent in any way on religion (in fact religion detracts from genuine morality); that I do not hold any objects to be sacred; that my sense of awe and wonder are with this world not directed towards a supernatural being or sacred objects; that I do not pray; that the point and purpose of and meaning in life is the meaning we give it; and finally that I am not a member of an organization which shares these thoughts. I therefore think that I can be correctly described as non-religious.

I return now to the question of why I oppose non-theistic religions as well as theistic ones. The reason is that non-theistic religions share with theistic religions almost all of Alston's "religious-making characteristics". Religionists of all stripes have, without a shred of evidence, an unfounded assurance that the particular doctrines or dogmas they believe in are the absolute truth and other religions (or even other sects of the same religion) are false, leading to social divisiveness, exclusivity, sectarianism, animosity, violence, and war. It doesn't take a great deal of historical knowledge to come to that conclusion. From prehistoric tribal conflicts, to pre-Christian civilizations at war with one another, to the crusades, witch hunts, and massacres of the Middle Ages, to the post-Renaissance inquisitions, to modern day atrocities all over the world but particularly in the Middle East, the story continues – violence and human suffering caused, at least in large part, by religious zeal and intolerance. On this account alone, religion is reprehensible.

But there are also other reasons for opposing it. Because of its reliance on faith and dogma without reason and evidence, religion necessarily undermines rationality and the achievement of our full human potential. This is so not only for theistic religions but also for other "philosophies of life" or near-religions, such as the Buddhist traditions, as well. Practices such as yoga and meditation to relieve stress and mitigate suffering and anxiety are potentially laudable and uncontentious. But when these practices are bound up with a host of unfounded and unsupportable doctrine, and then infused with ritual and sometimes even prayers or sacrifices, then these non-theistic movements take on the trappings of theistic religion and can and do become questionable and contentious.

These near-religions are potentially pessimistic views of the world, and in my view inhibit the potential for human development. Belief in the inevitability of human suffering can lead to resignation to and acceptance of preventable evils and miseries. Instead of this head-in-sand type of escapism, why don't we spend our time, effort, and resources as well as our emotional and intellectual powers in attempts to eliminate self-inflicted and natural evils around us. Escapism is not the answer in coping with evil and suffering, rather it is the avoidance of accepting responsibility of using our reason and rationality to improve the human condition. We can and should use our rationality and reason to improve the human condition and maybe we can get to the point where there is actually less suffering. Efforts spent in accommodating suffering is effort wasted in eliminating suffering.

Theistic and non-theistic religions alike seem to me to make false claims about the real world, to assert as true highly speculative metaphysics. These beliefs and attitudes are wrapped up in rituals and practices that include the non-sensical and ridiculous, all of which serve to undermine the development of our full rational human potential. It is for these reasons, and more, that I do not subscribe to any religion and consider myself to be non-religious.

Leaving Damascus

As I sit here in my study and re-think my non-theism, I am satisfied that non-theism is very much straight-forwardly rational and normal. The Bible and other so-called sacred books are totally unreliable as revelations of the Divine. Proofs for the existence of the Christian God, or any god, just don't work. The concept of the Christian God is largely incoherent at best and at worst, downright silly. It has been suggested that since the Enlightenment, particularly since Hume and Kant, there is little left to discuss in the debate about God; nothing left but to announce the death of God[145] and religion and declare the world open to a new humanity. "Contemporary atheistic arguments are [nothing more than] mopping up operations after the Enlightenment."[146]

When I leave my study and travel just an hour away to visit my siblings in the Fraser Valley, the 'bible belt' of southern BC, I am always totally amazed that they have hardly moved an inch, if at all, from their childhood religious beliefs and commitments. They think that they have changed and become modern, not only by adopting modern technology but also by moving on some social practices such as using cosmetics or going to movies, but nothing significant has really changed. They still think that they will literally be seeing Dad and Mother and all their other loved ones soon up in heaven. They still tithe and attend church regularly. They still give to missions to spread the word of God. They still pray for a change in weather, for better crops, for safe travel, for the demise of other religions, for the salvation of sinful souls, for the poor, for the sick and the down and out. And they thank God out loud and in public for the food that *they* worked so hard for. It is only that I do not want to hurt them that I don't speak out against this, though I suppose that I am doing exactly that right here and now. I feel that it needs to be done for the good of all.

---

145 As Nietzsche famously did.
146 Kai Nielsen, *Philosophy and Atheism*, p 224.

How does one be a compassionate iconoclast?

I just can't bring myself to kick out the crutches from under those who seem to need them. I just can't bring myself to engage them in debate about their religious beliefs. They are such fine people in so many ways. I can't imagine myself trying to shatter their delusions on which they so desperately yet falsely depend. When I do visit my still religious family, I keep the peace and just play along with the absurdity and walk away thinking that I have lost yet another opportunity to try to advance reason and rationality, though also thinking at least I was kind and non-abrasive. If amiability is the result, does it really matter what our philosophical and religious differences are? I used to think not, but now I think that it does indeed matter. Perhaps we non-theists are even obliged to ruffle a few feathers in the name of the common good (though I suppose that one has to exercise great caution as that line of thinking when used by religionists often leads to violence or war).

My family, though always nice to me face to face, are troubled by my state of apostasy. In their terms I am a rebellious reprobate, having gone astray and fallen into the hands of the Devil. I have succumbed to temptation and become evil. I don't feel evil. From my point of view, I am the lucky one who found a way out of the trap of debilitating doctrines and ridiculous rituals. I believe that I have found genuine morality and decency, complete with freedom of thought and action. Is it worth it to take on the struggle against such polar positions, knowing that success in changing either position is unlikely and significant conflict almost assured?

We are facing a period in history in which there is actually an upsurge of religious fanaticism, intolerance, and violence when we really need to be going the other way. If we are to maintain peace in the internet age, as differing cultures come into more and more contact with each other, religious people need to find ways of modifying their views to become more tolerant of other religions and non-theists. Sadly, it seems like the opposite is happening.

The risks from terror and war, largely stimulated by religion, are very real. I for one do not want to go down to destruction without having done all I can do to advance reason and rationality over blind faith and irrationality. That means that I, and others, need to overcome our worry of offending people and come out of the closet, so to speak, and declare our stance vis-a-vis religion and why we oppose it. Furthermore I feel obliged to tell the world that I am happy and proud to be a non-theist. Hurting friends and family who cling to religion, by knocking down their beliefs without a good reason would be cruel, but I think I have good reason. A little so-called collateral damage in the war against unreason and irrationality cannot be avoided.

As I have noted several times in this memoir, I feel very fortunate to have achieved freedom from religion. To my knowledge, I am the only one of us ten siblings in my family to have done so. I am also only one of a very few among my classmates at SMCI and PBI to have done so, such is the strong power of indoctrination. I would therefore like to point to some factors that have contributed to this good fortune.

Some of these factors are personal characteristics that I either inherited or somehow developed on my own early in life. Right from my early years, I was a bit of a maverick, not afraid to wander off course doing my own thing. For example, I enjoyed skiing through the woods and open fields all by myself on cold January Saturdays, checking my trap line for skunks, while the rest of my siblings remained inside. In my youth, I was known for having a spirit of self-reliance and independence (not always encouraged by the religious mindset). I had the courage to do unusual things and the courage to speak my mind which went hand in hand with my sense of independence. I also possessed, and still do, a tenacity to finish even difficult tasks and to get to the bottom of things. Even though I had them, I was not very comfortable with doubts and thus I could not tolerate the discrepancies and contradictions that I found in the Bible. I had to resolve my doubts even if that meant discomfort and acknowledging heretical ideas. I believe too that I had a sense of integrity in that I just didn't and couldn't delude myself very much into believing some iffy proposition just because everybody else did. These and other personal characteristics helped me to get unstuck from religion. However there were also favourable circumstances that helped enormously.

One such circumstance was meeting and talking with that liberal theologian in the limo on the way back to BC from Three Hills, Alberta, the right person to talk to at exactly the right moment in my religious devolution. I had just finished my studies at PBI and the continental tour with the PBI musical / evangelical group in mid-September, 1954. If you recall, I had decided to hitch-hike all the way home to Chilliwack, get a job for a few years, save up some money and then head off to theological seminary to finally rid myself of all my nagging doubts regarding my faith. How remarkable and timely it was that I would meet this defrocked cleric and have a chance to sit with him and discuss liberal theology for two whole days. He and those discussions would be in my thoughts for years to come.

Another lucky circumstance was my admission to Normal School in Vancouver. Here, as I have already related, my focus shifted entirely away from religion to education. This redirection in life went very smoothly, partly because my new role as

David and Cornel, on Granville St., Vancouver, circa 1958

teacher was not that far removed from being a minister and partly because I had already developed and honed my public speaking skills at PBI. Being in a new city, far from the people who shared my faith, far from pointing fingers and accusations was certainly a help, and the fact that I was literally too busy to attend church or observe other religious practices also significantly contributed to my dissolution of faith. It was the first time in my life that I did not attend church regularly, nor have any religion pressed on me. It was the first time that I was away from the flock and I found it more liberating than frightening.

At Normal School I also met David Janzen, who became my lifelong and closest friend. David had been expelled from the same church congregation in which I was still a member because he had announced his disbelief to family and church elders. He was, when I met him, a declared atheist. I was not. Though, of course, I had my pockets of disbelief. Even though David and I were roommates, partners in student-teaching, and generally close friends, we seldom, if ever, discussed religion. David helped me in my religious struggles not by challenging my beliefs directly or contributing specific insights but rather by just being a good person and a good friend who stood by me without judgment. He didn't ever tell me that I didn't need religion to be a good person, he *showed* me, and that was all the more powerful. I was lucky that he too came along at just the right time in my journey.

Another huge factor in the unraveling of my religious faith was attending secular University and particularly the discovery of and careful study of philosophy. Ideas that I had hardly dared to think before were openly discussed. I learned to think more clearly and how to express my vague thoughts, to put them out there for others to challenge and debate. Often these thoughts didn't make much sense but sometimes they did; and when I did have lucid moments, it was very satisfying. How different and eye-opening it was to have everything open for debate without having strict limits imposed. That freedom of thought together with a wider array of knowledge of history, literature, and other disciplines gave me the opportunity to examine Christian doctrines thoroughly. And, not too surprisingly, as I genuinely examined those doctrines that I had followed so faithfully for so long, I found them to be less and less rational.

Yet another factor that may have played a part in the slow death of my faith was the compilation of benefits that I experienced as I dropped, piece by piece, the prohibitions and requirements of the church. It was almost like what psychologists would call classical conditioning and I even started to salivate every time the bell rang. How pleasant it was to be able to sleep in on Sunday mornings after working hard all week and the previous night until 2 a.m. I could hang out with my friend, David, go to movies and do other innocent yet formerly illicit things without even feeling guilty! After Normal School and during my early years of teaching I learned how to dance. What wonderful clean fun dancing is! I was always taught that it was entirely sinful and therefore strictly forbidden. During those years I could afford many new diversions: bowling, driving my own car, downhill skiing, going to concerts, travelling, and more. Had I kept my faith, I would have forgone all of that.

I think Mennonites could compete or even come out ahead of the Catholics when it comes to using guilt to keep the faithful faithful. There is, of course, a place for guilt in the life of a moral being, in the sense of genuine remorse for a wrong done and a feeling of obligation to make restitution; but here I'm talking about massive, oppressive, needless, and pointless guilt, some of which still sticks to me to this day. Most of it, however, vanished along with my faith. My biggest reward for leaving religion behind was not the money I was earning or the entertainments that I could now afford and indulge in; it was the cessation of guilt.

Along with the cessation of guilt was the cessation of fear – fear of hell, fear of missing the Rapture, fear of missing my calling, fear of death, fear of authorities, and fear of freedom itself. From my early youth to that fateful year of 1954-5 when my faith started to evaporate, guilt and fear had plagued me, as no doubt plagued and continues to plague countless millions of others. By the end of the 1950's, I was able to declare myself a non-believer and with that most of my fears were dispelled as I made my exit from Damascus for good.

CHAPTER NINE

The Road Ahead

Vision for the Future

As I closed the last gate on my way out of Damascus, there gradually appeared to me a vision of the 'new Jerusalem', our little plot of heaven on Earth. It was not a clear vision of a city replete in all its splendour and detail, but rather glimpses of some of the central features of what was to come. It was a city not built by God but by human hands for human purposes, inspired by human imagination and governed by human morality and law. Outside of Damascus moral codes are not posited by supernatural beings foisting their will on us. We are the creators of our own moral code arising from inborn and cultivated moral intuition and sentiment. Outside of Damascus there are no supernatural explanations for causes and events. There are only reasonable and rational explanations of a human kind or there are no explanations at all. It should not be surprising that the vision of this new city is a thoroughly human one.

Essentially we are all humanists of one kind or another. We can and ought to think for ourselves, choose for ourselves, and generally act by and for ourselves. Whether we choose to build magnificent temples to imagined gods to mollify our fears and to satisfy our egos; whether we waste away our lives waiting for the Rapture;

whether we pollute our only planet and atmosphere, endangering not only our survival but also all forms of life, just to satisfy our greed; whether we choose to bomb each other into oblivion because of petty hatreds and jealousies; or whether we choose to rid ourselves of religious delusions and embrace the task of taking responsibility for our own lives and actions – these are all human choices expressing our way of being human.

There is no escape from being human and living out our lives according to our choices. That is after all our existential condition. If I express my humanity by following a religion, that is my choice; but it remains a choice made by a human being. If I choose to express my humanity by rejecting religion and following reason and rational morality, that is my way of being human. In my vision of the new city, I see religion and attendant bigotry in retreat and reason and good will in ascendancy.

In the broadest sense, my vision of the future is one that could be shared by almost everyone. When it comes down to it, who really doesn't want to preserve the human race, and other species, to preserve the planet in a condition fit to sustain life? Who doesn't want to be healthy and happy, to have the opportunity to create, to know, to understand, and to achieve self-fulfillment? We can build a New Jerusalem, a little bit of 'heaven' here on Earth, here in the only place where we know for sure we can live.

Where many people differ is in the approach to bringing all this about. What exactly are health, happiness, and self-fulfillment anyway? The disputes are in the details. Even reasonable, educated people will not always come to the same conclusion. However, I believe, or at least hope, that as long as we keep researching, discovering, thinking clearly and discussing openly, instead of closing our minds and opening the arsenal, we will make progress toward a shared definition of 'heaven on Earth' and the means to achieve it. My vision for the future, this 'road ahead', is open for criticism and dialogue, for it is not set in stone, not pre-ordained, and we as the human race have a lot of difficult and important choices to make if we are to survive with dignity and respect for all.

While my glimpse of this new magnificent city is only fragmentary, some of the architecture has already come into view. Some of the features, such as public education, health care, democracy, and environmental protection are springing up and growing, having been cultivated only relatively recently in human history. These are all conceptually and institutionally in their infancy (particularly environmental protection) and we must work long and hard to flesh out their potential. As I see it, public education is the show piece in the architecture of the new city.

Public Education

MUCH OF MY ability to break free from the clutches of religion, much of my freedom of thought and indeed much of my happiness could not have happened had I not had access to the courageous, enlightened, and dedicated thinkers and writers that I encountered through books and public education. I can think of no public policy more enlightened, more forward looking, of more personal and social benefit, and more civilizing than free public education for everyone. Even here we have to be on guard though because not everyone understands the very important difference between education and indoctrination. It is a shame and a transgression against universal human rights that there are still so many places in the world where not only is public education not provided but books are burned, communication with the world community tightly controlled, and education itself cynically regarded as a threat.

I can't imagine my plight had schools not been available to me. They were immensely important in my journey. Nor can I imagine living in a society without general public education. Many countries aren't as far along the path of education as we are, but nonetheless public education, even here in Canada, is still a work in progress. Even here we have to guard against taking it for granted, keep funding it, and keep it evolving in the right direction.

One lingering, sometimes growing, misconception about education is that the main job of public schools is to provide job training and to ensure socially acceptable behaviour. While those are laudable goals, and it is appropriate to include some utilitarian aims in the curriculum, real education is so much more than that.

The primary objective of public education, or any education, is to achieve a general state of enlightenment, no more, no less. This is decidedly a conservative conception of education, echoing Matthew Arnold's views on education as the transmission to the next generation of the best that has been thought and said. Recently, a similar view was proffered by Andre Comte-Sponville who argued that, "Only by transmitting the past to our children can we enable them to invent their future; only by being culturally conservative can we be politically progressive."[147] School curriculum should introduce the student to all the various forms of knowledge[148] such as logic, philosophy, mathematics, science, social science, history, art, literature and ethics. Students need all of these tools if they are to examine life in a complex world and make wise choices not only in career but also in all facets of life. Education is not only a utility, though it certainly is that as well, but achieving a certain state of mind worthwhile in and of itself. This notion of education as a normative concept was explored in the sixties and seventies by R.S. Peters whom I was fortunate to study under and have as my PhD supervisor. His ground breaking work is not surprisingly also reflected in my work.

This emphasis on knowledge and understanding in breadth and depth is at the core of this conception of education which Peters and I, and a great many other educators, share. I believe it is this that all people of the planet have a right to. That is what I mean

---

147   Andre Comte-Sponville, *Little Book of Atheist Spirituality*, 2006 (transl. 2007), p.27.
148   I didn't include 'religion' as a form of knowledge in this series because there is no religious 'knowledge' per se. We can and should learn *about* religion but in terms of public education that can be covered in courses like social studies, history and literature.

by education being a 'normative' concept. It is this kind of education that will enable people to resist indoctrination, to overcome delusions of various kinds and to give them a fair opportunity to be successful in both career and in all facets of life.

Another misconception of education is that there can be many different kinds of education, depending on parental choices, societal wishes, and local preferences. If there is a specific agenda, the prospect of getting a good general education is greatly diminished if not entirely eliminated. It is true that there are many ways to *deliver* education, with many varieties of curriculum, teaching methods, extra-curricular activities and so on, but there can be only one goal. If this is correct, and it is my considered professional opinion that it is, namely that the core of education is knowledge and understanding in breadth and depth, then education is much more universal than it would appear at first glance. That is because knowledge itself is universal in character. There is no Christian mathematics, Muslim chemistry, nor Jewish physics and so on. Science is science; logic is logic; reason is reason. The universality of these is well established. When one takes away cultural, religious, or any other kind of bias, then one can see that real education is by nature secular and universal.

I am suggesting that the term 'secular education' is actually a redundancy and that 'religious education' is a misnomer. There is some point in using the former to distinguish from the latter but ultimately both are misleading. Indoctrination is a large part of religious 'education' but that needs to be exposed as invalid when it comes to real education, for to inculcate doctrines by limiting questioning and discussion is reprehensible. The practice of indoctrination needs to be removed if one is to achieve education. In fact I would argue[149] that even parents do not have the right to indoctrinate their children, particularly if they use public funds and tax breaks to do so. On the contrary, children have the universal

---

149 For a detailed discussion see my essay 'Constraints on Parents' Rights Concerning the Education of their Children', published in M Manley-Cassimir, *Family Choice in Schooling*, Lexington Books, Lexington, Massachusetts, 1982, p. 71.

right not to be indoctrinated just as they have the right not to be physically harmed by parents or anyone else. 'Religious education' is not just another form of education, deserving of public support and public funds. The indoctrination that goes on in the name of 'religious education' is *not* education and has no place in the ideal of universal free public education.

Yet another misconception regarding education is that public schools are and should be free of value judgments and remain morally neutral. That should not be and is not the case. That public schools are not value free surely must be obvious. Every day when teachers and educational administrators choose what to teach and how to teach it, they are making value judgments, based on what they think is *valuable* for the student, what the student *ought* to learn. There would be no point in compulsory education if we educators didn't think that we could provide something better, something more worthwhile, than what could be accessed randomly on the streets or on the internet. There is no escape from making value judgments for teachers, administrators, or for that matter parents.

The public school is also not neutral when it comes to moral values. Public schools, in fact any school or institution, could not even operate if they didn't subscribe to some basic universal moral principles, namely justice (fairness); liberty (freedom to think, to speak, and to debate); honesty (truth-telling, keeping promises, not cheating); non-malfeasance (not harming others nor preventing others from learning); beneficence (helping those that need it, being kind and respectful to others) and so on. We can and should make a determined effort to provide moral education as part of the overall offering.

I have spent a good deal of my professional life on the question of what constitutes moral education and how it is to be brought about so I will not repeat here all my thoughts on these matters.[150] Here, I will just note that there is a universal body of ethical rules

---

150 Interested readers may want to read my paper 'Moral Education as the Achievement of Virtue' in *Melbourne Studies in Education*.

and principles available that any rational person can and must subscribe to if public moral education is to be served. The public school must not shy away from moral education simply because of an unclear understanding of what ethics is.

The public school system (here in Canada at least and I would strongly suspect elsewhere) suffers not just from these and many other misconceptions but also from neglect of various kinds: underfunding or cutting back on well-reasoned existing programs (such as arts or physical education), unclear goals, shortage of quality teachers, unequal quality of the schools themselves, top-heavy administration, and unimaginative architecture of the buildings themselves just to name a few. The list of deficiencies and threats could go on and on. Here, I only wish to indicate the type of issues that need attention. Even here in a place where our education system has a good reputation, we have a long way to go before we reach the goal of truly free, universal public education. The American policy of 'no child left behind' may be short on the details of how to achieve education for all but it seems to be at least the right sentiment. Until we reach that goal, public education still requires a lot of work and fine tuning.

At the same time that education is a value in itself and also utilitarian (a stepping stone to the achievement of other goals such as employment, physical health, social finesse and so on), education is also central to moral understanding and therefore moral behavior, a properly functioning democracy, and genuine social justice. It should therefore not be surprising that I have placed education centre stage in the new republic.

If public education is paramount in the New Jerusalem, then of only slightly less importance is public and universal access to health.

Health Care

ANOTHER GOOD IDEA that is only half-realized, even here in Canada where we have a reasonably good reputation for it, is free universal health care. A recent WHO study found that Canada, once a world leader in health care, doesn't even rank in the top ten countries worldwide when it comes to health care; and small poor countries like Cuba consistently rank ahead of rich powerful nations like the USA when it comes to the quality and universality of health care. A healthy body to go along with an informed healthy mind should be everybody's birthright.

The idea of universal health care is still relatively new and obviously has not been adopted by every country, even rich ones that can afford it, the USA being a prime example. Why the Americans are so reluctant to buy into this idea is incomprehensible to me. Nevertheless, some excellent progress has been made on this front. There are no doubt problems associated with any public health care system yet invented but this is not the time and place to solve all of those. What I would like to do is suggest that it is immoral for the rich and healthy to hoard their riches while innocent poor children, or anyone else, suffer for lack of medical care simply because they cannot afford it.

The irony here is that it is probably even economically advantageous to share the wealth when it comes to healthcare. Is not a healthy work-force more productive? It is likely that the cost of down-time and/or loss of efficiency due to treatable health concerns is more costly than health care. I haven't seen the numbers but it seems to me entirely possible. However, that is not really my point; my point here is one of ethics not just cost-benefit, though it may well be the case that both the bottom line and morality can be served at the same time by public health care. Preventable human suffering *ought* to be addressed on moral grounds regardless of affordability; it's just a nice corollary that it may well be cost-efficient as well.

Democracy

SOME FORM OF democracy is very likely the best form of government to allow universal moral principles, of the kind alluded to earlier, to be realized. Ideally, the laws under which people live should actually reflect the will of the majority and this tends to happen much more frequently in a democracy. In order for democracies to function as designed there needs to be an educated electorate and the free flow of ideas and information in all directions. Not only should the electorate choose their representatives but those representatives need to be accountable to the people.

In many parts of the world, and increasingly so, nations have expressly written into their constitutions the requirement of a democratic form of government. I think that this is a good development as the basic idea of democracy, of rule by the people for the people, is a sound one. It is encouraging that many nations are going in this direction but we are still experimenting with various forms of democracy and there is much work still to be done before the ideals of true democracy are realized. However, one has to be ever vigilant against 'tyranny of the masses' and even in a situation where a majority rules, minority rights must be protected. For a democracy to function in a way that actually protects moral principles, it requires careful balance and compassion. It has to be more than 'winner takes all'. I would like to suggest two ways that democracy can be improved.

First is the matter of revamping the policy of the simple majority, winner-take-all procedure for electing representatives. There must be a more fair and more accurate way to reflect the will of the people. Perhaps proportional representation, giving seats based on a percentage of popular vote, like they have adopted in some parts of Europe, as opposed to one and only one winner per geographical area like we do in Canada. We must learn to avoid situations where a large segment of the population, sometimes even a majority, have their concerns ignored by a government elected from a minority of the people because of the proverbial 'first past the post' electoral system.

I would also like to suggest that a better informed electorate and limits on election tactics and spending would be an improvement. Despite vast amounts of money spent on electioneering, the public all too often doesn't even know what a candidate actually stands for and why. Too little money and effort is spent on actually informing people and much too much is spent on intentional misinformation (spin) and childish hate-mongering and mudslinging. Instead of actually debating the issues, the focus of getting elected is all too often about out-spending the other candidate, image manipulation, and cheap appeals to base emotions. Often, to get elected, all one has to do is spend more money and spread more lies and that is pretty far from the democratic ideal.

What can be done is to limit spending and control electioneering in the interest of fair play and equality. Even in so-called 'mature' democracies like Britain, Canada, and the USA, there are still significant problems with how we carry this out. We tend to operate more like oligarchies, with only the very rich running the show, rather than real democracies. Real equality is a nice concept, and it gets some lip service now and then but it is rarely actually achieved. The rich corporations buy the media, together they manipulate the government, and the government makes rules that favour the corporations. And so the cycle goes; the rich get richer and the poor are left to fend for themselves in a very unequal system. For the most part that is how our 'democracies' function. In fact, it doesn't even seem to be getting better (i.e. more transparent, more fair and more ethical), it seems to be getting worse.

Because money influences voter patterns so significantly, and because there is such disparity of wealth, it seems necessary to enact more control over the amounts spent on elections in the interest of a more level playing field. The US Supreme court just recently ruled against such controls on election spending, essentially allowing vast amounts of wealth[151] to pour into and potentially poison

---

151 These extremely well-funded political power blocks have come to be called 'super-pacs' (PAC, being an acronym for Political Action Committee). An attempt to limit

the political process. Democracy, despite being attempted for a while as a laudable concept, is still in its infancy. Let's just say that democracy is a worthy goal but is still a work in progress, even here in the so-called 'first world'.

Environmental Sustainability

IT GOES WITHOUT saying, or at least it ought to, that environmental sustainability is an absolute must if we are going to thrive or even survive as a species. My vision for the future includes plans for environmental clean-up, improved environmental protection, and curbing our voracious and wasteful consumption of finite resources. Our shared land, atmosphere, and water resources have already been severely polluted. People are suffering and dying *now* from such pollution and the problem will only get worse, much worse, if we can't change our ways dramatically. Individuals need to change their lifestyles and governments need to enact better laws and impose penalties to facilitate and encourage this.

Unfortunately, space and time do not allow me here and now to go into details, but fortunately environmental issues are now being widely discussed and debated. Much information and good science is available for consideration. From Rachel Carson's, *Silent Spring*, to E.F. Schumacher's *Small is Beautiful*, to Al Gore's, *An Inconvenient Truth*, to Naomi Klein's *This Changes Everything*, there are numerous good books available to pursue and study. Lack of information, however, is less of a problem than lack of will to act on the knowledge we do have. That is why laws and penalties might be good motivators to help us along until the ethics of environmentalism clicks on and sinks in.

---

their funding was thrown out by the courts and so they have become hugely wealthy and influential political power brokers.

Redistribution of Wealth

AFTER ENVIRONMENTAL degradation, which directly threatens all of our health, the redistribution of wealth, many informed people would say, is the biggest problem on Earth. In country after country around the world, the rich are getting richer and the poor poorer. It seems we are going in reverse with regard to establishing and maintaining equality of opportunity and rewards for work and risk. Not only is the perverse distribution of wealth an economic problem, it is a moral problem (in that it just isn't fair), and it is also a serious political problem by eroding the proper functioning of democracy. And not only that, economic disparity undermines education, erodes environmental sustainability efforts, and creates problematic social divisiveness.

For a while, and in recent history, it appeared that in some democracies such as Britain, the US, and Canada egalitatirianism was on the rise. In the 1950's and 1960's middle classes began to grow in leaps and bounds. It seemed, at least for a while, that everyone who worked could have a comfortable life, not too far out of touch with their neighbors. However, that trend seems to be reversing, and in a large way.

These days, approximately 90% of all the wealth of the USA is in the hands of fewer than 10% of the people. Is that the will of the people? Is that fair? Is it because the rich work harder, are better educated or are more enterprising? Hardly. Throughout history the rich and powerful have been loath to give up their wealth and power voluntarily, often resulting in violent uprisings and revolution. However, we democratic nations have the potential to put methods in place, other than violence, to bring about political and economic change; our will to do so, however, seems weak.

The sickness of our democratic system is feeding the disparity of wealth instead of fixing it and the disparity of wealth is further eroding the effectiveness of our democracy. Reforming tax laws would be a quick and efficient means of righting some of the outrageous disparities but those are almost always met with aggressive opposition from very powerful rich lobby groups. Ironically and sadly it seems many people who would benefit from a redistribution of wealth are the very ones opposing it, because many of whom have been brainwashed into thinking that this kind of 'socialism' is bad for everyone and somehow threatens their core freedoms.

Why anyone, no matter how talented or hard working, needs more than a million dollars[152] a year in income is not reasonable or fair. Income above that amount should be taxed at close to 100% and redistributed to the poor or at least spent on better health care and education. Other measures, like succession duties, could also help in the redistribution of wealth. It is ethically desireable to even out the world's gross disparities. We still have a lot of unfinished business before we can truly call ourselves enlightened or even fully democratic.

The United Nations, great in concept, is also still in its infancy. Its potential for keeping the peace and solving problems of poverty, disease, and education on a world-wide scale has barely been tapped. While the UN has the potential to be a great tool for humanity, its structure and governance needs to be revisited and revised and its mission redefined to include a permanent international police force. Membership in the UN should be mandatory for all nations. The costs of operating it should be shared commensurate with the ability of individual states' wealth and size. In the UN we have an idea, an institution with the potential of significantly advancing our common humanity but there remains a lot of work to be done here too.

All this unfinished business – universal public education, democratic governance, health care, fairer distribution of wealth, caring for our planet and international cooperation – amounts to only a small number of issues out of many that have emerged in the last few hundred years. These are big concerns all needing continuous revising, renewing, and reinventing. There are, however, also in my vision for the road ahead, smaller projects for the betterment of humanity that need attention.

---

152 I chose an arbitrary amount in 2011 US dollars. It could be much less.

Projects for the Planet

WHAT FOLLOWS is a list of projects that I have been or would like to be working on to make the world a better place for all. Of course I could list many more but these are a brief selection of my hopes for humanity and include some pet peeves:

1) The complete separation of church and state (actually this is not such a small project).

In many western democracies the idea of separation of church and state has been adopted officially but only enforced sporadically and only to some degree. In some cases, as in the USA, this principle is enshrined in the constitution. The First Amendment, Article One, of the Bill of Rights, famously states that: "Congress shall pass no law respecting an establishment of religion, or prohibiting the free exercise thereof."

What this actually means was clarified in the Supreme Court's 1947 ruling in Everson vs. Board of Education:

> The 'establishment of religion' clause of the First Amendment means at least this: Neither a State nor the Federal Government can set up a church. Neither can pass laws which aid one religion, aid all religions, or prefer one religion over another... No tax in any amount, large or small, can be levied to support any religious activities or institutions, whatever they may be called, or whatever form they may adopt to teach or practice religion. Neither a State nor the Federal Government can, openly or secretly, participate in the affairs of any religious organization or groups or vice versa. In the words of Jefferson, the clause against the establishment of religion by law was intended to erect 'a wall of separation between church and state'.

I have not seen this principle stated any clearer than that. The problem is that very few countries have this principle articulated in their constitution, and where it is included, as in the USA, it is not followed owing to little to no enforcement.

In the USA "Religio-political changes now threaten church-state separation as never before."[153] In his article 'The Tax Free Ride', Austin Miles finds that, "...because the churches are tax exempt, the average citizen pays an additional $925 a year in taxes to support them. The churches own 81 billion dollars' worth of tax-exempt real estate in Texas and 1.3 billion in Los Angeles County alone."[154] The point is that even though it is clearly spelled out in the Constitution and by the Supreme Court, the separation of Church and state in the USA is just not enforced and barely exists at all.

Here in Canada, we don't even have the principle of Church-State separation in our constitution. We adhere to the principle, to the extent we do, under a sort of gentleman's agreement. We have similar tax exemptions for religious institutions in our country. How much I pay in extra taxes to fund churches I do not know. Perhaps every citizen should be given a 10% tax-free 'tithing allowance' and then we could all support whatever cause we want. I for one would use the money to support the elimination of the favourable position of the Christian church, and all churches, in our society. To give everyone the same exemption would at least be more politically palatable to some than eliminating a long established and expected practice of allowing church only tax exemption.

Meanwhile, in both the US and Canada, millions and millions, perhaps billions, of dollars of public money are spent in support of religious schools. I think that many people don't even know that their tax dollars are going towards indoctrinating people in various faiths in the name of public 'education'. I find it particularly trou-

---

153   Tim C. Leedham (Ed), *The Book Your Church Doesn't Want You to Read*, E World Inc., 2001, p.332.
154   Ibid., p.341.

bling in this day and age to be *required* to pay for the loathsome practice of religious indoctrination with public funds, especially when this is done in the name of 'education'. What is more, until recently the public education system in BC and I suspect across Canada and elsewhere actively supported the Christian religion by requiring Bible reading and the reciting of the Lord's Prayer in classrooms. That has changed now, but the full separation of church and state is still a long way off, even here in Canada.

2) Prevent, or at least minimize the effect of religious indoctrination of children by their parents or their surrogates.

In his otherwise excellent book, *The God Delusion*, Richard Dawkins makes an urgent plea not to refer to children by their parents', or any, religious affiliation as a counter measure to children's indoctrination. He proposes that there are no such people as Christian children or Muslim children and so on. While I share Dawkins' view that indoctrination of children is indeed reprehensible and is a problem that needs to be addressed, I think that the proposed remedy is neither very effectual nor is his characterization of the problem that accurate. Much depends on what age of child one has in mind. I myself was a Christian by age eight when I got 'saved'. Perhaps Dawkins forgot that part of the Bible that says "Except ye ... become as little children, ye shall not enter into the kingdom of heaven."[155]

The Christian mind-set is the mind-set of a child. If religion is indeed without foundation, as both Dawkins and I believe, then children are as well-founded in their religion as adults are. Growing up will not change that. Children have as much evidence for their faith as they ever will have, namely none. There cannot be an evolution of faith on the basis of accumulating evidence; there can only be greater degrees of unreasonable commitment to tenets of religion as a result of further social pressure and further indoctrination. The problem of early parental indoctrination is not eliminated by refraining from referring to children by their religious affiliation.

---

155 Matthew 18:3.

Attempts to curb parental indoctrination will be seen by many parents as a violation of their existing right to religious freedom. Curbing religious freedom to some extent is precisely what is required to solve the problem of childhood indoctrination. So what is needed is a re-examination of the very notion of religious freedom and one could wish that Dawkins would lend his estimable powers of mind to that examination. As things now stand even the UN charter states that when there is a conflict between the state and the parent vis-à-vis the education of the child, the parents' right is supreme. But is it? Do parents indeed have the right to decide their children's education? *Should* they have that right? Or does the child's right not to be indoctrinated (which Dawkins, I think, and I agree is fundamental to obtaining a genuine education) supercede the parents' rights? I have argued elsewhere that indeed there are restrictions of parents' rights regarding the education of their children.[156]

We need to seek a balance between a parent's right to express and act on their religious beliefs in the home and community (and thus perforce strongly influence the children in their care) on the one hand, and on the other hand a child's right to obtain an authentic, unbiased, open-minded general education (without parental indoctrination preventing that). To achieve that balance (just to hint at some possibilities) we may have to legally prohibit certain parental practices concerning the coercive application of religion such as forced attendance at religious services, or punishments for breaking religion-based rules. Another possibility would be to mandate a certain number of years attending secular public (state) schools, in which courses on comparative religion would be compulsory. It would be interesting and valuable to know exactly how many people there are right now in Canada (and elsewhere) who are schooled (though not necessarily educated), hold degrees and powerful political offices who have never attended a secular educa-

---

156 See my article 'Constraints on Parents Rights Concerning the Education of Their Children', in M. Manley-Casimir (Ed.), *Family Choice in Schooling*, Lexington Books, Lexington, Massachusetts. 1982, p.71.

tional institution. I suspect that there are many. This is not acceptable in a multi-cultural democracy. But it happens because we have not yet solved the problem of childhood religious indoctrination and because we have given away too much under the rubric of freedom of religion.

3) Dying with dignity is another important social issue clouded by religion that I would like to see discussed and then put into legislation.

This is another area where the religious and secular positions clash. Convincing arguments can be made for the legalization of assisted suicide, allowing terminally ill people to end their life with dignity and less suffering. It has been said that we treat our dogs better than our own species when it comes to end of life suffering. However the Christian position on any kind of suicide is that it is against God's will and therefore cannot be tolerated and no amount of logical argument seems to be able to penetrate that position.

I am not afraid of being dead, but the process of dying is another story. If I should fall into the class of those old people that suffer terribly from an incurable disease, I should not like to be forced to stay alive against my wishes. I should have the right over my own life, and so should others.

4) Effective population control.

It takes no genius to grasp the idea that population expansion cannot go on indefinitely in a world of finite resources, but once again logic clashes with religion. In the past, wars, disease, natural disasters, limited food supply, and other such factors have worked to keep human population in check. We have relied too on discovering new uninhabited lands, improving food production, and inventing new technologies to permit population expansion without too many deleterious effects. In recent history, knowing that overpopulation is a growing problem, we have found ways to slow population growth by birth control and family planning. The Chinese have even made much publicized legislation limiting most families to a single child.

Many of us have finally concluded that we cannot with impunity keep on breeding uncontrollably. If we are to get anywhere in this complex but critical issue we cannot keep allowing religious leaders to dictate to the world on matters of birth control. It is outrageous that the Pope, for example, should try to influence the people of Africa on the use of condoms. I don't pretend to have all the answers but at the very least we need to make birth control and abortions freely available to keep unwanted children from being born. No child should be born without being wanted by the parents. Whether or not there ought to be national and international restrictions and sanctions legislated for the control of birth, I am not prepared to say. What I can say is that this is yet another case where churches have wrongfully and without warrant claimed for themselves a privileged position, and may indeed be doing much more harm than good.

5) Eliminating the privileged position of religion in society.

As we have touched on briefly already, even in countries where there is no official state religion and where the concept of separation of church and state has been advanced somewhat, there is still a huge bias in favour of special status for church and religion. In the USA for example, one of the very few countries to have actually formally adopted a position of no official state religion and separation of church and state, the chances of getting elected to public office if you are an atheist are almost nill. In a recent survey in a local American newspaper[157] they found that 51% of respondents were prepared to vote for a woman for President, 49% a black American, but only 9% would vote for an atheist! While one must guard against making too much fuss about a small local survey, my guess would be that the results reflect general American attitudes fairly accurately. Even President Obama, a confessed Christian who very publically goes to church with his family on Sundays, isn't Christian *enough* for a large section of the American electorate. Imagine the great thinkers, people such as Bertrand Russell, David Hume,

---

157   *Desert Sun*, circa 2007.

Charles Darwin, Immanuel Kant, Richard Dawkins and so on, not even having a chance at public office, simply because they publically disclosed their non-theism!

Somehow in the mind of the public, despite a lack of any kind of evidence, there seems to be a connection between non-theism and untrustworthiness, and vice-versa. To put it in stark relief, to try the shoe on the other foot to see how it feels, suppose we were artificially to turn the tables by making a general rule that no confessed Christian (nor any other religious adherent) is fit to run for public office because they are not of sound mind and character, believing as they do in superstition. That is the kind of prejudicial voting patterns that avowed non-theists face. Again, we can see that in practice, there is in fact not much division of church and state, even in the USA where it is written into the constitution.

It is bad enough when the privileged position of the church infiltrates the attitudes of the electorate, but when the state openly favours religious groups over secular ones (as in tax breaks and funding for religious schools) that is really not acceptable. The state also favours religion by exempting people from compliance with the laws on religious grounds, such as not having to attend public school or serving in the military. When my brother-in-law exempted himself from military service during WW2 he could easily do so by pointing out that pacifism was part of his religion. In contrast, when Bertrand Russell, an affirmed atheist, argued against war with Germany, he was fired from his post at Cambridge and sent to prison for sedition. "In 1940 he [Bertrand Russell] was appointed to a professorship at City College of New York, but after a public outcry he was deemed 'bereft of moral fiber' and unfit to teach, and fired before his first class could convene."[158] There is little doubt that this was because of his atheism and his views on love and marriage.

It is time for non-theists to come out of the proverbial closet and declare themselves equal citizens and time for their persecutors, the theists, to desist. With reason and rationality as their watchwords, with universal human rational-based ethics as their moral compass,

---

158   From the NNDB website: http://www.nndb.com/people/954/000044822.

with well thought-out ethically based politics, it is time for non-theists to take centre stage in education and politics. It is time for the intellectually honest to step forward and be heard and heeded. With faith as their only guide, with absolutely inflexible doctrine on social issues, with God-centred revenge and thoroughly outdated scripture-based ethics as their moral compass, with the arrogant attitude of the superiority of faith over reason, with indoctrination as their 'educational' tool, it is the theists that are actually unfit to lead or teach on many levels. If they must put into practice their intolerance and lack of rationality, then the theists are morally obliged to withdraw from public discourse and retreat into the privacy of their homes and churches. If we actually want a free and fair democracy, it is time, in fact long overdue, for the privileged position of the church in society to end.

6) Introduce legislation against 'faith' healing and the neglect of children motivated by religion.

It is not possible to cover all the details here but suffice it to say that much needless mental and physical harm, even death, has been caused, or at least not prevented when it could easily have been, because of 'faith' healing. For example many people have died because of refusing blood transfusions on religious grounds. Perhaps one has that right as an adult but who gets to decide for a child? There has been some advancement in the concept of the state protecting children from their parents' misguided ideology but there are still many places where simple decency and common sense is trumped by religion. I would urge more people to study this pernicious problem and bring it to the attention of legislators.[159]

7) Eliminate privilege by birth.

Here is another humanistic project that has started but is still really unfinished business. From the disappearance of the God-like Pharaohs of Egypt and the emperors of China, to the decline of

---

159 Possible readings: Victor Stenger, *Has Science Found God*, (p241) or SM Asser & Rita Swan, 'Child Fatalities From Religion Motivated Neglect', *Pediatrics*, 1988, pps625-29.

absolute monarchs in Europe, worldwide much of the long standing practice of extreme privilege, power, and wealth based on birth alone has ceased or is at least in full retreat. However, much remains to be done. Even in mature democracies where the concept of 'meritocracy' is bandied about, rarely is this concept fully realized. There are still many people in many places that have much better housing, food, and water, access to health care, education, training, access to political power and anything else that money and influence can buy, simply by right of birth. They are born into positions of wealth and power, often because their parents and their parents' parents were wealthy and influential. The cycle continues. It must stop if we are going to continue to think of ourselves as 'civilized'.

I do not want to argue that people should not work hard and enjoy the fruits of their labour. There is nothing wrong with being reasonably well off and comfortable, but I do want to argue that the cycle of immense hereditary wealth and power must be broken through legislation that allows for very little inheritance. People should enjoy the wealth that they themselves create not the wealth created for them by somebody else. The world is unfair enough in the random distribution of health, talents, intelligence, appearance, and other hereditary traits, without adding more unfairness created by human decision and action. We simply must on moral grounds create a more level playing field and actually embrace and enact the concept of meritocracy, where all people have a somewhat equal chance at achieving wealth and power based on their individual talents and efforts.

8) Encourage ethics and etiquette for a healthy planet.

Vancouver, my hometown, prides itself on being environmentally friendly and aims to be the 'greenest city in the world'. However nice that sounds, we have a long way to go to realize that. Our mayor cycles to work, looks over a vegetable garden from his office, and dreams of Vancouver as a showcase of green living. I share his dream, but we have to get beyond symbolic gestures and greenwashing. At last count only roughly 4% of Vancouverites regularly commute by bicycle and this is supposed to be a leading

Canadian city in terms of cycling and environmentalism in general. In reality, Vancouver is clogged with car traffic, the worst in all of North America, recently eclipsing even Los Angeles.[160]

The centrepiece of Vancouver's attempt to be a green city, is to encourage high density living. Yaletown, the area in which I live, is supposed to be an example of model city planning, and indeed people around the world are taking notice. Vancouver already has a wonderful natural setting and the architecture here is supposed to mesh with that, with great ocean views, parks, and the ever-popular 'seawall', a wide cycling and pedestrian path that rings the shoreline. Rather nice, but the buildings themselves are far from ideal. We have to get beyond what looks nice.

In addition to the problems of architecture and building practices there are also problems of interpersonal ethics and etiquette. Someone badly needs to write a book on that, perhaps with a title like *The Ethics and Etiquette of High Density Living*. Problems like unwanted loud music, toxic perfumes and cleaning agents, pet control, and other similar issues cause not only annoyance but in the long run constitute significant health concerns. Only when we develop both better buildings and establish better social ethics will we be able to live together in high density happily and in good health.

Some other projects that I don't have space to fully explore here but nonetheless would like to see taken on in the future, mostly pertaining to Canada, though there are some similar issues elsewhere, are:

9) Establish a Federal Department of Education for the purpose of reviewing funding for schools and universities and setting national educational standards.

10) Eliminate the Department of Indian Affairs. It is time that our First Nations people fully integrate into the Canadian family, time to completely re-think our relationship with aboriginal peoples.

---

160 According to the most recent TomTom Traffic Index.

11) Reinstate and improve the gun registration.

12) Amend the constitution to formally separate church and state (similar to the US amendment).

13) Renegotiate NAFTA (free trade) to include Europe and Asia.

14) Reintroduce FIRA, our Foreign Investment Review Agency.

15) Introduce a universal child-care program.

16) Ensure that our Parliament buildings, and other public infrastructure, are not used for religious practices and purposes.

17) Make our Members of Parliament disclose their spending and be more fiscally responsible.

The wish list could go on and on as I have here merely pointed at the proverbial tip of the iceberg. I hope it is at least sufficient to indicate what kind of world we could create if we leave behind our dependence on religion or at least don't allow religion to interfere with the building of a just human society. This 'New Jerusalem' that I symbolically envisage arises out of a moral vision. There is no doubt in my mind that there is such a thing as a universal human ethic, rich enough, practical enough, and acceptable enough, to guide us forward without having to defer to a supernatural being.

The New Jerusalem

AS PREVIOUSLY mentioned, I, unlike Paul on the road to Damascus, had no sudden flash of insight, no epiphany, no instant revelation that suddenly illuminated the road ahead. Rather, my vision for my future and the future of mankind was acquired slowly over a long period of time as a result of schooling and education, trial and error, long periods of reading and studying, travel, and observation. Likely not in my lifetime, and perhaps not even in my children's lifetime but maybe in my great, great grandchildren's time I can see a world where true democracies flourish, where the power-hungry moneyed few don't buy elections and influence, where the will of the people is truly reflected in the practices and laws of the land, a world of equal opportunity where true meritocracy can take hold and people are rewarded based on their efforts, talents, and risks, rather than their lineage. I see a world where a more even distribution of wealth benefits everyone.

I see a world where every child has a relatively equal opportunity to engage in real education, where the concept of 'no child left behind' becomes a reality and not just a slogan, and the freedom to pursue their own personal dreams through the perfecting of their own talents. I see a world where schools are more than job training centres, where learning a variety of subjects is deemed worthy for its own sake. I see a world where teaching and learning are both highly respected.

My 'New Jerusalem' would be a place where every person has free access to the best available health care, where the medical profession (and their patients) place as much emphasis on prevention of disease and the promotion of healthy living as it does on curing problems after the fact. Physical education, health, and nutrition must become more prominent in public education if we are to achieve that. Mental health issues must be destigmatized, better understood, and included as part of normal health care and maintenance. I see a world where the right to good health is accepted as a fundamental human right.

I see a world where going to work is a pleasure, where everyone, or nearly everyone, has a job that suits them. And if someone can't work for whatever reason, we ought to share the wealth for the benefit of all. The workplace doesn't need to be a battlefield between competitors, between unions and corporations. Already technology allows for significantly less work to produce all we need and that trend will likely continue. Why then are we still struggling, working longer and longer hours instead of fewer and fewer?

I see a world where we have made significant progress in the development of a world government armed with an international police force to deal with international issues such as climate change, air and water pollution, population control, violence, and more.

Further on down the road, I see a world where science has eliminated most if not all diseases, and social changes and financial balancing has ended hunger and poverty and the endless suffering that goes along with that. I see a world where we have understood human motives and idiosyncrasies better to improve education. And with that education we can perhaps bring ethics and rationality to the forefront, curbing our greed and tendencies towards violence and war. Perhaps we can even perfect interstellar space travel and discuss the possibility of discovering and colonizing new worlds.

Finally in the far distance, I can see a world free of religion. What such a world would be like is difficult to say with great specificity; but it would be along the lines indicated in this chapter. In my mind it would be a better world. There is though considerable disagreement, even among non-believers, whether or not the world would be better off without religion. Both great good and great harm have been attributed to religion.

Some would argue that religion has been very good for humanity by way of providing social cohesion, civility, art and architecture, scholarship and learning, solace and comfort in hard times, and more. It can hardly be denied that religion has at some points in history given some people in some societies a better life.

Others would argue that religion has brought a great deal more harm than good to humanity by way of divisiveness and social disharmony, conflict, brutality, war, ignorance, fear, unnecessary guilt, and impediment to progress in education and science.[161] In

---

161 One example of religion preventing science from benefitting humanity is a quote from Timothy White, President of Yale University, in 1795, who opposed small pox vaccinations by arguing that if God had decided from all eternity that an individual's fate was to die of smallpox, it was a sin to interfere with the divine plan through a man-made trick like vaccination.

this way religion has inflicted on humanity what Matthew Arnold called "the eternal note of sadness" heard long ago by Sophocles and described as "the turbid ebb and flow of human misery"[162], still heard around the world to this present day.

We can only surmise what kind of life would be possible in a worldwide humanist society free of religion, for we have only few and partial, if any, historical precedents. However, I am persuaded that religion has done much more harm than good and that the way forward for mankind is non-theism and non-religiousness.

My view that the world would be better off without religion does not entail that I favour and advocate stamping out religion by force as has been attempted in recent history in the Soviet Union, Albania, and elsewhere. I do think it important to retain the right of freedom of religion (though constrained to mitigate the problem of indoctrination). I think it would be unwise, cruel, and counter-productive to try to suppress religion by force. Rather, I think it advisable and productive to *educate* our children and youth out of religion. Enlightenment may yet lift the dark cloud of religious violence and fanaticism that has haunted humankind throughout the ages.

The assertion that religion satisfies a deep craving and meets a basic human need is not true at any fundamental level. I would suggest that the 'need' for religion is artificially created by clerics and maintained by indoctrination. Religion takes advantage of human weaknesses and propagates a lot of beliefs that exaggerate the fear of death, artificially creating a yearning for redemption and salvation. These and other religious doctrines promote and sustain an artificial need and dependency. In this way the clergy keep control and power over the laity. Leave people alone without arousing their latent fears, without pressing doctrines on them, and they will do perfectly well if given proper education. Religion is not a basic need.

Non-theism is a milestone in the development of humanity. We, the human race, can finally overcome our propensity to become deluded when we bring ourselves fully to acknowledge that there is no

---

162 From Matthew Arnold's poem, 'Dover Beach'.

grand designer and admit that we are free agents to decide our own destiny based on human moral principles. Only then will it be possible to improve the lot of mankind and achieve the dream of peace on Earth. Only then will we build the New Jerusalem. Meanwhile we must join forces with those architects of reason who have gone before us and until our last breath fight ignorance, greed, and delusion. So with that as my goal, my pen as my 'sword' and our whole planet as my 'England', I join with Blake in his declaration:

> I will not cease from mental fight,
> Nor shall my sword sleep in my hand,
> Till we have built Jerusalem
> In England's green and pleasant land.[163]

---

163   From 'Jerusalem' by William Blake in the preface to the epic poem 'Milton', (1810).

APPENDIX 1

Geneology Chart

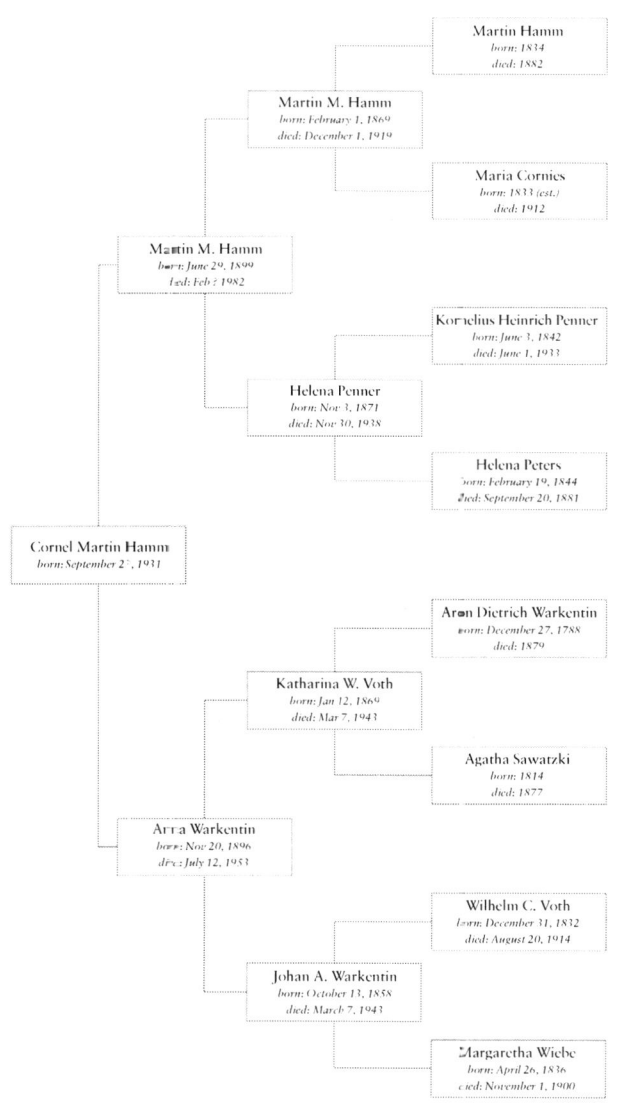

- 369 -

APPENDIX 2

Grandfather's Death

ON FRIDAY, November 28, 1919, we were gathered as a group of young people in the summer kitchen at P. Harms' practicing spiritual songs for Christmas. Suddenly Mr. Harms opens the door and announces that in Orloff they are murdering people and burning homes. News has come that Mr. Peter Martens and many other men have been shot and hacked to pieces. The bandits are now on their way to other villages. Quickly we all rush home to prepare for flight. The whole village was afoot. The worst was expected. Everyone prepared to flee, but where should they go?

Arriving at home, every preparation was made to flee. Only one wagon was loaded with the most essential survival items. The horses were harnessed. Father and I buried a chest with our best clothes in the barn. It was midnight, but no one thought of sleep, at least not of going to bed as usual. For a week already few had dared to take off their clothes for the night. One was much more concerned what the espionage had to report. From four directions in the surrounding area reports came in every three hours. Three successive shots were a signal for rapid flight.

Finally morning dawned. We had been spared. However, we could no longer feel safe even during the day. Then we hear that the worst atrocities have been carried out in the villages of Orloff, Tiege, Muensterberg, Reinfeld, and Gnadenfeld. In Muensterberg nearly 100 people, including the old and young, parents, siblings and children have been slain and hacked to pieces in horrible ways.

Many are fleeing from our village, some to the "Chutor" (large farm outside the village), others to Russian villages, not knowing where they will be safest. We also hitch our hoses and drive to the school, where we are to pick up the teacher's family on our "Droschke" (carriage). Father had promised it to them. But there others from Schoenau persuaded us to return, on the one hand, because it will be no benefit to us, and on the other, because it is assumed that the robber bands have left Sagradowka.

It seems that nothing serious happened during the day; but who suspected or knew what was being planned on the other side of the Colony? As darkness fell, the fires still burning in the villages that had been attacked came more clearly into view. We climbed the windmill and from that height could see that the whole village of Muensterberg was ablaze. Also in Tiege we could see the flames. But our nearest villagers had been spared so far. News also came to us that the "band" had left Sagradowka and had headed in the direction of Apostolowo. People calmed down a little more. Dad and Teacher Peters talked at twilight about holding a church service. It was on the street, and I was there. Dad said, "When our loving God ploughs so deep we must sow the seed." The service was to be held next morning, Sunday, in the school house. Sunday was chosen rather than Saturday, so as to celebrate Mother's birthday in a quiet manner. This was also the year of our parents' 25th Wedding Anniversary.

Going back, as already stated, the danger seemed to be more or less over for now. Tired from recent experiences, people came to rest a bit more. Only the watchmen could not be withdrawn. It is late, and I also go to bed. Franz, my brother, has ridden out to be on watch. At 4:00 am he returns and also goes to bed. Everything seems to be in good order.

Suddenly Dad comes into our bedroom very excited and reports that he had heard gunfire. It was still very dark, and also very foggy. But many were already up. At our place, the ducks for the noon meal were already in the oven. Quickly we, the first awakened, dressed and rushed with Dad onto the street to find out what was going on. We run to the end of the village, where many have already gathered. Here the matter is clarified. Two of our spies on horses meet a pair of riders at the east end of the village, this side of the dam. The fog prevents them from recognizing the pair immediately. They were... (Russian word) outriders of a band of 70 men. They called out to them – but no answer – and the pair take flight. Our watchmen pursued them and fired several shots. These were the shots that had been heard. But only up to the dam did they dare to pursue them. There the danger we were in was revealed, for the whole meadow was full of bandits, so they said.

With great haste our men rushed back and cried, "Take flight! Take flight!" The whole village was thrown into panic. Some, only a few, wanted to resist. But what good were a few "Kugelspritzer" (shotguns?) in this situation for almost all of the weapons of the "Selbstschutz" (Self-Defence) had been taken away. Many gave up hope of saving their lives through flight. But most of them quickly hitched their horses and drove at break-neck speed to the west end of the village out onto the pasture toward the "Kornswald" (crown forest). This we did as well. If we had not promised to take along the teacher's family (J.Peters), we would have all made it in our "Droschke". But then how should these get away? It had been arranged that Franz and I would follow on the other wagon. But when the "Droschke" was the first prepared to leave, Dad stood beside it, wondering whether I shoudln't go with Mother, the siblings, and the teacher's family, and he with Franz on the other wagon. "Well Martin, you get in!" he said. These were the last words he spoke to me; I've never seen him again.

I drove to the school house and waited for the teacher's wife and children. Since they did not come immediately, I went in and ordered them out and rushed them to get into the "Droschke", since there was no time to get dressed. They hadn't yet realized how grave the situation was. Accidentally I stumbled across a stick, which I grabbed to use as a whip. Once all were aboard we were off at the fastest gallop toward the west end of the village and away, with many ahead of us and a few behind.

Perhaps the reader will wonder how we all had time to flee. Here is the explanation. Earlier already a false rumor had spread that in Schoenau there was an organized cavalry of 70 men. Because the "puslemka" (?) was still being persecuted, the "band" was mislead even more. The bandits feared to enter the village blindly and so proceeded to form a chain around it. This gave us an advantage; we gained time. Otherwise, few would have escaped. As the chain was being drawn on both sides from east to west, most escaped before it could be closed on the west. Another circumstance helped the fleeing to escape. The gun shots of our young men had delayed the forming of the chain on our left, so that we had an escape to the "Kronswald" (crown forest). Only the bandits on our right pursued us.

The flight itself is indescribable. Driving our horses as fast as they could gallop, with bandits on their horses close behind, spraying us with bullets. Lamenting, screaming, crying to God and gun fire, all at the same time. Our driving was hindered greatly by the mud, as the ground was not frozen enough to carry the weight. In addition, only one way was open for us, southwest toward the "Kornswald" across the pasture of a "Chutor", where, alas, there were puddles almost impossible to cross. How would we have fared if I had not found that stick on the school yard? The horses strained themselves to their limit, as if they too were aware of the danger. Despite this I had to beat them mercilessly, so that in a few minutes my hands were blistered. I also cried to God to save us. I told someone to quickly grab the reins, should a bullet hit me. At the same time it almost seemed to me as if I already felt the sword thrust in my back. The double-tree on one wagon broke, so that they could not go on. They were our neighbors with their son and children. The son quickly mounted one of the horses and fled that way, while another managed to grab the tail of his horse and ran behind. The parents who stayed behind were shot. Another wagon also did not get away. The people scattered on the steppe, hiding in stooks left from the summer. A few saved their lives this way; others were stabbed where they were found. Finally we reached the forest, where our pursuers gave up the chase. Praise be to God, we were saved this time.

But what a scene rose behind us! The smoke rose from our village as it did once from Sodom and Gomorrah. But that was not the worst! Where had our beloved father and brother Franz stayed? We had not seen them anywhere. Had they also escaped with their lives? No one could tell us. Almost everyone had someone missing. Now we drove slowly, so that the horses might get rested up, through the forest to Friedensfeld. But here, also, we did not feel safe. The residents of Friedensfeld and of the other villages not yet plundered also took flight. They drove to the Russian villages. Most went to Michajlowka, where we also went. It was hard to find lodging there. The Russians were ill-disposed toward us. What would become of all this? We had no idea. Only one refuge was available to us, and blessed was the one who found that refuge. We were persuaded that since God had saved us thus far, He would continue to help us. Many turned their lives over to God here.

We stayed at the Russian village from Sunday evening to Wednesday morning. For promises that we would reward them richly, we were given lodging by a thoroughly unsympathetic family. By day we occupied ourselves with trying to assess our condition. Many were brought together here with their loved ones. Parents found their children and children their parents. Greetings after the trauma of a few days were like those after long years of absence. Every familiar face coming into view was like a new gift. But where did Dad and Franz stay so long? Finally, on Tuesday morning, someone brought the tragic news that Dad was no longer alive; but someone had seen Franz. What grief for us and our mother! The only comfort was to know that he was with the Lord. Though he had died a horrible death, it was all over now. He was now where he will be reaping what he had sown. Oh how much we would have loved to keep him here, for he was not only our earthly father but our spiritual father. How he was loved by all as one who cared for their soul. "What is Schoenau worth now" said one from Schoenau, "if Mr. Hamm is gone?"

Since nothing further was heard about the "banda", we, and some others, returned Wednesday, December 4th. On our return through the forest we got an awful scare. Suddenly we saw, about half a mile ahead, a troop of riders approaching us. We feared they were bandits

Appendix 2 – Grandfather's Death

and turned back in wild haste. The faster we drove, the closer they came. We already abandoned hope, since before us was the crown land's ravine that we could not cross. We look back and see, to our great joy, that the riders are beckoning us. Now the Goertzens and we take courage again. We recognize in the riders our Germans, returning from burying our loved ones. Now we are told distinctly that Dad was murdered and has been buried. Was it too, perhaps, that we did not get to see his distorted, wounded, and hacked-up face? We shall see him again in his transformed state. Thank you, dear Saviour, that you have bought us and that we now have this living hope.

We enter our devastated village. Not all the houses have been burned down. Many have been spared completely, including our whole "Wirtshaft" (farmyard?). But who valued earthly possessions these days? It almost seemed immaterial whether one's place was burned down or not. Our indescribable loss was the death of our beloved father. The first few nights we spent at our beloved friends, the Goertzens, because we were all afraid to stay in our big home. On Thursday morning we already surveyed the whole village, going from yard to yard. Everywhere things were still smoldering – it gave one an eerie feeling.

So we also came to our yard. I am not certain anymore whether there was another beside Janzen, Goertzen and me. A wild scene met us in our house. Beds, books, papers, and furniture were strewn everywhere in all the rooms. The cattle had been let go by those who stayed to save them from starvation. Suddenly, while we're in the barn, my brother Franz enters. It seemed as if we hadn't seen each other for years. So many things had happened in just a few days. It was a heart-felt greeting. But he looked so shaken. He had experienced more frightful things than we had. I asked him if he didn't want to make his deicision for the Lord now. Upon this he confessed, to our great joy, that he also had become a child of God. But he still had frightful inner struggles to overcome... ...Little by little he told us what had transpired since we had left. But we dared not to ask him too many questions. He would have preferred to keep quiet about the whole affair, since so many feelings were aroused when he talked about it.

His story, in brief, was that after Dad had sent the "Droschke" on its way, he rushed to prepare the horses and wagon for his and Franz' escape, hoping to catch up with us. They were already outside the village but did not know that only one escape route was available, and so they, with some others, turned north-west rather than south-west. As a result, they ran right into the hands of the bandits. Immediately under death threats they had to hand over watches and other valuables, like money. As captives of the bloodthirsty bandits, with much weeping, mourning and lamentation they had to return to the village, suspecting what likely would follow. On his last journey, in this hour of his death, my dear father still spoke words of comfort to many and pointed souls in despair to the Saviour. He also was allowed to experience and rejoice in my brother Franz finding peace. For himself he spoke the words of Paul in Philippians: "For me to live is Christ, and to die is gain." He was not the first of those taken captive to have to lay down his life. That lot fell first on my two uncles Jacob and Johann Wiebe. Then on the street in front of Heinrich Loewens our dear father was murdered in a horrible way. When he dodged the first sword thrust, his godless attacker hollered at him, asking whether he was afraid to die. "No", was his reply, and since escape was impossible, he obeyed the command to take off his coat; whereupon he had to turn his back toward his godless attacker. Shortly before this he had read his Bible. "Franz, do not look this way", he had said, "Greet the family, obey Mother, and love each other." Then the monster had struck him repeatedly with his sword in the scruff of his neck. Father had fallen forward and so, half dead, had struggled with death for a long time. Later another bandit had shot him to take him out of his misery. Franz had not been able to look away while this murder was in progress. Even before this beloved departed one had breathed his last, Franz had been ordered to remove his boots. Then he had to obey the command of the murderer to hitch up the horses. The goods which were not taken away were burned. Franz had had to give up his coat, and in its place had been given an old soldier's coat. This coat contributed to his not being recognized and being considered one of them. However when several drew attention to him while he was leading the horses, he suddenly dropped everything and ran as fast as his legs would carry him, without looking back, into the smoke of a burning building, where he hid himself and so escaped.

After an hour and a half of robbing and killing the bandits moved on. A few days later the inhabitants who had been spared began to return one by one to their village. Everyone had gone through dreadful experiences. Even today the ruins there are a grim reminder of those days of terror. Would that be the last time such disaster would come upon our people? The prospects are dark today in Russia for our loved ones there who could not emigrate. Oh that they could also come here, and that soon we could all pass over into that land where Jesus sits enthroned, and were our dear father has gone before.

– Martin Hamm, LaGlace, Alberta, 1927.

ACKNOWLEDGEMENTS

FEW BOOKS these days are written single-handedly and mine is no exception. So I am happy here to express my gratitude to a number of people who helped me bring this work into being.

First and foremost, my extreme gratitude goes to my son, Colin Hamm, who, over a number of years, acted as typist, editor, agent, and more. I got a rough, very rough, hand written copy to him just before my 80th birthday on September 23, 2011. Thereafter I became legally blind and physically indisposed for over two years. During this time, Colin kept the project going while I recovered from my disabilities and was again able to join in on the many revisions. Without his help the book would not have materialized. Thank you, Colin, ever so much.

Even before Colin came into the picture, my high-school friend Harold J. Dyck, with whom I reconnected in Vancouver after his illustrious career in the civil service both in Regina and Ottawa, became an important player in the production of this work. While he was writing vignettes about his life, I was writing vignettes about mine. We read these pieces to each other and offered criticism. He said to me that he had not ever read an autobiography of a philosopher of education, and it occurred to me nor had I. So I thought that it might be worthwhile to write one, and he urged me on. Without his urging and encouragement it is very unlikely that I would have produced a manuscript for Colin to work on and for me to revise and complete. Thank-you, Harold, for your generous help.

Appendix 3 – Acknowledgements

A number of friends and acquaintances helped in the project by agreeing to have a look at a pre-publication manuscript and offer their comments and criticism. Foremost among these was Lynda Philippsen, whose expertise as a book reviewer and English teacher enabled her to provide me with many very helpful suggestions for improving the work and eliminating horrible howlers and embarrassing errors. Her thorough reading and criticism of the manuscript helped immensely in its improvement. Lynda, thank-you.

Others who gave me helpful suggestions were David Janzen, Norman Robinson, Helen Knight, Harold Dyck, Mary Hamm, and Finola Finlay. Thank-you all.

I wish to thank also Betty Hamm, widow of my deceased brother Peter Hamm, for giving me permission to quote from Peter's *Reflections on My Journey*, which I liberally did.

I am also grateful for permission from Helmut T. Heubert and the Mennonite Historical Society to include in my work a copy of W. Schroeder's map "Mennonite Colonies in South Russia".

INDEX

1931, year of my birth 33-37

ACHOTE 277
Alston, William 332
Anabaptist 19
Argue, Ken 243, 245
Aristocratic, restaurant 205, 208
Arnold, Matthew 344, 367
Atlanta 176, 214
autobiography 9-11, 378

Barker, Dan 185, 324
BC, moving to 88-89, 93
Beaver Cove, logging camp 165-170
Bible
    discrepancies and contradictions 162, 183-188, 315, 337
    in public school 242
    literal interpretation of 19, 59, 64, 98, 110, 152, 305, 307
    quotations 34, 66, 100, 135, 137, 139, 141, 162, 163, 174, 176, 182, 183, 195, 201, 305, 319, 356
    story of Saul on the road to Damascus 62
billeting 194
Blake, William 368
Borosenko 14, 16, 24
Braden, Harding 189-191, 199
Bruce, Will 189, 194-195, 200

Canada 15, 19, 24, 27-28, 33-34, 47, 70, 80, 129, 131, 147-148, 189, 196, 248, 250, 252, 284, 343, 347, 348-349, 350, 355-357, 363
cancer, squamous cell 277
Catherine the Great 19-20
cattle, backgrounding 271
caution 266
Charlie Lake 280, 283-284
Chilliwack 68, 88, 91, 92-147, 154, 204
Choir, Vancouver Bach 79, 221
chores 40, 69, 77, 84, 87, 89, 95-96, 105, 107, 108, 109, 110, 113, 126, 134, 136, 158, 193, 216, 238, 263, 266, 275, 290

Chortiza River 20
Christmas 25, 26, 33, 48, 54, 82-84, 95, 164, 175, 214, 225, 228, 231, 294, 370
Church, separation from state 354-356, 359
Church, Trinity Baptist 217, 218, 226
Church, West Point United 225, 226
conceptual clarity 249, 306, 315-318
conscientious objection 19
conversion 24, 60-64

Dad 24-28, 28-30, 31-33, 36, 37, 39, 43, 69, 70-71, 74, 85-87, 88, 157, 252, 305
Damascus 61-64, 146, 185, 302, 304, 310-311, 315, 316, 325, 335-340, 341, 364
dancing 22, 128, 145, 216, 224, 340
Dawkins, Richard 62, 139, 312, 323, 356-357, 360
Dearden, Robert 246, 256, 283
Dearing, Ruth 161
Dehy 263, 268
delusion 62, 104, 139-140, 189, 306, 311-315, 318, 323, 336, 368
democracy, a work in progress 343, 347, 349-351, 352, 358, 361
deprivation 82
diary 102, 104-115, 119-122, 126, 142, 152
disbelief
    accretion of 181, 218, 318-326
    pockets of 161, 173, 176, 196, 203, 210, 304, 305-307, 315-316, 339
Discontent, poem 214
doctor, playing 43
doctrine 50, 60, 61, 64-65, 69, 110, 122, 143, 146, 149, 161, 177, 181, 197, 200, 202, 315-318, 333, 334, 336, 339-40, 345, 361, 367
Dreiband 22, 23
Dyck, Harold 378, 379
Dyck, John 157

education
    elementary 208, 211-218, 223, 224
    moral 209, 244-247, 252, 270, 275-276, 329, 331, 346, 347
    parents' rights 270, 357
    philosophy of 233, 235, 241-244, 246, 250, 254, 257, 282-283

public 47, 176, 197, 221, 255, 328, 343-348, 353, 356, 365
secondary 220-227
secular 188, 204, 345
Ehrman, Bart D. 163, 187, 323
Elliot, Murray 243
emigration 24, 26-27
Emmerson, R.W. 219
environment 343, 351-352
etiquette 153, 302, 363

farming
  auction 27, 90, 269
  Dawson Creek 260-270
  life 20, 25, 41, 70, 86-88, 92, 96, 103, 154
  machinery 29, 260-262, 266, 282
fear 17, 71, 118, 242, 298, 330, 340-341, 366-367
Feldkirch, Austria 231
fire, at Paul's place 172
fleece, test 130-142. 312, 321
Frederick the Great 19
Friesen, Mrs. C. 35, 72
Frost, Robert 198

Gdansk 14, 19
Geddart, George 154
Geddart, Jake 94, 154
German, language 13, 18, 39-40, 57, 70, 72, 76, 95, 99, 109, 123, 221, 223, 231
grade Twelve 122-130, 133
Grande Prairie 46
Grassy Lake 157-160
Great Depression 31, 35
Green, Ruth H. 186
guilt 116-119, 121-122, 124, 133, 144, 155, 180, 210, 222, 279, 299, 340, 366

Hamilton, Mary 228-235, 238-239, 243, 245, 249, 253, 257, 261, 272, 276-277, 379
Hamm
  Anna (mother) 14, 20, 25-26, 30, 35, 36, 38-41, 68, 69, 71-76, 82, 85, 114, 178-179
  Anna (sister) 31, 75, 76-77, 88, 97, 107
  Colin 37, 239, 250, 252, 266, 271, 298, 378

Cornelius 13-15
Devin 297
Frank 31, 75, 77, 88, 97, 108, 123, 154, 156
John 26, 66, 70, 75, 76, 86, 88, 91
Lena 26, 27, 75, 87, 89
Margaret 69, 75, 79, 97
Martin (brother) 29, 42, 66, 75, 76, 88, 91, 205, 261, 276, 289
Martin (father) 24-28, 28-30, 31-33, 36, 37, 39, 43, 69, 70-71, 74, 85-87, 88, 157, 252, 305
Martin (son) 234, 235, 239, 250, 252, 266
Mary (sister) 26, 75, 87, 89, 91
Mary (wife) 228-235, 238-239, 243, 245, 249, 253, 257, 261, 272, 276-277, 379
Nigel 297
Peter 12, 15, 16, 18, 31, 35, 36, 37, 39, 71, 72, 74, 75, 78, 97, 100, 123, 132, 156, 161, 164-165, 205, 379
Shiraya 297
Walter 39, 66, 71, 75, 79, 102, 104, 108, 156-157, 174
Hammstead 297-298
Hampstead, London 230, 250
Harris, Harley 217, 218
health hare 348-349, 353, 365
high density living 301-302, 363
Hirst, Paul 246, 283
honeymoon 192, 229, 232, 236
humanism 332
humanist 252, 330, 341, 361, 367

iconoclasm 336
indoctrination
  definition 50-51, 140, 343, 345, 346
  methods 64, 99, 225, 241, 356, 367
  my childhood 55, 60, 98, 99, 140, 143-144, 304, 337
  prevention 356-358, 361, 367

Janz
  Abe 41
  Annie 35
Janzen
  Aaron 29
  David 208, 238, 339, 375, 379
  Jake 55, 90
Johnson, B. and B. 179, 214, 232, 235

Konrad, George 47

La Glace 28-33, 33-91
Langley 270-274, 277, 282
leaky condos, Greater Vancouver 299
lesson, demonstration 233
logging 165-166, 168-170
Lowe, Mrs. L. 47-49

Machnos 17, 25
Mango, Ray 10
Maxwell, L.E. 95, 114, 120, 148-149, 152
McAllister, Howie 233-234
McLean, Donald 239-240
McNaughton, Walter 55-56
Meadows, L. 241
Melita, ship 28
Mennonite, central doctrines of 18, 19-24, 88
Metcalfe, Miss 41-43
Molotschna 14, 20, 24, 26
Moral Education, The Domain of (book) 270, 329
moral principles 245, 310, 346, 349, 368
Mother 14, 20, 25-26, 30, 35, 36, 38-41, 68, 69, 71-76, 82, 85, 114, 178-179
movie, Goodbye Mr. Chips 179

New Jerusalem 302, 341-342, 347, 364-368
New York City 198, 232, 234-235, 249
Nicodemus 56, 305
non-theism 226, 258, 325, 326-328, 328-331, 331-337, 360-361
Normal School 13, 123, 175, 197, 205-211, 223, 338

open mindedness 189
oral, exam 247, 255-257
ordnung 69
other worldliness 20, 22-23

Palm Springs 195, 274, 290, 294-296
PBI, Prairie Bible Institute 120, 133-134, 147-151, 160-173, 173-180, 180-189, 189-204
Peace River Bible Institute 55-56
Peace River, region of (peace country) 86, 132, 259, 260-269, 284

Penner, Cornelius 14, 292, 293
Penner, Philip 103
Peta 39
Peters, R.S. 243-248, 250, 255-257, 270, 283, 344
philosophy 76, 182, 183, 188, 218-220, 221, 223, 233-235, 241-246, 246-253, 253-260, 339
pioneering 31-33
Pisesky, Mike 178
Plato 219-220, 308, 310
Plautdietsch 39, 40, 279
Pollyannaish 38
population, control 358, 366
prayer, in public schools 242
privilege, by birth 318, 359-362
proof, burden of for God's existence 327
publishing 270
punishment, physical 43, 66, 221-223

race, mile 112-114
Ratzlaff, Lloyd 65
reason
  and faith 50, 60, 64, 138, 140, 141-142, 143, 182, 184, 305, 317-318, 321, 322, 324, 334
  embeddedness of 307-311
  power of 139, 141-142, 245, 306, 322, 334, 336, 342, 345, 360, 368
religion
  a basic human need 129, 367
  acquisition of 65-66, 99, 100, 115, 225
  concept of 50, 64, 141, 258, 307, 308, 310, 330, 332, 333, 335, 342, 356
  freedom from 65, 130, 184, 203, 210, 219-220, 226, 252, 304, 306, 311, 314, 320, 321, 325, 328, 329, 334, 337, 339-340, 343, 364, 366-367
  privilege and position in society 328, 336, 354, 356, 357-358, 359, 360, 361
  types of 332
religious mindset 120-121, 130-142, 337
retirement 289-300
Ripple Rock 166
Rogers and Hammerstein 229
romance 232, 272, 278-281
Russian Revolution 17, 23, 294

Saint Paul 62-64, 162-163, 319, 364, 376
Salzburg 231, 247
saved, getting 57-66
Savery, B. 219, 244-245
Sawatzky, B. 57-58
Sawatzky, Walter 151
Schoenau 17-18, 20, 24, 26, 371, 373, 374
scholarship, money 212, 224, 234
school
  CHS (Chilliwack High School) 93-96, 102-103, 111, 122-124
  La Glace School 41-45, 77
  Lord Byng Secondary 239, 240-244
  Old Post 45-50, 55, 77, 94
  SMCI (Sharon Mennonite Collegiate Institute) 97-104, 105, 108, 110, 122, 123, 128, 143, 179, 337
  Sunday 52-54, 56, 57, 69, 94, 95, 109, 115, 124, 170, 172, 177, 304
  Vancouver Secondary Teachers Association (VSSTA) 242
  Vancouver Technical High School (Van Tech) 237-240, 260
search questions, at PBI 150, 152, 161
self-sufficiency, at PBI 148-149
self-enactment 11
separation, marriage 272
separation of Church and State 354-356, 359
servants, unto all (class motto) 173-174
Sharon Mennonite Collegiate Institute (SMCI) 97-104, 105, 108, 110, 122, 123, 128, 143, 179, 337
Siberian work camps 25
siblings 13, 26, 37, 40, 43, 66-68, 75-79
Siebert, Abe 52, 86
Siebert, Nick 89, 204, 207
sightseeing 198, 235, 250, 257, 276
Simon Fraser University (SFU)
  early years on staff 253-260
  education faculty undergraduate directorship 285-289
  job application 250
  later years 270, 273, 274, 277, 278, 282-285, 289
Simons, Menno 19
sin, the 'big' one 115-122
Smart, Elizabeth 201

Sointula 170-171, 177
Stroll, A. 223
Sunday School 52-54, 56, 57, 69, 94, 95, 109, 115, 124, 170, 172, 177, 304
surrender, to God 139, 146, 154, 160, 161, 200, 312-313
Szell, George 231

Tchaikovsky 164
teaching
  elementary 175, 211-218
  secondary 220-227, 237-240, 240-244
  theory 50, 174, 204, 208-211, 233
  university (SFU) 253-260, 282-285, 285-289
Three Hills, Alberta 142, 147-204, 338

United Nations 353, 357
university
  Columbia 233-236, 237, 242, 243, 244
  of BC (UBC) 161, 171, 205, 211, 213-220, 221, 223, 224, 233, 239, 243-244, 246, 321
  of Melbourne 274-278
  Simon Fraser (SFU) 250, 253-260, 270, 273, 274, 277, 278, 282-285, 285-289
  Washington State 227

Voth
  Alexander 29, 55, 57, 59, 114
  Cornelius 14, 20
  Katherina 16, 26

Wall
  Justine 47
  Peter 46
Warkentin
  Anna 25
  Cornelius 14, 20
  Dietrich 14
  Johann 14, 16, 17, 26, 293
  Katherina 16, 17
  Peter 27, 28
wealth, redistribution of 352-354
wedding, Edmonton 189-191
Weinberg, Steven 290
West Coast Children's Mission (WCCM) 165
Westlynn Terrace 236

Williams Lake, B.C. 261
Williams, David 238
Winona Lake, Indiana 175, 199
witnessing 71, 154-160, 180
Wordsworth, William 183

Yaletown, Vancouver neighborhood
 299, 300-302
Yarrow 88, 95, 97-98, 102-103, 109,
 122, 126, 143
Yeats, W.B. 273

Zagradovka 14, 16, 17, 20, 24, 26,
 27, 293

CPSIA information can be obtained at www.ICGtesting.com
Printed in the USA
LVOW11s2142080416

482823LV00001B/2/P